2014 BEST INDIE BOOK

NOTABLE INDIE

For complete reader reviews visit the reviews page at NanaMizushima.com

"Her story has resonances with our daily media accounts of the displacement, wounding, killing, and rape of women and children in violence around the world...
Mizushima is to be commended for providing Western readers with this chilling account of some wrenching human aspects of the end of World War II."
— *Professor Emeritus Joyce Lebra. first woman Ph.D. in Japanese History in the U.S. (granted by Harvard/Radcliffe)*

"*Tei* reminds us of what the Syrian and other refugees must be experiencing today in similar circumstances. It is a story without any boundaries for all time."
— *Caroline Matano Yang, Former Executive Director Japan-US Educational Commission (Fulbright Program)*

"Tei's story is impossible to forget, a bone-achingly sharp and beautiful reminder of my privilege."
— *Ansley Clark, poet*

For more information, visit:
NanaMizushima.com

Tei

A MEMOIR OF THE END OF WAR
AND BEGINNING OF PEACE

———————

By Tei Fujiwara

Translated from the Japanese
by Nanako V. Mizushima

TONNBO BOOKS

CONTENTS

PART I

THE HILL OF TEARS

PART II

THE TOWN WITH A CHURCH

PART III

THE VOICE OF BEELZEBUB

The Story of Her Story

Boulder, Colorado
April 2014

Almost seventy years ago, Tei Fujiwara wrote a memoir about her harrowing journey home with her three young children. But the *story of her story* is what every reader needs to know.

Tei's memoir begins in August 1945 in Manchuria. At that time, Tei and her family fled from the invading Soviets who declared war on Japan a few days after the United States dropped the atomic bomb on Hiroshima. After reaching her home in Japan, Tei wrote what she thought would be a last testament to her young children, who wouldn't remember their journey and who might be comforted by their mother's words as they faced an unknown future in post-war Japan.

But several miracles took place after she wrote the memoir. Tei survived and her memoir, originally published in Showa Era 24 [1949] became a best seller titled *Nagareru Hoshiwa Ikiteiru* (Shooting Stars are Alive). Over the following decades, millions of Japanese became familiar with her story through forty-six print runs, the movie version, and a television drama. Empress Michiko, wife of the current emperor, urged her people to read Tei's story.

Why should Westerners read this translation of her story? Tei wrote about men, women and children caught in the middle of the world's most devastating war and how they coped. The suffering, endurance, and struggles she described reminded the defeated Japanese of their strength, their spirit, and hope in the future. Her sense of humor, compassion and love helped defuse anger and despair. She brought back a basic sense of trust towards former enemies, but also a honest new look at her own countrymen.

In many ways, Tei was a typical Japanese housewife, but she was also extraordinary. The memoir begins with a well-educated but sheltered young wife of a civilian scientist, who is a mother of three young children. Her keen insights in 1945-46 – on the Koreans, fellow Japanese men, women and children, as well as the Russian soldiers and the American GIs – give us rare glimpses into a part of the world few Americans know.

Why did I translate Tei's memoir? My initial reason for translating her book was personal. My parents both grew up and lived in Tokyo during the war. My father was 22 years old and my mother was 13 when the war finally ended after four long years. WWII devastated the lives of millions of Japanese civilians living in Japan as well as in Manchuria and other parts of Asia. Tei's story resonates deeply with my parents' generation.

Her memoir and family also influenced my family in unexpected ways. Tei's younger son, Masahiko, became a mathematician, and came to the University of Colorado as a Visiting Scholar, where my father taught in the physics faculty. My parents enjoyed taking care of any visiting Japanese, and often invited them over to our house to stave off homesickness. I met Masahiko at one of the social gatherings at our home. I was 13 at the time but vividly remember meeting the young professor.

Over the next years, my family visited Tokyo several times. I heard first-hand, stories of how people survived and struggled after the war. The stories of the Fujiwara family as well as those of my own family encouraged me to study in Japan, obtain a Masters degree in International Affairs from Columbia University, and work in international educational exchange over the next several years. This included several years as the Educational Information Officer at the offices of the Fulbright Program (Japan-U.S. Educational Commission) in Tokyo, and as the Japan Correspondent for *The Chronicle of Higher Education* newspaper.

The impact of Tei's story on her own family life is also fascinating. After her memoir became a best-seller, Tei found herself in the public spotlight and dealing with the complexity of life after the war. At the end of this book, I included the afterwords she wrote in two of her later editions of her memoir.

Her husband, a former meteorologist, became an award-winning historical novelist himself, under the pen name, Jiro Nitta. Her children also wrote essays and books. In 2005, Tei's son Masahiko Fujiwara wrote a book, *The Dignity of a Nation*, which has sold more than 2 million copies.

For Tei, this memoir was the achievement of a lifetime. She wrote it because she thought she might not live long enough to pass her story on to her children. In an interesting twist of fate, she has lived longer than most of us ever will. As of this writing, she is alive and well, ninety-six years old and living quietly in a senior home in Tokyo. Although Alzheimer's has taken its toll and she no longer speaks or writes publicly, she still shares weekly meals with her three adult children, and her grandsons.

I feel fortunate to have had the privilege of translating her memoir while she is still alive. Her words are still as fresh as when she wrote them over sixty years ago. Tei's story has also helped me in my own life as a mother of three children. By coincidence, I also have two boys and the youngest, a girl, about the same spacing in age as Tei's three children.

When I first read her memoir, I was a full-time mother of

three young children, adjusting to life in Colorado after living in Tokyo for two years, and in Jakarta for a year. Although I faced completely different challenges—divorce, financial hardship and starting over—her words encouraged me, inspired me, and gave me perspective.

My mother helped translate this memoir, by reading out loud passages from the book, and explaining what life was like in 1945 Japan. We spent many afternoons reading and discussing Tei's stories, and we worked together to create the glossary in the back of this book. My mother and many of her Japanese friends say they have read and reread this book. When she introduced this book to me in the midst of all the turmoil in my life, I knew this was more than a casual book recommendation. The emotional impact of this memoir hasn't diminished, even after sixty years. Often, during our afternoon talks—my mother would stop in the middle of a chapter she was reading to me—because she couldn't continue. Her voice would break, quaver and die off to a whisper as her eyes filled with tears. Memories of the end of war and the beginning of peace are still very much alive.

Nanako V. Mizushima
NanaMizushima.com

Historical Background

Since I am not a historian, I will present only basic information and anecdotes from my own family who immigrated from Japan after the war ended. I hope these snippets will help the reader better understand the background for this memoir. Tei and her family traveled through Manchuria and Korea, both former colonies of the Empire of Japan which existed from 1868 to 1947. For more detailed information, please see the list of Resources, the Glossary, and East Asian experts in your area.

My great-grandfather, Masamichi Mizushima, served as a general in the Russo-Japanese War (1904-05) which gave the victorious Japanese significant influence over Manchuria and Korea. The Japanese military at the time was instrumental in expanding the Japanese Empire which extended over Manchuria, Korea, Taiwan and other parts of Asia. But like many members of the former samurai class, he grew disenchanted with the military, and encouraged his son, (my grandfather), Seizo Mizushima, to study and begin a career outside the military. Education, not family background was the key to success in the new Japan. My grandfather Seizo was the first civilian in his family, and he built a successful dental practice in Tokyo during the prosperous, liberal *Taisho Era* (1912-26).

Several members of my family went to the United States to study and seek their fortune during that time. Well-educated young men like Tei's husband and Seizo's son (my father), were also eager to learn from the West. My father's uncle, a medical doctor, followed in the footsteps of other Japanese scientists who went to the United States, but a tragic car accident killed the ambitious doctor and his wife in Stockton, California. My relatives were dismayed to hear how poorly the Japanese and the Japanese-Americans were treated in the U.S. at that time.

The Great Kanto Earthquake of 1923 killed over 140,000 people in the Tokyo-Yokohama region, set back the economy, and increased social instability. My family survived the earthquake but remembered the anti-Korean sentiments — thousands of Koreans living in Tokyo were killed by panic-stricken Japanese who believed the Koreans had poisoned the drinking water. Conservative military leaders fanned such xenophobic feelings toward foreigners and the West, and they began silencing the liberals, imposing more restrictions and military control.

As my grandfather Seizo saw the growing militarism in Tokyo (In 1932 young fanatic military officers assassinated the Prime Minister), he was probably relieved when his sons took academic paths away from military school. The *Kenpeitai* (secret military police) forbade political meetings, censured student meetings, confiscated foreign books, and tortured dissenters, including my father's friend who never recovered. The *Kenpeitai* were known to be brutal , particularly in Korea.

By the time Tei's husband moved to Shinkyo City, Manchuria in 1943, the Japanese army had been at war with China for three years. Manchuria was an important source of raw materials for Japan, a resource-poor island nation. Although my father and many others in the educated community knew the U.S. would defeat Japan, the militarists, particularly the army, pushed for war, especially when the U.S. threatened Japan's oil supplies.

My father escaped widespread military conscription because

he could do scientific research—such as on alternative fuels. Tei's husband was also one of the educated who was not drafted. Tei and her husband were part of a thriving economy in Manchuria. Over 850,000 Japanese lived in Korea and more than 2 million in China. In Shinkyo, where Tei and her family lived, the Japanese made up almost a quarter of the population. Modern factories, and institutions such as the Meteorological Institute where Tei's husband worked were well established.

Tei begins her story in August 9, 1945 as they fled from the invading Soviets who declared war on Japan right after the U.S. dropped the atom bomb on Hiroshima. The Japanese military abandoned the civilians, leaving them completely vulnerable. More than 11,000 Japanese settlers died as they fled, about a third by committing suicide.

Hundreds of thousands of Japanese men were captured, including Tei's husband, and were sent to the Soviet forced labor camps, the infamous *gulag*. After the end of the war, the *hikiage* began, the massive reverse migration of millions of Japanese soldiers, civilians, women, and children back to Japan.

Most of Tei's memoir takes place in what is now North Korea. Long before the Russo-Japanese War, Japanese merchants settled throughout Korea, seeking economic opportunity. Westerners were also in evidence on the peninsula. Tei saw a church and a hospital left behind by Protestant and Methodist missionaries who arrived in Korea from the United States and Canada beginning in the 1880's. By the time Tei arrived, these missionaries were gone, replaced by the Japanese military. Tei's group stays in the house next to a shinto shrine which was burned down, most likely by locals who resented the Japanese and their regulations: the abolishment of the Korean language in public schools and public functions, the pressure for Koreans to adopt Japanese names, use Japanese language, and bow to Japanese shinto shrines.

When Tei finally reached the shores of Japan in 1946, the situation was not much better—food shortages and the spread of the black market. My relatives experienced malnutrition and vividly remember the U.S. emergency food packets which saved many lives. It was no wonder that Tei thought her memoir might be her last testament. Her world in 1946 looked bleak and uncertain.

Tei's memoir is about a year that was the confluence of tremendous change—the end of the most devastating war the world had experienced, and the beginning of tremendous social change for Japan and the rest of the world.

For her personally, her memoir documents the end of her innocence. Just as Pandora found when she opened the box, Tei found hunger, pain, suffering, cruelty and all the evils man could inflict on man. But also like Pandora, Tei finds one last spirit still remaining in the box—hope.

Nanako V. Mizushima

March 2014

Translation Notes

I am not a professional translator or an academic, so the reader may wonder how I came to translate this work. First, my language background in a nutshell: My parents both immigrated from Japan as adults. I was born in the United States, but spoke Japanese at home and attended school in Japan several times for stays ranging from half a year to a year (*yochien*, middle school, and college). I vividly remember learning English when I began kindergarten in Boulder, Colorado. I lived in Japan for a total of about ten years, spread out over several visits.

I enjoyed reading many Japanese-to-English translated works through my middle school and high school years, but found many of them to be difficult to read. I have consciously tried to avoid the stiff style I encountered in some of those translations. Once I reached college age, I did not major in Japanese but I did study Japanese at the University of Colorado, and in the Master's program in International Affairs at Columbia University. (My major was economics as an undergraduate, and international affairs, with a focus on modern Japan, at Columbia University.)

Much of the Japanese I learned was through living and working in Japan. Besides attending Japanese schools, I worked for a large Japanese steel company (*Nippon Kokan*) for two years, the Japan-US Educational Commission for four years, the *Chronicle of Higher Education* for a year, and was the busy mother of three children who attended local Japanese schools for two years. Many of my relatives and friends are Japanese.

I do have professional experience as a Japanese-English interpreter (translating the *spoken* language) with two companies here in Colorado. I was an interpreter for a Japanese heart transplant patient in Denver, other Japanese medical clients, and an American engineering company with Japanese clients. I find translating written work more difficult because I am limited to written characters. Fortunately, I can ask family and friends to clarify the Japanese vocabulary. Now, I mainly communicate in Japanese with my parents.

I don't have the linguistics background to explain the intricacies of my translation process. My goals are to be accurate and translate the emotional intent of each sentence. In any case, I hope that most readers are going to be more interested in the story rather than my translation process. I am going to cheat here and quote a professional translator, Professor Jay Rubin, who translates Haruki Murakami's works and is much better than I am at articulating the translation challenges.

> The Japanese language is *so* different from English …that true literal translation is impossible, and the translator's subjective processing is inevitably going to play a large part.

I try to write in a natural style which is enjoyable to read. I believe the translation should be invisible, just as the camera is invisible in a good movie. But the reader should be aware that this is *my interpretation* of Tei Fujiwara's story, not a literal translation. What is the difference, you ask? I will give you a specific example from Jay Rubin's work mentioned in his book *Haruki Murakami and the Music of Words* (ISBN 1 86046 952 3 (tpb). A paragraph from the Professor Rubin's translation of Haruki Murakami's "The Girl from Ipanema":

> When I think of my high school's corridor, I think of combination salad: lettuce, tomatoes, cucumbers, green peppers, asparagus, onion rings, and pink Thousand Island dressing. Not that there was a salad shop at the end of the corridor. No, there was just a door, and beyond the door a drab 25-meter pool.

Professor Rubin notes that a literal translation of the same paragraph would actually look like this (foreign non-Japanese words are italicized):

> High school's corridor say-if, I *combination salad* think-of. *Lettuce* and *tomato* and cucumber and green pepper and *asparagus*, ring-cut bulb onion, and pink-color's *Thousand island dressing*. No argument high school corridor's hit-end in *salad* speciality shop exists meaning is-not. High school corridor's hit-end in, *door* existing, *door's* outside in, too-much flash-do-not 25-*meter pool* exists only is.

The differences in grammar between Japanese and English make translation between these two languages challenging. Professor Rubin's example is from a Japanese book which is widely regarded as more American in style than most Japanese books. So the reader can imagine Tei Fujiwara's book, written in the 1940's, is going to be even more difficult. Here are a few notes for this translation:

• Please see the **Glossary** at the end of the book to see the original kanji (used by Tei Fujiwara) of names of people and places. If I had a choice, I used the simpler pronunciation of a name.

- I purposefully left out Tei's husband's first name since she only refers to him as "my husband."

- I used Western ages for people (a person becomes one year old after a year has passed from the date of birth.)

- I inserted pronouns and gender and titles to clarify the identity of the speakers. And used Mrs., Mr. and *Dancho* as the form of address instead of the gender neutral *-san*. I used *-chan* as the Japanese do, when addressing children.

- *Okusan* (literal meaning Madam) is the form of address commonly used when talking to Mrs. Fujiwara and other married women.

- I used the original map from Tei's memoir with the Kanji characters. These are the 1940's Japanese names of the cities and towns. I added a larger map for readers unfamiliar with the region.

- I added a few details to clarify the context of the story and the identities of the people, but did not change any of the events of Tei's story.

- The Glossary in the back provides additional information.

Acknowledgements:

This translation would have been impossible to produce without the help and support of many people. I wish to thank Tei Fujiwara's family for giving me permission to translate her work. I am especially grateful to my mother, Yoneko Mizushima, who introduced this book to me, encouraged me to translate it, and provided essential help over many months. My father, Masataka Mizushima, was able to explain many of the details and vocabulary of that time period. Becky Tarr was a patient and wonderful reader of my earlier drafts, as well as a good writing buddy. Members of the Tuesday Fiction Writers group were gracious enough to look at the earlier drafts, and gently critique my writing and story-telling style. John Shors, historical fiction writer of novels such as *Beneath a Marble Sky*, gave me the go-ahead when I needed that initial encouragement, and provided many helpful comments. Ansley Clark, creative writing instructor at the University of Colorado, gave me useful advice. Aaron Klass also critiqued the earlier draft. Professor Faye Yuan Kleeman of the Department of Asian Languages and Civilizations at the University of Colorado helped create the thought provoking discussion questions provided at the end of the book. I am especially indebted to my husband, Robert Forshay, for his patience, support and valuable feedback.

I hope readers will contact me if any errors are found or any additional information is available. I thank you for having the patience and interest in reading this translation. Most of all, I hope readers will forget that this book is a translation.

Nanako V. Mizushima
NanaMizushima@gmail.com

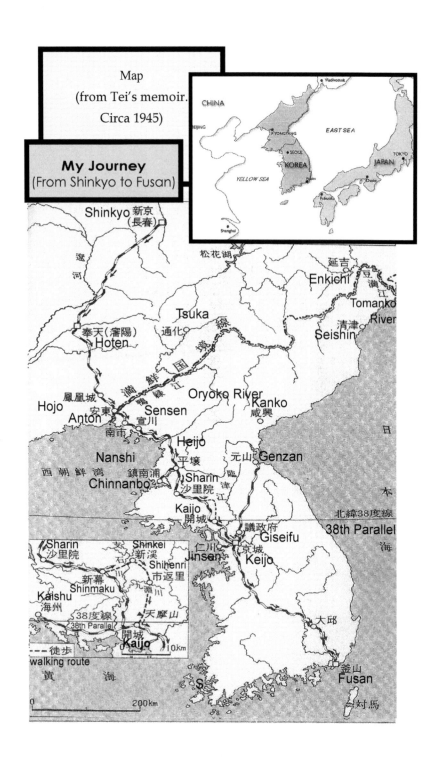

Map
(from Tei's memoir.
Circa 1945)

My Journey
(From Shinkyo to Fusan)

CHINA

BEIJING

PYONGYANG

SEOUL

KOREA

YELLOW SEA

Fukuoka

Shanghai

EAST SEA

TOKYO

JAPAN

Osaka

Vladivostok

Shinkyo 新京
(長春)

松花湖

遼河

Tsuka
通化

延吉
豆满

Enkichi

Tomanko
River

奉天(瀋陽)
Hoten

満鮮国境線

清津
Seishin

Hojo

鳳凰城

安東
Anton

南市

宣川
Sensen

Oryoko River

咸興
Kanko River

Kanko

日

満

Nanshi

西朝鮮湾

平壤
Heijo

鎮南浦
Chinnanbo

元山
Genzan

Sharin
沙里院

臨津

38th Parallel
北緯38度線

本

Kaijo
開城

議政府
Giseifu

仁川
Jinsen

京城
Keijo

海

Sharin
沙里院

Shinkei
新渓

支石

Shihenri
市返里

新幕
Shinmaku

九溪川

Kaishu
海州

38度線
38th Parallel

開城
Kaijo

天摩山

大邱

--- 徒歩
walking route

0 10Km

黄 海

S

釜山
Fusan

対馬

0   200km

PART I

THE HILL OF TEARS

CHAPTER ONE

Four Kilometers to the Train Station

Shinkyo City, Manchuria
August 9, 1945, around 10:30 p.m.

I heard a loud knocking at the front door. The children were asleep. My husband and I were talking about getting to bed soon because we had stayed up late the night before.

"Mr. Fujiwara! Mr. Fujiwara! We're from the meteorological station!" a young man shouted from outside.

My husband and I opened the front door to find two young uniformed men holding rifles.

"Sir? Are you Mr. Fujiwara? Please come immediately to the office," said one of them.

My husband asked, "What is going on?"

"Sir, we don't know the reason but everyone is being called to an emergency meeting. Please cooperate and come right away!" The two rushed off to the next house to continue their mission.

When I closed the door, I felt light-headed. My intuition told me that I shouldn't let my husband go into the pitch-dark night by himself. "Are you sure you want to go out alone?" I asked.

Right after I said that, I peered into my husband's eyes to try to extract what vital knowledge he had. I was sure that there was something he didn't tell me, something he hid about what was going on with the war. The last two or three days, uneasiness clouded his eyes.

"Don't worry. I want you to wait for me," he said. Then he sighed. "It looks like the day has finally come," he added and he opened the door again. "Here. Listen...it definitely isn't the same old Shinkyo City we know."

I turned my attention to the night and listened carefully. In the distance I heard cars running, people's nervous voices, and other restless noises. A big change was about to happen. It was like an omen, vibrating all around us in the dark night air where the new moon shed no light. "Has the day finally arrived? Is this it?" I asked. I sat down in the dark, narrow hallway as all of the strength drained from my body. I clung to the bottom of my husband's jacket and trembled.

"*Baka!* You fool," he scolded me. "What are you doing? Hurry; you've got to get everything ready so that we can leave this place right away."

"Leave here? Leave our home — to go where?" I asked.

"I don't know myself. I don't even know yet if we're really leaving or not — but we've got to prepare ourselves; we've got to be ready."

He hurriedly wrapped his uniform leggings around his trousers and rushed out. The meteorological station where my husband worked was in the suburbs south of Shinkyo, in a place called Nanrei. From here, it was going to take at least thirty minutes for him to get there by foot. Even if he turned right around, it would about an hour before he got back home.

I went upstairs and tried to decide what to do. From the second-floor window, I saw confirmation of my fears. Even though there was an official blackout order, scarlet points of light flickered between the window shades of the neighbors' houses.

Tonight, it wasn't just my home. Everywhere, in every home, terrible thoughts ran through people's minds. Turmoil and fear spread, like a plague. The shadows in the windows moved about hastily, as if they were in a panic. "I've got to do something," I told myself and opened up our emergency suitcase.

Inside, our winter clothes — children's and adults' were neatly packed. What about emergency food? Some packages — sugar, hard biscuits, and canned goods were already packed inside. If we have to leave Shinkyo tonight and go who knows how far — other than these things — what in the world should we take? As I thought about this, my heart pounded faster and faster, and soon any semblance of rational thought fled my mind. I couldn't think.

Under the mosquito netting hung in the center of the eight-*tatami*-mat room, I saw the faces of my children, all sleeping together on one bed — limbs and bodies intertwined as if they were one creature. How could we possibly leave this house and get very far with these children? My two boys — Masahiro was five years old and Masahiko was only two. My baby girl, Sakiko, was a newborn who had just turned one month old. As I nervously packed and unpacked things in and out of the backpack and suitcase, I was overcome with dread, and my eyes welled up.

"I'm not strong enough for this. There was nothing I could do by myself," I thought. A woman alone with her children. All I could do was wait for my husband to come back. As I sat quietly, various sounds outside seemed to press in on my home from far away. Looking out again from the window, I saw the unfamiliar sight of the headlights of many trucks reflecting off the white walls of our housing compound along the Daido Daigai Road.

My husband came home. His pale face was so tense that he seemed like a different man from the one who usually stood before me. "We've got to get to the Shinkyo Station by 1:30 this morning," he said.

"What!" I cried. "Shinkyo Station?"

"We've got to evacuate by train," he said.

"Why?" I asked.

He explained the situation quickly in terse sentences. The military families of the Kanto Army were already moving. The authorities had issued an order; families of the civil servants must do the same. There was the real possibility that Shinkyo City would be engulfed in the turmoil of this war. I thought, "Did that mean the Soviets were invading the city?" Any Japanese who remained would be risking his life. We had to leave right away. Other families besides those of the meteorological station were also preparing to leave. We needed to evacuate immediately.

He said, "We've been assigned to a train. In just thirty minutes…we're supposed to leave. Hurry!" My husband instructed me as if he were ordering the troops,

"Of course, you're coming too, aren't you?" I asked. There wasn't time to argue with him any more than this. I felt that as long as we were all together we would somehow survive. I looked at his face.

"I will take you as far as the train station but I've got to stay here," he said.

"What! You're leaving me?" I was shocked. With fear and

anger rising in me—like a woman who had lost her mind—I hurled harsh words at him. As I screamed, I barely heard him say, "I still have work to do..." and something about "...as a man in my position, I can't leave without first finishing what needs to be done..." But he was overwhelmed by my anguish and stopped talking. He looked into my eyes. As I noticed my silent husband gazing at me, I realized that there was nothing I could say to change his mind. I stopped.

He put his hand on my shoulder as I crumpled in tears.

"Now hurry. Think about the children," he said.

With those words, I regained my composure. I'm a mother...a mother who has to save her children by running away. I became resolute. There was no room for crying now.

Once more, from the beginning, I organized our belongings. But with three children, how much could I carry? With just the essential things—the children's winter clothes—the bags were full. I put two-year-old Masahiko piggy-back in a sling across my back while my husband tied Sakiko, papoose-style, on top of his backpack. In both hands he carried the other bags. Masahiro was just old enough to walk, carrying his own small bag. That was how we decided to get to Shinkyo Station.

As we opened the door, the cold night air blasted our faces and took my breath away. We had the children wear as much as they could. Since I was also dressed with layers of winter clothes, the dry cold wind blowing in from the Manchurian plains felt just right. From the many vegetable plants I had in our yard, I picked a couple of tomatoes and put them in my bag. My husband kept saying, "Hurry, hurry," while I thought about how I wanted to properly pay my farewell respects to the neighbors, Mrs. Maeda and Mrs. Sato. But tonight, the six houses in our compound were dark and empty. Where did they go? I said good-bye to them silently as we walked out toward the Daido Daigai Road. As I looked back once more at our home of two years, I saw only a dark square shadow, and it looked like a pile of dirt.

Shinkyo Station was four kilometers away, straight on the Daido Daigai Road. But before we had even walked one kilometer, I was exhausted. My poor body had given birth to Sakiko just a month earlier, and I was in no condition to carry a toddler like Masahiko. I tried to catch my breath around Daido Park, but was overcome by a sadness that I have never felt before in my life. In front of us passed a truck heavily loaded with the military families and their luggage. There were parents like us who were fleeing, holding onto the hands of their small children. How could it be that just two hours earlier, my family had been living here in such peace? My husband and I had often admired the vast Manchurian night sky. Why do we now look at that same starry sight with such fear? What could a woman with children do? We passed the thickets of the park and, almost horizontally in front of us, a large shooting star flew across the sky.

I felt as if an icy blade were plunged into my chest— hopelessness bled into my body. I said, "Let's go home. If I am going to die anyway, I'd like to die at home."

My husband said nothing and kept marching. He took out his pocket watch and tried to look at it in the light of the stars. I knew he wanted me to keep walking. There were still three kilometers to go. I thought if I kept walking like this I would collapse, a body already weak from loss of blood.

"Please. Please...let's go home," I pleaded one more time. But I knew that I was making an impossible request.

CHAPTER TWO

The Separation

Shinkyo Station was a mass of people stumbling in the dark. There were supposed to be about fifty in our assigned group, the *dan*. It was a minor miracle that my husband and I found them, huddled in front of the government travel office in front of the train station.

"Good. We made it," he said.

But I didn't see anyone's face that I recognized. I collapsed, so thoroughly exhausted that I couldn't do anything. The families of the Kanto Army formed nervous lines around us that steadily snaked into the train station. We were told that our group's departure would not be until seven that morning, long after these military families left on the first trains. I spread out a single blanket on the bare dirt ground, and together with the children, curled up into a circle to sleep. The only comfort I had was the knowledge that my husband was near us until we had to leave.

An uneasiness, the unfamiliar sensation of being surrounded

by so many people, grew like a web in my brain. In my sleep, I must have breathed in the soot-filled air. A fit of coughing woke me from the desperately needed rest. It was dawn. Now we were surrounded by a crowd that had grown through the night; how did we sleep without being trampled? My husband was nowhere to be seen. As I looked for him I was relieved to see faces I knew right in front of us — Mr. Daichi and his family! Their kind, friendly faces lined up near us was reassuring. Between Mr. and Mrs. Daichi sat their teenage daughter, Seiko who hid her pretty face in her father's shoulder. Mrs. Daichi held their baby. It turned out that my husband had gone to the office to get more instructions.

The chief of our General Affairs Section, Mr. Shibata, was busy trying to organize our group. "Is Mr. Fujiwara back yet?" Mr. Shibata waited anxiously for my husband's return. By the time my husband came back, it was already past seven. Now we were told that our train would depart at nine.

"What did the director say?" Mr. Shibata impatiently asked.

My husband said, "He told us to make our own decisions on how to select the men."

The two of them moved away from me and began discussing matters in lowered voices so that I couldn't hear. But I knew they were deciding which men would accompany us on the train. By us, I mean the women and children. Four men were selected. The families of the lucky four joyfully crowded around their own husband or father.

"Who should we choose as *dancho*, to head the *dan*?" Mr. Shibata looked at my husband's face.

"Mr. Tono would be good," I distantly heard my husband say.

Mr. Shibata hesitated, then said, "Hey, Mr. Fujiwara. Why

don't you go on with this group? You've got three young children… I can explain everything personally to the director later. Even if you stayed behind with us, it's just a matter of two or three days anyway."

My husband didn't answer. I stood up unsteadily and went closer to him. "Dear…please come with us," I said.

My husband looked at me accusingly, as if to blame me for embarrassing him. "I will not go," he said very clearly to Mr. Shibata. Then he shouted so that everyone could hear, "Mr. Tono. Mr. Tono, you've been selected to head this *dan*."

I couldn't believe it. I witnessed my husband sacrifice his own family. For what? For the sake of appearance, for the sake of honor. He did what he was expected to do in his position, I suppose. Back then, all I could do was cry like an ordinary, helpless housewife. Tears poured down my face.

Night gave way to morning, and Shinkyo Station became clear in the light. The station was much more crowded than it was when we arrived in the middle of the night. Lines and lines of people formed, most of them women and children. Japanese soldiers ordered everyone about with hoarse shouts and barks. My husband brought a bundle wrapped in our large *furoshiki* cloth, the cloth I used to wrap my packages. He must have picked it up from our house on his way from the office.

"You might end up throwing this away but if this bundle stays at the house, it won't do any good there either," he said.

It was mostly clothes. In my husband's other hand hung a basket full of my freshly picked tomatoes. Seeing my fresh vegetables made me happier. As the children and I ate the sweet, juicy tomatoes, I watched my husband's eyes — red, bloodshot eyes that hadn't had any sleep at all. There was one hour left before our train was supposed to depart. It was a terrifying sixty minutes.

The motorcycle sidecar that was supposed to fetch Mrs. Tono, our *dancho's* wife, came back loaded with baggage belonging to someone, I don't know who. But Mrs. Tono was not aboard.

Mr. Shibata shouted something at Mr. Daichi. People argued, discussed, bickered. I listened distractedly, no longer capable of caring. At eight o'clock we were allowed onto the train platform. Then we were assigned to an open freight train car with the number thirty-five painted on in black and white. It wasn't a passenger car, just a freight car used to transport logs or rocks with no roof overhead, no seats.

My husband dragged us onto the car, with our children and our bags. But by the time we got on the freight car, the 'good seats' on the car floor were already taken by the nimble people. We were left with the worst spots, in the front—right where the train's steam engine would shower us with smoke and coal dust.

Mr. Shibata then called out, "All right, men, we've got to get back to the office!" They were leaving us.

My husband loved two-year-old Masahiko with a special tenderness. He was a lively little boy who looked just like his father. My husband picked him up and put his face close to his son's. He spoke using his usual paternal tone. "Masahiko-chan, remember your Daddy's face, all right? Don't forget me, all right? Do as Mommy tells you. Okay? Listen to her; listen to her well. All right?" He nuzzled Masahiko's frightened face and set him down beside me.

Then he turned to our eldest son, Masahiro, who stood in a daze. My husband knelt down, faced him, and placed his hand on his small shoulder. "Masahiro, how old are you?"

"Five," he said in a small voice.

"That's right; you're five years old. So you're old enough to understand what Daddy has to say. Listen to me carefully, Masahiro. You are going on this train with Mommy, your little brother, and the baby to a place that is far away. Daddy has to stay behind in Shinkyo. I am not going with you, so you need to do as Mommy says and be a good boy."

Masahiro obediently said, "Yes, Daddy:"

My husband then turned to look at me and simply said, "*Dewa tanomu yo* — I leave this matter in your hands," just the way he asked me when he needed me to do an ordinary task, and then he stood up. It was a man's job to be strong, not sentimental.

This might be the last time I would see my husband. The last time I would see him alive. I couldn't possibly utter the word 'good-bye' — not like this. I stood up and said gently into his ear, "Please stay alive, dear. Stay alive. Do whatever you have to do, just please stay alive." I whispered this over and over into his ear.

Without saying a word, he took out his watch from the pocket of his tailored government jacket and gave it to me. It was his precious Longines pocket watch.

"*Kodomotachi wo tanomu yo*," he said, asking me formally to take on the responsibility for the lives of our three children, a terrible burden to place in my hands, and then he turned his back to us — to get ready to jump off the train car. Just then, a small towel tucked into his waist brushed against his hand. He stopped, came back to us, took the towel out, and put it around Masahiko-chan's head and face.

"Don't let him get sunburnt. He'll get too hot." He said this without losing control over his emotions. A father worried over his son. Then without hesitation, he took a big leap off the freight car and lightly landed on the station platform. He ran to catch up with the other men.

Long after I lost sight of him in the crowd, I kept looking and looking, hoping that he would reappear. The cold Manchurian wind penetrated me, and sliced my heart.

CHAPTER THREE

The Open Freight Car

When I leaned against the outer railing of the train car and held completely still, loneliness pushed up against me, then engulfed me like a huge, dark ocean wave. I had just lost that one person I could lean on, my husband. Now how was I going to survive? As I thought about this, I couldn't stay still any longer. I looked around me.

Dancho Tono waited to see if his wife would make it in time. He stood up and looked anxiously into the frightened crowd on the train platform. She was nowhere to be seen. At ten, the train started moving. I was relieved. At least, something was happening. I thought, "That's good, the train will keep moving, keep going all the way to my homeland, Japan..." Japan? How silly I was! How childish. As the train started moving everyone turned back toward the station and started waving their hands. I knew that my husband was gone. He wouldn't be standing on the platform anymore. But along with everyone else, I started waving a handkerchief at the crowd remaining on the platform. A throng of faces—all turned toward us but not a single familiar person—no friends or anyone I recognized.

Somebody cried out, "*Shinkyo sayonara*, Good-bye, Shinkyo!" I wondered what the person who shouted that was feeling. I felt empty, devoid of emotions.

My children. As the train moved forward I thought, how can I keep the smoke, the flying soot and cinders from smothering them? Both of the boys, Masahiro and Masahiko, were exhausted. Unlike their usual selves, the two boys just sat there silently, in a daze. Baby Sakiko slept, her tiny face nestled in the sling against my body. How could I protect her against the coal dust? I tried to take Masahiko's hand towel to cover her face. He suddenly broke out of his trance and pulled back with unexpected strength on the towel. He cried, "No, don't!" He cried out so piteously that I let the towel go. Masahiko blinked his round eyes, fighting back his tears, and held on tight to the towel that his father had draped around his head.

"Poor child. Let him hold onto that small token of his father's love a little longer," I thought. So I opened the rucksack and found a dry cotton diaper that I pulled out and placed over the baby's face. Without warning, my tears came. I turned my face toward the wooden wall of the train to hide. I cried and cried. I was not alone in my grief. A number of the wives wailed and joined me in sorrowful chorus.

I closed my eyes. In my mind, I took myself back to the life we had before last night. Our cozy brick house—the home we enjoyed until only yesterday. From the second floor I looked out to the yard where I had planted vegetables; the sight calmed and soothed me. The rocking and swaying of the train receded into a faint backdrop. This train was just a dream. I wanted to wake up from this nightmare. Oh, don't forget! There was a little red kimono I made for Sakiko up on the top shelf of the closet. I wanted to try it on Sakiko once. My precious baby daughter was sleeping peacefully under the south window. How strong was that sensation that Sakiko was still sleeping upstairs...

Suddenly I was jolted out of my vision. Sakiko hadn't been fed since yesterday. My breast milk had stopped since last night, since the nightmare began. "My baby will surely die," I thought, "if I can't feed her." My tears started again.

Dancho Tono stood up and announced, "Attention, everyone, please." His voice pierced my aching head. He spoke formally and introduced himself as *dancho*—our formal group leader, "Let's call our group the Meteorological Station *dan*. As your *dancho*, I will be honored to accompany you all." He bowed formally to us.

The wind chopped up *Dancho* Tono's voice. I strained to hear his words "...rules for our group...must stay together...take care of those with many children...do not not wander off on your own, check with me before leaving the group..." *Dancho* Tono's thick eyebrows twitched with concentration as he gave his directives.

As the morning turned into midday, August reared its ugly head. Beneath the burning hot sun, people began to dry up and — just like vegetables, they sought shade and water.

The children began to incessantly demand water from me. From time to time the train stopped at a small station and, with Sakiko in my sling and a canteen in my hand, I got off the train to try to get water, but always, strong men and women pushed in front of me.

Miserably, I returned to the train empty-handed. But even

more troubling was washing the baby's soiled diapers. If it looked like the train would stop for a while, I tried to rinse out the diapers at the station's water pump. But as I stood in line, with my baby and the diapers, men shouted at me, "Don't do anything dirty near the pump!" as they carried buckets of water back to the train. Finally I found a small fetid, foul-smelling pool near the station and hurriedly tried to clean the diapers in the blue-black muddy water.

When I got back to the train, my two thirsty boys cried, "Mommy, did you get water?" I didn't know what to say to them.

"I'm so sorry. I couldn't get any." Saying this, I sat back in my seat, and looked reproachfully at the hot sky with a sigh.

Suddenly, I noticed a young couple, seated a few rows in front of us. They poured water out of a full jug into a pan. The splash of water sounded heavenly. The young man grunted with effort as he lifted the heavy pan. "He'll share that water with us," I thought hopefully. But then he put the pan in front of a round-faced woman sitting next to them.

"I've never washed my face in a cooking pan," the round-faced woman joked to the young man as she put both hands into the pan and began splashing water onto her face. Then without any hesitation, they threw the water off the side of the train.

When the train stopped at a larger station, a group of the Japanese Wives Association brought in dozens of *onigiri* (seasoned rice rolled into serving-size balls). They also gave us stewed acorn squash. The children were delighted and ate with gusto. But I was so terrified they would ask me for water afterwards that I had no appetite at all. I just thought, "Were these women feeding the refugees on each train—every train as it came through from where we came? Why don't they save themselves while they could?" No one knew anymore what would happen to us or Japan.

As we left Hoten, the sun was in the west. And for the first time that day, I saw the shadow of our train on the side of the tracks. Then I remembered. Hoten was the train station where we first arrived here, in April of 1943. My husband was transferred here from Japan. We had come from so far away, but I remembered Hoten as a much more beautiful and quiet train station back then. At that time, Masahiro was our only child. Now I thought, "Here I am again. At this station. An exhausted mother with three children riding on a open freight car — where are we going this time?"

We were all afraid. Where are we going? Where could we escape? Rumors spread among the panicked passengers. We would go east to Tsuka — but that turned out to be untrue. Would we go straight south from Sokato, or would we double back then go south? Would we go west to Tairen or go towards Korea? The train had come to a point where someone would have to make a decision. I was too tired to care which way we went. I leaned my back against the wall and closed my eyes. Then someone said it was decided. We would go south to Anton and then on to Korea.

"Oh, what a beautiful sunset," said a woman who was standing near me. I raised up my head. The huge sky was filled with spectacular shades of red and orange and purple. Our first night arrived. I gathered the children as close to me as I could, and tried to go to sleep. We were alone. Countless stars began to emerge in the darkening sky, and they remained fixed in their places, unlike us. How small I felt beneath that massive dome.

When I woke up, the train had stopped, and dawn was on the horizon. We were at a station called Renzankan. As far as I could see, green fields of maize lay under a thick layer of mist, flat as a blanket on top. The train started moving again as the sun rose. It would be another hot day like yesterday. But compared to the day before, I had a little more energy. If my children and I were to survive, I knew I had to change. I wasn't afraid to be more pushy anymore. I got better at haggling and managed to get water, some melons, and tomatoes. I nursed Sakiko. At Ryu-kaga there was rain which drenched our clothes. I busily wrung out the sopping wet things, laid them out to dry around us, and somehow, someway the four of us got through another day. By the time the clouds clustered on the horizon and turned purple, our train neared the border.

The men gathered together in the middle of the car and began discussing something. They appeared to have made a decision. *Dancho* Tono turned to everyone and said, "Soon the train will pass through Hojo. We've thought of a way to send a message back to Shinkyo. The Hojo Meteorlogical Station is located right next to the railroad — so when our train goes by, let's all raise our voices to let them know we've gotten on the train. Then they can send a telegram back to Shinkyo for us — to let them know we've made it this far."

I suddenly stood up with renewed energy like a rescued woman. My husband must be still in Shinkyo, so worried about us. This was the one line of communication I had left with him. I grabbed one of the drying white diapers to wave, and stood with everyone on the side of the train car.

Soon we saw the red building of the meteorological station. The familiar weather monitoring devices on the rooftop. But our train was moving so fast. We would pass this little station too quickly. The steam from our train glittered in the setting sun and looked beautiful.

When our train was less than fifty meters from the weather station building, we all faced the building and yelled as loudly as we could. "*Oooi, Kanshoo-jo, oooi, kansho-jo!* Hey - Weather Station, Weather Station!" we called out to the people in the building. But no one came out of the building. We couldn't tell if anyone was there or not. Just as we gave up, I saw the four metal cups of the *Robinson* anemometer gaily spin round and round, as if to mock me. I was so angry. What's the use?

As I sat down, full of disappointment, another night arrived. We didn't know where we were going. We were frightened people with only uncertainty ahead. Then the train started making a loud "goro-goro" sound, the sound of metal wheels going across the long steel bridge which spanned the Ooryoko River. We entered northern Korea.

The people in the train started talking excitedly, "We'll stop soon and reach our final destination." But there was no sign that was happening. The train kept going on and on.

Just as I had done the night before, I sat up, lost in my world without time or place, and not sure if I was asleep or awake, when the train stopped at a station, one that was larger than most. The sign said "Nanshi." While the train stopped, the men representing every *dan* jumped down from each car, and joined together to talk. We were then told for the first time that the final destination would be—Sensen. We wondered, "Sensen, Sensen, what sort of a town is Sensen?" What would be waiting for us there? We started to get ready to get off the train. All I could think about was how I desperately wanted to sleep.

CHAPTER FOUR

The Day the War Ended

I woke up early and found myself lying on the cold floorboards of a cement building, on the edge of town where we arrived the night before. I lifted my head, so as not to wake the children, and tried to see where we were. Everyone was fast asleep—dressed as they were when we all collapsed upon arrival. The morning sun shone on the children and intensified their ghastly faces, white with fatigue beneath ugly streaks of coal dust.

Sensen Agricultural School took us in to join about three hundred Japanese refugees already here—mostly women and children. As the sleep slowly dissolved from my eyes, my first thought was, "I must wash Sakiko's diapers."

I slowly rose from beneath the single blanket that covered us, unwrapping my arms from around my three children, who remained asleep. I crept outside and after going up a little ways on a dew-covered farm road, I found a clear small stream and followed it up into the middle of the woods where a beautiful western-style red brick-building stood. When I went past the front of the building, a lovely view suddenly appeared.

It was a pretty town. More sturdy western-style buildings, perhaps a school or a library stood next to what looked like a church tower. Below that, several neat dwellings lined up, all of them still dark in the thin morning light. Mountains embraced this valley while a river ran through the middle of a town laid out in a square. A single lonely train track crossed the river, then wound around and disappeared into the mountains.

Behind our refuge, this school where we slept, the men were building a simple kitchen. They had set up a cook stove, a place to put the pots, and a communal serving area. Later that day they prepared a mixture of half soybeans with half white rice and made *onigiri* to distribute twice a day. But the soybeans must have gone bad. After eating, almost all the children got upset stomachs, and most of the adults ended up with a most unpleasant diarrhea.

A cow looked up at me in curiosity. Thank goodness, there was a cow at the agricultural school. Those of us nursing babies each received a small portion of her milk. We mothers were helped a great deal by this cow, but there were so many of us that the milk was not nearly enough. Those whose breasts stopped making milk became desperate as their babies became weaker and weaker.

Once we settled in, I dragged myself several times a day to the river to do the laundry. Sometimes I heard planes flying overhead and each time, I followed the contrails and wondered, "What will happen to us?"

On August 14th, around noon, a single plane began circling high in the sky. "There must be some good news," we fervently hoped, and rushed outside to wave at the plane. As if to answer our signal, the plane scattered handbills. But they only contained a message from a senior officer of the Japanese Kanto Army asking, "Where are our families?" They only care about their own.

August 15th was a clear day. I was carrying Masahiko on my back, sitting under the poplar trees when — suddenly — bells started pealing. I could hear the footsteps of the agricultural school students as they gathered in their school yard. There must have been four or five hundred of them. A bald man we recognized as the headmaster stepped up to the speaker's platform. I watched and waited for something to begin.

Then the headmaster waved his right arm at me, as if to tell me to go inside the school building. I looked around to see who he had waved at. There was no one behind me. He waved his hand again in big movements. I gave up on my day's excursion and began slowly climbing up the hill back to our building.

Then suddenly, like a wave coming towards me, I heard strange sounds. I turned around and those sounds quickly became cries and moans. A male student with a white shirt and crewcut cried so sharply that icy shivers went up my spine. Without any further thought, I hurried back to our schoolroom. Something must have happened.

That was when I first heard the news. "The war is over," announced *Dancho* Tono, his face pale and drained. As I watched his tears drop one by one to the ground, our nerves stretched to the breaking point. One woman burst into hysterical wails. Her cries sparked all of us. So many times, I wept since leaving Shinkyo. As I began to cry this time, I thought, "Where is my husband? Where is he hearing this news?"

Another fear quickly grew amongst us. "Would we all die now? What is going to happen to us?" Japan was defeated. Our world was coming to an end and something catastrophic would happen very soon. The evening of the fifteenth we prepared to flee as quickly as possible. Terrors of the worst kind filled our imagination. I sat with Sakiko strapped onto my back. If we had to run then I'd throw away everything I had in my pitiable rucksack. I took out the Longine watch my husband gave me and looked at it in the moonlight—it was past midnight. I had Masahiro and Masahiko go to sleep with their white cotton shoes on, ready to run at a moment's notice. I watched their restless legs tangle together, then untangle as they slept.

The wait for morning was exhausting. I was stiff from sitting up for so long with the baby on my back. When dawn finally arrived, we were so frightened, our own shadows spooked us. But nothing happened. While the boys slept, I got up. Severe diarrhea sapped me of any strength I had left. But I continued, dragging myself up through a thick fog to wash the diapers.

Outside the school, crowds of Koreans passed by, they waved flags, and there was a festive mood flowing about the town. They were celebrating the end of Japanese rule. We felt nervous and uneasy for the rest of the day, especially when all the *dancho* ordered us to stay inside. The children and I huddled quietly in the classroom.

As the hours ticked by, we grew hungry. A few bold women from our group ventured out to climb the hill beyond out building where cornfields and apple orchards lay. They managed to get food from nearby people. But I was so afraid, too afraid to do as they did, so I watched them with envy as they came and went. I had money, but since I couldn't go out, I tried to satisfy the children's hunger by feeding them strings of lies.

When I separated from my husband, I had a three thousand

yen certificate from the Bank of Manchuria and my post office savings book. But in this town, the Manchurian money was useless. I had managed to get to the post office once to get Korean bank certificates. Using them, I bought a few vegetables from the town market. But living in a group like this, there was little tolerance for individuals. When I approached our common cooking area to try to cook our own food, the men yelled at me and drove me off. I had no choice but to give up.

All four of us had diarrhea. Masahiro, my oldest, and I had it the worst. I knew we needed to eat *okayu* — rice gruel — but we didn't have any. From the window I saw the Japanese Kanto Army families, their strong men, stripped to the waist, mixing big pots filled with *okayu* and good-smelling soup. The military families had a lot of supplies and we saw their storage containers filled with canned food, sugar, and various other items.

I envied them as they ate and enjoyed their food. It became obvious that those of us in the Meteorological Station *dan* were the poorest of the Japanese refugees here at the school. Why had our group not saved as many supplies? Why were we so poorly treated? I wondered. My husband was one of those who were treated as second-class citizens by the Japanese military authorities.

My life was soon reduced to walking a small triangle — from the corner of our room to the toilet, and then from the toilet to the small stream at the top of the hill where I washed the diapers, and then back to our corner. Back and forth. Back and forth. My diarrhea worsened. Then as Masahiro's fever rose, he could no longer walk. I put him on my back and carried him along that triangle over and over.

In the toilet, I tried to check to see if there was blood in our stool, but the others waiting in line behind us complained for us to hurry, so I rushed out with Masahiro's feverish, limp body in my arms. When we returned to our 'home,' I found Masahiko and Sakiko bawling, and the neighbors glared at me. Their eyes burned white-hot with hate as they wallowed in their own misery. I stopped talking to anyone the whole day. I scolded the children to be quiet and swallowed the bitter phlegm in my throat. As diarrhea tortured my body, walls of agony closed in on me, and the fever burned away everything in my mind. Everything except the desire to go home. The desire to go home and thoughts of my husband.

CHAPTER FIVE

Meeting My Husband Again

It was very late at night on August 15th, when there was a sudden commotion at the front gates of the school. I had already put Masahiko and Sakiko to bed, and was still up mending the split seams on their clothes when I heard loud voices. I put my sewing down and crept down towards the front door to see what was going on.

"They're from the meteorological station," one of the women said as they stood in the hallway. I gasped and hurried into the entryway. Beneath a dim light, I saw several men. Among them, I immediately recognized Mr. Narita, a meteorologist from my husband's office. I ran about looking, "Where is my husband?" But I didn't see him. I sank with bitter disappointment against the metal bannister. As if I had lost any will to live, I just stared at the faces of the men from our meteorological station as they lowered their rucksacks to let people see what they brought. Then suddenly, Masahiro, my eldest, said in a strange voice, "There's Daddy!"

I jerked awake and looked where Masahiro was pointing. My husband was separate from the other men—he kneeled at a table—surrounded by a crowd, and was writing something. When he finished writing, he talked with the *Hoantai*, the Korean police who had brought our men. I grabbed Masahiro and crumpled to the ground in tears.

There were eight men who returned to us that night. With these men, now there were eleven families restored, made whole again. But six men did not return—their families sat desolate as the rest of us rejoiced. I touched my husband's rucksack and asked if I could take it. He shrugged as if he didn't care. "Go ahead," he said. There was a mountain of things for us to talk about, but when we took his bag to our 'home' in the classroom, he gently touched the cheeks of our sleeping children, Masahiko and Sakiko. Then he laughed, and took out a wrapped present for Masahiro. He started to go talk with *Dancho* Tono, to catch up, and I stopped him to say, "Be sure to thank *Dancho* Tono. He's been a good leader despite his missing wife.

He nodded his head, again surveyed my 'home,' our family's sleeping area on the school room floor, and strode over to *Dancho* Tono and they talked quietly for some time.

I was delighted as I went through my husband's bag. He brought a new blanket for us! And his winter underwear. I was so happy with the thought that we would sleep under a warm blanket that night. Happy families here and there laughed and talked late into the night. But I noticed the six families left out of the happy reunions. They sat apart from us—dejected and silent. I waited for my husband to come sit by my side. I was so happy and relieved, and repeated to myself, "My husband is back." I wanted to chatter about everything—all my complaints, my worries.

Although I knew I would sound silly, I didn't care anymore. "I can talk with him." I pulled out the Longines watch I kept in my clothes to show him.

"See. I still have it," I proudly said. The pocket watch swung on a heavy black silk rope. He took the watch and put it up against his ear to listen, to drink in its nostalgic ticking. When I tried to untie the watch to give it back to him, he refused. But that watch didn't mean anything to me now that I had my husband's breathing to replace its sound. The hands of the Longines pointed to two a.m.

I think my husband hadn't expected to ever see us again. In his bag, there were no clothes for the children or me, but I found a small square package wrapped in cloth. Out of the cloth, photos fell out. He had taken them out of our photo albums. Photos from our wedding, photos of the children, about ten photos in all, carefully tucked away.

That night, as soon as he curled his body around the children, he fell asleep. Grateful for the warm blanket that he had brought, I silently thanked the universe before I lay myself down on the other side of the children. His sunburnt face glowed in the moonlight shining through the window. After I gently lifted my side of the blanket to slip in next to the children, I fell into a deep sleep, so deep it felt like several nights rolled into one.

CHAPTER SIX

Shall We Go South?

I couldn't rouse myself out of bed the next morning, maybe because I was too drunk with happiness — my husband was back. I
didn't want to get up. I wanted to let him take care of me again —
to *amaeru* – that delicious feeling of losing myself in him. I was
so happy that I could relax, even a little. But two days after he
arrived, there was a change in our group. *Dancho* Tono learned
his missing wife was in Chinnanbo, a town further south, and he
decided to leave our group to go find her.

Who is going to be our next *dancho*? This was wartime and
we couldn't depend on the usual procedures we followed for this
sort of thing. They would probably select someone based on a
his former job. Out of the eleven men, the ones most likely to be
chosen were Mr. Narita and my husband In addition to these
two, there was Mr. Oe who was ten years older and used to be
a manager. So there were three candidates. Watching the eleven
men seated in a circle in the middle of the room, intently talking, it
looked like the *dancho* job was going to be handed to my husband,

but I prayed that he would turn the job down.

Mr. Narita was a weak, scholarly man and I dismissed him, thinking, "He's not much use in this situation." Next they talked about my husband. I was worried sick that he would end up with the job because I knew my children and I would end up secondary to any *dancho* responsibilities. They kept talking through the morning but still hadn't made a decision yet. When my husband came back to talk with me during their break, I told him to not accept this job, "Never!" He didn't say anything but just nodded.

In the afternoon, it was decided. The new *dancho* would be Mr. Oe, who was older and known for being a tough boss. Next in line—*fuku dancho,* the assistant head, would be my husband. I was uneasy but grateful that he wasn't picked to be the *dancho*. *Dancho* Oe and *fuku-dancho,* my husband, they were announced to the other Japanese.

Everyday at one p.m. representatives from all the refugee *dan* met at an elementary school in the center of town. When *Dancho* Oe and my husband, the *fuku-dancho,* got back from these meetings, we gathered round to hear the latest news. But who knew if the information was really reliable or not. I thought a lot of it was gossip, or just more propaganda from the government. I waited anxiously for my husband to get back because he sometimes managed to pick up some apples or Korean rice cakes on the way back.

The information from these meetings made everyone uneasy. There was always talk of something terrible about to happen to the Japanese—the hated former colonizers of Korea. More and more Japanese fled south when the trains began to run as they did before. I thought we should take the chance, too, and go to Jinsen in southern Korea, rather than stay here northern Korea with people I didn't know. The former head of the meteorological station, Mr. Wadachi, his wife and others would be down south.

I had the feeling that if we could somehow get to Jinsen, we could escape this terrible situation. "Now. Now, we should go south," I urged my husband. When he was extremely worried, a deep wrinkle would appear between his thick eyebrows. He said, "But what about the other families who get left behind?"

"But in this situation, we don't have the luxury of thinking about other families," I said.

"That's just your selfish logic," he shot back. "It's true that if we go south, we would be saved. At Jinsen, there's not just Mr. Wadachi, there are a lot of people I know from the Korean meteorological station. That's true that we would be better off than we are now. But, who's going to help these other families get home?"

"What are you saying? There's a great *dancho* here, and there are a lot of older men who could do the job," I said.

"You don't understand," he said. My husband became very serious.

Did he intend to endanger the lives of all five members of our family and have us stay in this dangerous place? All because of his sense of responsibility, his devotion to other Japanese refugees, and his willingness to meddle in their problems?

I told him, "Times have changed. The meteorological station is gone. And you are not a manager of a section. You have no department. If there's any connection, it's just the people who were civil servants, who were in the same bureau. Why should your freedom be held hostage by forty-nine strangers? How is that a reason for staying behind?"

I ignored Mr. and Mrs. Mizushima who sat next us. Mr. Mizushima wiped his glasses, but he was obviously listening in on our fight. I pressed my husband even harder. But he dug in his heels, and ignored my pleas. "The section chief, Mr. Taya, asked me to look after these people. If I go now, this *dan* will become a mess," he said.

My husband's idiocy, as he went on and on about his duty and his obligations finally got to me. I shouted, "You're just thinking about yourself. You have a twisted, one-sided prejudice against your own family. Stupid ideas about your own superiority and sense of justice are all you care about!"

"What? Superiority?" he angrily sputtered.

I shot back, "That's right. I don't know what Mr. Taya said to you but you've gotten so full of yourself, you think you are the only honorable person here. I'm sick of your thinking. Do whatever the hell you want," and I turned away from him.

Out of the corner of my eye, I saw Mrs. Mizushima cover her mouth. She trembled and clung to her husband as I spit out my words. My husband didn't try to argue. He finished his dinner quickly and gazed at the group as everyone got ready for bed. His eyes focused on two or three families in particular, those with children. The Mizushima's leaned their heads close together, to gossip about our fight, no doubt. From time to time, they glanced back at us. My husband finally noticed them.

"I'll think about it tonight," he said.

After that he didn't say a single word.

When he ended his silence the next day, he began talking with *Dancho* Oe about going south. They decided that those who wanted to go south should be allowed to do so. He said, "Let's ask everyone what they want to do." At the next group meeting, the idea of going south was brought up. Many were pessimistic. They said, "The more we move, the more dangerous it will be. If we just stay where we are for another month, we can go back to Japan with those from the north." There were many who believed this nonsense.

We devoted the day to deciding what the *dan* should do but the discussions just went around in circles, with no end in sight when we went to sleep that night. The next day, the *dan* still couldn't reach an agreement and I grew irritated with all the waffling. The morning of the third day, my husband made an announcement to everyone. "Not as your *fuku-dancho,* but as an individual and a family man, I've decided to go south. If anyone else wants to come with us — we leave tonight." After saying that, we began preparations to leave. Then the people who were so opposed to him suddenly changed their minds and began preparations themselves. Soon everyone joined in the preparations.

Mr. Kimoto and another man ran to the train station to check on the departure times. One man told us a train would leave at 6 p.m. that day. But as we hurriedly packed, Mr. Kimoto came running back from the train station and said, "Mr. Fujiwara, it's no good. Starting today, the trains are not allowed further than Heijyo, in northern Korea, which is only a little ways south of us."

I felt that whatever we decided to do was going to determine our fates. (I think this was August twenty-fourth.) They said the 38th Parallel was closed and trains would no longer be allowed through. We stopped packing and were stunned into silence. My husband remained quiet and gazed out toward the eastern sky for a long time.

CHAPTER SEVEN

A New Worry

When it looked like we couldn't get through to southern Korea on the train, there was talk of going back north. Some, like the Manchurian Railroad people, tough Japanese engineers who lived in Manchuria for many years, thought that once the Soviets finished their rampage, the situation would be better up north than it was down here in northern Korea, surrounded by angry locals. Many of these people did go back but there were a few of us who still thought it would be better to somehow get through the 38th Parallel before they closed it down completely.

As it became clear we had to move somewhere, I cut up our blanket and made coats for Masahiro and Masahiko. The uncertain days passed into September. Our *dan* was ordered to leave the Agricultural School and move into an empty house on top of the hill outside town. We stuffed the bags of forty-nine people onto two ox-carts we borrowed from the school. We avoided the middle of town where we might run into Koreans eager for revenge, and instead walked around the village to the hill. But it was soon obvious that we wouldn't be able to get the two ox-carts up the hill.

We collected our bags off the carts and carried them up. The house at the top had a small wooden sign, "Sensen *samusho*," a reminder of its past life as a Japanese *shinto* shrine, one of many built by the occupying Japanese government. The shrine itself had been burnt down recently, perhaps by an angry mob celebrating the end of the Japanese occupation. But the residential building next door had miraculously escaped the fire. This house had Japanese *tatami*, rice straw mats laid inside. How nostalgic! There was nothing else inside. The thought of sleeping on comfortable *tatami* mats made us feel safer. Beyond the remains of the *shinto* shrine, a mountain range rose into view.

In terms of size, the house contained an eight *tatami* mat size room, two six mat rooms, and two small four-and-a-half mat size rooms. Our group divided up into these five rooms. There was a kitchen and two toilets. Although the pump didn't flow very well because we were at the top of a hill, if we left a bucket under the pump for the night, by morning there was a good amount of water in the bucket.

At night we saw the lights of the town below. Sometimes we even heard sounds from the town. But besides that, we had an interesting view. We saw below us everyday, open train cars going south overloaded with people. Mostly Koreans passengers, but we still wondered, "When can we go home to Japan?" As we obsessively wondered what to do, whenever we saw anyone on the trains who looked Japanese—we asked ourselves, "Has the *hikiage* repatriation started?"

After seeing some Japanese on the trains, my husband went to see if he could verify who and from where these Japanese might be. We felt better sleeping on *tatami* mats, outside of town and although we were a group of forty-nine strangers, it was refreshing to hear the sound of laughter from time to time.

We were fortunate to find a large number of *futon* quilts left behind by other Japanese who had already left. Many of these *futon* were wet and half rotted but when we dried them out, some of them could be restored back to decent shape. I took two of the quilts and used them for our bed. Around our house on the hill, wild white chrysanthemums blossomed with a few yellow ones scattered amongst them.

Our children regained their strength. Avoiding the main roads, the men went to town everyday to buy food. They bought back something that looked like *hoshi-zakana* dried fish and some *hango*, small metal pots for cooking. We cooked vegetables and fish. We bought and baked sweet potatoes, roasted corn and ate. My breasts swelled and I nursed Sakiko once again. We even talked about daily life, mundane things like, "Three ears of corn for one yen. That's cheap…or that's too expensive." Using wood we picked up on the mountain, we cooked the food and felt good.

We were seventeen families, almost fifty people all together, in the five rooms. Living so close together, we had a new worry. Where to keep our money? We decided to hide our money tucked in empty cans — near the roots of trees, under rocks. Each family hid their money, not only from outsiders, but also from the other members of the *dan*. There had already been several thefts. My husband and I decided to divide our money into three parts, and to hide it outside and inside.

Everyone had to contribute to a pool of money to cover group expenses. It was frightening to think what would happen if someone inevitably ran out of money, and could no longer contribute their share. I wondered, "Would the rest of the *dan* look after the impoverished members?" I tried not to think of that. For now, we depended on the money from Manchuria. Later, we might go our separate ways but for now, we had to live together.

Once every ten days, we withdrew our Manchurian money and exchanged it for Korean bank certificates. One hundred yen became fifty yen. Japanese money was no longer accepted and we were running out of funds. The men went out to work everyday, doing anything to earn a little money. My husband got up early and come back late, exhausted after a full day of manual labor, but all I could offer him at the end of the day was one ear of corn or maybe an apple.

CHAPTER EIGHT

Corn Husks

That day my husband was working at a mountain three *ri* away (about seven miles). We women had finished washing clothes at the river at the bottom of the hill, and were on our way back when I saw a group of Korean men digging about. They were close to the spot where I buried some of our money. From the window at our sleeping area, our money was hidden beside a far rock, next to the third deciduous tree. But now a man in a hunting cap came up the hill, and as he dug here and there with a small shovel, he approached that tree.

Mrs. Daichi who was standing nearby said to me, "*Okusan* (Ma'am), he's about to dig up your money!"

I shushed her to be quiet and held my breath. That man dug around the roots of a tree below my tree. He stepped closer to my 'safe'. I couldn't help myself and let out a small cry, "Ahh." He stopped, rested his arm on his shovel, and looked up at us. At the same time, there was a loud noise from nearby, and a large rock came rolling down. Underneath that rock, a small can appeared.

"Oh, no. Someone's money's been discovered," we all knew. The man with the hunting cap shifted his body and turned around to look. Maybe he thought that newly discovered place was more promising. In any case, he rushed over to that area, away from my 'safe'. Several men focused their attention on that rock and began digging around its former resting place. They were obviously thieves but there was nothing we could do about it. We were just refugees, and could only helplessly watch.

Then a whistling sound drifted up from below. Somebody from the *Hoantai,* the local Korean police, came up the hill on a horse. Thank goodness. The thieves quickly disappeared. But Mrs. Sakiyama's money was gone. In our group, she was probably the worst off or close to it. Her husband never returned, she was pregnant, and she had two young boys to care for. Of course, I hoped that wasn't all of her money. I assumed she did what we all did. Divide the money into at least three parts before hiding it. Mrs. Sakiyama was usually morose but it was still terrible to see how she tried to hide her anguish. She refused to be comforted as she stood alone in her pain. I was relieved my money was still safe. I glanced at Mrs. Daichi and thought, "Wait a minute! How did she know my money was hidden there?"

I asked her, "Mrs. Daichi, how did you know my money was there?"

She smiled and said, "Oh, I'm not the only one. Everyone knows."

The morning my husband and I hid our money, the fog was thick. We did it at mealtime when everyone was eating, I went to my room and was the lookout while my husband went to bury the money. I didn't notice anyone outside of the house. "How did everyone know where our money was?" Now I was frightened.

I quickly ran to the bushes, dug up the spot, and checked our 'safe.' Although it stunk of dirt, none of the money was missing. It was wrapped in paper and tucked inside the bottom of the *hango*. I had carried it with my husband's meal sitting on top and felt safe.

I sat staring at the *hango*, until my husband got home that night. Hiding the money in the house was dangerous. But hiding the money outside was dangerous, too. What could I do? Sewing a hundred yen bill in the seam of our clothes, in the collars, or inside the *obi* waist band, was too obvious — everyone knew about those hiding places. My husband and I continued to think about this problem everyday. He was so deep in thought that he no longer chatted with me.

One morning, during breakfast, he stopped eating. He was looking something outside through the window.

I said, "What are you looking at?"

There was only a corn husk someone had thrown away. When he was about to leave to work, he said to me in a low voice, "I figured out a way. I want you to collect as many corn husks as you can, and dry them."

"What are you going to do?" I said.

"I'm going to make *zori* sandals tonight," he said.

He must have some plan, I thought and did as he asked. I collected and dried corn husks all day. From that night, he started making *zori* sandals. He learned how to make them from Mr. Nagasu, a large, older man who came from a farming family.

Mr. Nagasu was curious. "Mr. Fujiwara, why use corn husks to make *zori*?" Traditionally, they were made of rice stalks.

"I did some research on this," my husband said. "Corn husks contain oil and on top of that, they have very strong fibers. They make stronger *zori* than rice stalks. And did you know that even if they get wet, they won't get soaked?" Saying such nonsense, my husband managed to deflect Mr. Nagasu's suspicions. My husband's first attempts were odd shaped *zori*, and Mr. and Mrs. Nagasu laughed at him because they looked so strange, but he didn't seem to mind. It was late when he got to the third pair, working all alone. Each man took a turn as night watch. That night, my husband took the first night shift and worked on his *zori* sandals. He made four pairs with the corn husks. He hid hundred yen and ten yen notes, folded into tiny strips inside the corn husks—altogether about a thousand yen for emergencies. I was impressed at his cleverness. "Not bad," I said to myself.

As he instructed me, I wore those *zori*, got them dirty and kept them along with the children's shoes, next to our rucksack.

And there was also my husband's precious Longines watch. We hid that, too. This was another good idea. I carved a hole in a large bar of laundry soap, then wrapped the watch in paraffin wax and placed it inside the hole. From another bar of soap, I carved out a chunk of soap to seal the hole. After carefully filling in the cracks with soap flakes, I warmed the soap bar. As far as anyone could tell, we had an ordinary bar of laundry soap—with a watch inside! I even dipped it in water and used it a few times to show everyone it was just soap. The corners were all rounded and smooth and I kept it inside a can. In these clever ways, we kept our valuables safe.

After we put these 'safes' together, I was relieved. No one seemed to notice what we did.

CHAPTER NINE

Where is My Husband Going?

In the yard there was a single small maple tree. This tree was in the shape of a sideways letter V and from the top, three branches sprouted from the same place. It was October when these maple leaves turned. We had to wear socks to bed, otherwise our cold feet woke us in the middle of the night, but the afternoons were still warm.

As I hung diapers to dry on the tree, I heard something. When I looked up, an airplane, one with markings that I had never seen before, flew north. A Korean man asked quietly, "Is Mr. Daichi here?"

I turned around to see the train station master standing there, half-smiling. Most of us didn't know what was happening in the war but Mr. Daichi found a source. On his daily walks, he became friends with this Korean station master. I wasn't surprised. Mr. Daichi was good with people—making anyone feel at ease. Every evening, he snuck down the hill and listened to the station master's radio and heard all sorts of news. This is where we heard:

the *hikiage*, the repatriation would begin in November.

I showed the station master up the hill to Mr. Daichi and, felt anxious — is there something new going on? By coincidence, I heard the same news about the November *hikiage* through my husband's distant relatives, an elderly couple who lived nearby, called Old Man Gomi and his wife. He used to be an elementary school teacher in northern Korea. They lived in a small place and started quietly bringing us things (mostly old magazines, paper and other useful things).

Around October 20th, Old Man Gomi came around and told us he heard through another Japanese group that the *hikiage* would be in November. "If it's possible, I wanted to ask if we could be included, to go home," he said. My husband tried to find out where that rumor came from but Old Man Gomi didn't know. Maybe it started with the station master's information? Old Man Gomi laughed and went back down the hill.

Around October 25th, there was more activity in the town and more trains started coming and going. Our hearts beat with excitement — maybe we could go home to Japan! When the men returned that night, sounds of laughter filled with hope floated through every room. The next day, we started preparing candy and other portable food. But, other than trains passing through the station, three or more times a day, nothing happened.

A gentle knock on the front door woke us from a deep sleep on the morning of October 28th. It was Mr. Daichi's friend, the station master again, but this time he asked for *Dancho* Oe and my husband to come outside together with Mr. Daichi. I felt uneasy. In every room, everyone woke up and we all quietly waited for the three men to return.

When they came back, I saw their faces were ashen, like those of the dead. I wondered, "What happened?" but our three men only said, "Hurry. Make breakfast," and went into the small room to discuss something in private. When my husband came out to get a piece of paper, I asked him, "What's going on?"

"I'll make an announcement soon — just get things ready," he said and rushed back to *Dancho* Oe and Mr. Daichi.

"Get ready for what?" I called out, but he didn't answer me.

When I went outside, an early-morning fog completely covered the town. It was eerie to hear all sorts of sounds — children crying, things being moved — through the thick grey mist. Then from the school below us, I heard the shouting of men. All I could do was pace back and forth. "Get ready? How?" I thought, but I did as he asked and repacked all of our things.

Sounds of a horse climbing our hill were followed by the appearance of a man from the *Hoantai* Korean Police. He asked for our *dancho* to come right away. I couldn't see where *Dancho* Oe and my husband went. Worried, I went out to wait. Out of the thick fog, my husband came back holding one of our 'safes', the tin can with emergency money. He hurriedly pulled out the money that was in the can.

"All Japanese men between the ages of eighteen and forty are to go to Heijo by train," he said. "I've got some money for myself. I'm giving the rest to you."

"What are you going to do at Heijo?" I asked.

"I don't know. We might be sent to Siberia," he said.

"Siberia?" I didn't know what to say. The world was ending. Clutching the money wrapped in paper my husband gave me, I sank to the ground.

"Please hurry. Get my things ready. I don't need money. Just the essentials," he said nervously.

He had to get back to his duties for the group, taking care of the bookkeeping, and giving final instructions to those staying behind. *Dancho* Oe came back. "Within thirty minutes, all men between eighteen and forty years of age are to report to the front of the school below us," he said. "Get ready right away." A black cloud descended on everyone—except for Mrs. Nagasu whose face lit up when they announced "men up to the age of forty." Her husband was forty-three. I hated the smirk on her face.

After they had their meeting, my husband came back. "This might be it. I may be leaving you for good," he said as he put on the black suit I had repaired. We sat down to eat but couldn't swallow the food. I stuffed the leftovers into a *bento* box for him. Looking through the clothes I packed in his rucksack, he said, "I don't need this...or this," and pulled out the winter clothes. I knew he was thinking of us. The *Hoantai* police came up to get our men.

"Hurry," they said while avoiding our eyes.

When I tried to get him to take the blanket, my husband fought back fiercely. "I'll manage," he said. I pleaded with him, crying. Finally, I got him to take five hundred yen.

The final moment came and we looked at our baby, Sakiko still fast asleep on our blanket. Gently touching her cheek, he said, "She's sleeping so well. She looks just like Masahiro when he was a baby." Then he turned around and gazed at our eldest son who was standing beside me. Masahiro was doing his best to be brave. "This time, Daddy might not come back. Listen to Mommy, all right? All, right?" my husband said. Masahiro nodded and put his hand on my shoulder.

Masahiko was on my lap, his face nestled against my breast. He was only a two-year-old, still in need of mothering. At this tender age, he had been forced to deal with the arrival of his baby sister, and the war. Masahiko was so thin, his eyes seemed even bigger. He was my husband's favorite and while I was busy with the other children, he took care of our middle child. One of their favorite activities was their walk to the bathroom every night. "Masahiko-chan, I want you to listen to Mommy, all right?" my husband said, but our son wouldn't let go of my blouse. Instead, he stared at his father with huge terrible eyes.

My husband then turned to me. "Go home to Japan. Take care of the children." There was so much to say but I couldn't speak. As tears trickled down my face, I finally said, "Take care. All right?...Don't get sick. All right?...Be sure to come back to us. All right?..."

Of our eleven men, those over forty years of age were: Mr. Narita, Mr. Daichi, Mr. Nagasu, and *Dancho* Oe. They would be allowed to stay with us. My husband and the six other men who were to be taken away from us gathered in front of our house. Facing us, one of them said, "Everyone...please be kind to each other. Take care of each other."

After each man spoke, my husband came over one more time as I held Masahiko. He gently touched his son's face. He used a favorite nickname and said, "Masa-chan, *sayonara*." My little boy, who until now had been silent, suddenly started screaming. I wanted to scream even louder than him.

The fog began to lift. An open freight car was taking our men, and we stood on the hill to see them off. The train started moving slowly. Mr. Mizushima's glasses glinted in the sun. I spotted my husband's black suit right away. He waved his handkerchief and I waved a hand towel back. He waved his handkerchief in a circle. I waved my hand towel in a circle. We said good-bye. The train picked up speed and then passed behind a hill. October 28th was one of the saddest days of my life.

CHAPTER TEN

The Hill of Tears

The autumn sun rose high as we stayed on the hill, silently crouched, even after we could no longer see the vapors left behind the steam engine of the train. The crowd at the train station disappeared, and everything had settled into a frightening lull. We wept silently as we faced the distant mountains. One by one, the women whose husbands had left, went alone to a rock or a grassy spot to grieve in private.

"Mrs. Fujiwara." When I turned around, I found *Dancho* Oe standing. As the head of our group, he had accompanied the men to the train platform.

"I was asked by your husband to return this to you." In his hand, *Dancho* Oe was holding a blanket and woolen underpants.

"Why?" I said as my eyes filled with tears.

"He was worried about you. He thought you would have a hard time," he said. "He also told me to give you this money." There was three hundred yen in his hand.

"What an idiot!" I scolded my husband silently. Going to

the *gulag* in Siberia, why did he give me back his most precious things? It's like some sort of love suicide. Maybe he thought if he left these things for the children, I'd be satisfied. But now every day, every night when I saw this blanket, I would be reminded of him. I was so angry at him for leaving me, I forgot to thank *Dancho* Oe—he stood there, waiting.

Finally, he said, "Mrs. Fujiwara, you might not know about it...a while ago, at the marketplace on the way back from a meeting, I lent your husband forty yen..."

"What...what about forty yen?" I mumbled. A look of annoyance flitted across his face.

"I lent him forty yen," he said.

"I don't give a damn about forty yen," I thought. I couldn't stand to look at his face as he tried to collect on a loan—to bring this nasty business up when my heart was breaking. I paid him the forty yen. The thought suddenly surged through me, "From today...I've got to be strong."

Near our *shinto* shrine house on the hill, the other women stood in a circle and looked towards me. They were the women who had always been alone, their husbands missing since we left Manchuria. From the hill, they looked down at the seven women who just lost their husbands, and whispered amongst themselves. I looked at them, then they averted their eyes, as if they had been saying something bad.

One of them, Mrs. Nagoshi, said to me, "*Okusan* (Ma'am), it's going to be hard for you now." She had one nursing baby and was the youngest wife in our group. Was she trying to be polite, or comfort me, or provoke me? I didn't know. I've got to be strong. I looked at the faces of my children. Masahiro, still stunned, came near me, and from time to time looked up at me, trying to understand what had happened. Masahiko-chan was angry—the pain of separating from his father overwhelmed him. I worried about Sakiko and went back to my room, the boys following close behind. It was unusual to find no one else in the room. She was asleep.

I picked her up and said, "Sakiko. Daddy is gone. Sakiko, he's gone." I rubbed up against her sleeping face and sobbed. I felt so miserable, but my three children understood me best. Masahiro, with his eyes full of tears, stared at me. For three days, I was in a daze. A voice, somewhere inside me said, "You've got to get a hold of yourself," but I could do nothing. Wherever I was, I was in tears, and consumed by heartache.

The four men left behind went back and forth to the main office of the Japanese Association. They talked importantly amongst themselves. Mr. Narita, who until now had been ignored, became one of the inner circle of men. When they announced that the age limit was forty, Mr. Nagasu was exuberant, and for two or three days, he worked energetically, and annoyed me by saying, "*Okusan*, it's no use crying. You must get to work." He bossed the women around and stuck his nose in the cooking pot, commenting on the food. Then on the night of the third day, he suddenly became quiet and his head drooped. I thought he was sick and asked Mrs. Daichi about him.

She said with a worried look, "It turns out that all of the men are doomed. Unless a man is really sick, everyone of them—up to age forty-five is going to be sent away."

"Is that true?"

"I think so. I don't know what to do." Her husband, Mr. Daichi would be sent away and their daughter, Seiko-chan, would be devastated. I don't know where that rumor came from but the remaining four men suddenly lost their spirit and began packing up their things. Four days after my husband left, I finally came back to my senses. There was no time to grieve, I knew I had to think about the future.

The morning of the fifth day after our seven men were taken away, the same station master knocked on our door, just as he had done before, to bring bad news. He announced that the remaining four men would be shipped away. The next morning at 8 a.m. the remaining men up to the age of forty-five gathered together at the school. Former *Dancho* Oe; Mr. Nagasu, no longer proud; and poor Mr. Daichi, held his daughter, Seiko-chan's hand. Mr. Narita, a weak man who was often feverish, couldn't move with the other men. Thankfully, because of his illness, the authorities let him stay.

I went through a repetition of the same horrible events of five days earlier, but this time I was the witness. *Dancho* Oe handed over the *dancho* responsibilities to Mr. Narita, then he talked in private with his older sister, Old Woman Oe. After three months as our leader, *Dancho* Oe was feared more than respected by us. Now he bowed his head, like a beggar monk, before us women and spoke. "Thank you all for everything. I ask you to take care of my sister," he said humbly.

I bowed my head to the man who at one time, forced my husband to apologize for some silly offense, with both hands on the floor. I hated him before for that, but now I felt nothing. Seiko-chan cried out in anguish, "Papa. Papa," as she clung to her father. The fourteen-year old girl couldn't be stopped by her mother and she held onto Mr. Daichi, crossing the hill with him. All of us were in tears watching them.

"Take care of yourself. Don't do anything rash," Mr. Nagasu

said to his wife and five-year old daughter, Hisako, as he kept turning his shoulders around, over and over, to see them as he walked down to the station. This once proud man was crying, and I felt guilty for my earlier feelings about him.

Dancho Narita, with his fever, struggled to keep his reddened face up and stand on the hill. We watched the train go past the hill again. This time, there were much fewer men on the train.

From our vantage point on the hill we heard Mr. Nagasu calling his daughter. His voice was cut by the wind, "Hisako... oh, Hisako...oh." His dark face strained to see his only daughter, and that voice...by the time the vapors floating horizontally from the steam engine faded, the train was on the other side of the mountain and his cries were gone.

I took tally of my group. Now we had:

Males: only *Dancho* Narita.

Females (Married women): sixteen.

Young single women: (Mrs. Kurashige's young sister, Kuniko), one.

Unmarried older woman: (Mr. Oe's older sister), one.

Children: twenty.

Total: thirty-nine people.

Under the leadership of our sick *Dancho* Narita, our small group of thirty-nine women and children would have to go forward beginning tonight, together with new tears.

CHAPTER ELEVEN

Making Ourselves Invisible

The locals called us *Nihonjin,* (Japanese) and none of us were upset because that was obvious. But if any of us called them *Chosenjin,* (Koreans) they got very angry. (It was the pent-up rage from many years of Japanese military rule.) In order not to provoke them, we decided to call them, "the people of here." But if we weren't careful, the words still slipped out of our mouths — *Chosenjin.*

The north wind that started blowing during the night kept gusting with the arrival of morning. We huddled in the corners of the rooms with rounded backs when the west-facing window shattered with a loud crash. We looked at each other. Another window broke.

A young Korean yelled something. When we peeped outside, we saw five or six kids, maybe fourteen or fifteen-year olds. They held rocks in both hands, and threw them at our windows. I rushed over to get Sakiko — any of these windows might be next.

Dancho Narita got up unsteadily and closed the northern window shutters quietly. Then all of us women and children hid in the darkened room. My children said nothing as they held onto me, letting their noses drip. If we could reach the *Hoantai*, the Korean police, maybe they would help us. But who was going to go from our house, down the hill to let them know? No one had the courage. If we went outside, were we going to be beaten? Maybe some thugs would kill us or worse…we were terrified. Even Dancho Narita trembled.

Through the cracks in the window shutter, we saw a white neck scarf of one of the boys. I tried to comfort Dancho Narita by saying, "*Dancho* Narita, maybe we could fix the broken window with a piece of paper."

He just said, "Those stupid kids."

After a while, we heard footsteps run over to our kitchen. Bang. Crash. There was the sound of metal banging into something. A boy said in Korean, "Hey, there's a *hango*." After some rustling, there was no noise. In a rush, we ran over to the kitchen.

Five of the *hango* that we had kept were taken. There was only one left. "If we don't have our *hango*, how are we going to cook?" Tears streamed down Mrs. Daichi's thin face. "And I had stuffed mine full of potatoes…for our dinner."

Seiko-chan pulled Mrs. Daichi's sleeve, "It's no use crying, Mama." And she went back into our room.

There were days when shifty-eyed Korean men hung around near the house. And days when boys drew nasty graffiti on our house. Some men came, saying they had messages from our men in Heijo. They banged on our door, claimed they had business with our men, and looked at us with suspicious eyes. The Koreans who were sympathetic no longer came near. If we passed each other on the street, they slipped the children an apple or a piece of candy. Most of those people were elderly. The young Koreans tried to not look at us as they passed by.

We didn't know what would happen if we ran across the Koreans who really hated us. They could do anything and we wouldn't be able to defend ourselves. We were terrified whenever we had to go outside, and shrank into ourselves in an effort to make ourselves invisible. The children learned this, too, and when they saw any townspeople, they covered their frightened faces and hid behind us.

CHAPTER TWELVE

Diamond Dust

November arrived, and there were nights where a cold north-west wind blew so hard it rattled the windows, and kept me half-awake until morning. Once there was enough light, we looked for branches the wind had torn off the trees — sometimes I found enough for an arm load. Later in the day, when the sun had warmed the ground, we went down in the hill to town. On the west side of the dirt road, apple stands started appearing.

These apple stands soon formed two red parallel lines all the way down to the train station entrance. From the mountains in every direction, hand-carts full of dried grass began to creep along the roads, dropping their loads into small haystacks here and there. Ox carts would then collect these haystacks into huge loads, and one by one, they lumbered between the lines of apple stands into the town center.

I guessed the dried grass was for the town's *ondoru*, Korean floor heaters. In the morning, smoke climbed from the many *ondoru* and make thin white layers in the air. Our lonely house at the top of the hill, where the men were gone, also let sad, bitter smoke out from the *ondoru* twice a day. Winter was coming.

Just after the middle of November, early in the morning, someone came knocking at our door. This felt ominous so early in the day. As we all got up, *Dancho* Narita brought in a Korean boy who was breathing hard and sweating. He had brought messages from the town of Anton, just north of us on the border with China. Mrs. Tomimoto, Mrs. Yamada, and Mrs. Sueyoshi got letters and money and they beamed with happiness as they read letters from their husbands. The messenger boy said, "Hurry. Hurry," while the three women wrote letters for him to take back to Anton. The boy looked worried, and kept looking out the door.

As soon as the letters were done, he grabbed them, and ran down the hill as if flying on the wind. After two or three such letter exchanges with Anton, four women with their children, ten people altogether, decided to leave us and go north to Anton to join their men there. A fine powder snow fell that day, and we saw them off. We called out, "*Sayonara.* Take care of yourselves," as the women and children disappeared into the snow.

Our group was now reduced to twenty-nine people. Once December came, the authorities decided that we would be rationed two Japanese *go* (about a cup and a half) of rice a day for each person. I was so happy at first. This rice would help us survive the winter. But then our *dan* decided to re-distribute this rice amongst us. For children under five, the ration was cut to half that of the others, in other words, just one *go* a day. The extra rice was saved to distribute to the women who worked for pay. With this new distribution system, the ones who suffered the most were the women with young children and babies: me - I lost two *go*, Mrs. Honda lost two *go*, Mrs. Sakiyama also lost two *go*, and Mrs. Daichi lost one *go*. We mothers with little children were the most desperate of the refugees. In this life, we endured and suffered the most. I wondered if this was my fate, determined from my date of birth. What is going to happen to my three, pale-faced sickly children?

Once the snow started, tiny ice crystals blew incessantly around in air. I'd seen this snow often in Manchuria where the temperature often dropped below freezing. The air was dry and the skies were clear. The snow particles stayed suspended and sparkled in the sun. It was breathtakingly beautiful. I had heard my husband describe such snow as "*saihyo*." But he also used another name in English, "diamond dust." That English name was so wonderful, I never forgot it. *Diamond dust*. There were times the snow really looked like that.

In my hometown Nagano, where winters were cold, there is a phrase we used — "ice drying". This refers to when the laundry is hung out to dry in the winter. It quickly froze stiff, but before you knew it, the clothes would be dry. In order to dry Sakiko's diapers, I hung them facing the sun. The wind pierced the red cracks in my hand like needles as I hung the wet cloths every day.

Now it was so cold the snow did not melt. When I walked on the icy road, my head would ache, throbbing with each step on the hard ground. Somehow my hunger made the frozen ground feel even harder.

Our toilet froze. The daily waste, instead of flowing down as usual into the pit, now froze in place, growing taller and taller. We shoved the waste down after we used the toilet each time, but finally, this grotesque 'tower' of feces and urine would not let loose, even if we hit it with all our strength. So we made a special toilet. We placed a large wooden bucket upside down and left boards on top beside the crude toilet opening to step on.

That way, we could move the toilet away from the icy mountains of waste.

But every morning, we took turns cleaning this nasty, frozen mess up. It was the most unpleasant chore we all shared. And those of us with small children bore the brunt of everyone's frustrations. Mrs. Nagasu, with her one five-year-old daughter, and enough money to pay for heating fuel, complained the most. Small children inevitably made the biggest messes so she haughtily said, "We need to have those with small children do more of the toilet clean-up."

CHAPTER THIRTEEN

The Child Who Doesn't Cry

We hauled winter fuel we bought at a distant mountain back up the snow-covered road to the top of our hill. One day, as a reward to ourselves, we decided to pool our money to buy special treats, *omochi* rice cakes, and eat them that evening. Everyone looked forward to having a small taste of home.

"Tamio-chan stole some *omochi*!" The children suddenly started screaming loudly, pointing at the little boy who was the black sheep in our group.

When I looked, I saw that in a corner of the room Tamio-chan was standing near the *furoshiki*-covered basket where the precious *omochi* was. He hid his right hand behind his back. With everyone staring at him, Tamio-chan didn't try to move away or show any signs of guilt. He didn't care what anyone thought, and quickly put the *omochi* in his mouth with a dirty hand.

His mother, Mrs. Toda, stood up white-faced. Without saying a word, she picked Tamio-chan up by his waist and carried him outside, where it was just beginning to get dark. We knew what would happen to that child.

Tamio-chan was really the child of Mr. Toda and his first wife. No one knew what had happened to the first Mrs Toda. Only that our Mrs. Toda became his step-mother when Tamio was three or four. He was five years old when I knew him, but looked small for his age. From his big knobby head, bright glinting eyes glared out of hollowed eye sockets and made everyone feel squeamish. There was nothing childlike or endearing about this strange, sickly little boy, and he never played with the other children. He snuck around the house, ignored everyone, including Mrs. Toda, and constantly prowled the rooms for something to put in his mouth.

Tamio-chan often stole food, and put his hand on anything that was edible. He picked up and ate anything lying in the corners of the room. Nasty things like potato peelings or soybean shells the other children had dropped while eating. Yet, to be honest, there was not a single person in our group who felt sorry for him. No one felt any desire to give him things. This child did not have a trace of any sympathetic qualities.

The most unpleasant thing about him was the way in which he would glare at us, with an insolent look which seemed to taunt us. He never laughed or smiled, and we never even heard him cry. But Tamio-chan must have felt pain. His hands were covered with swollen red marks where he had been punished. I wondered, "Did this child cry when his step-mother punished him?" Instead of sympathy for Tamio-chan, we resented Mrs. Toda for being responsible for this repulsive child. After the incident with the *omochi*, everyone complained to her again. Some even suggested it was her fault for not feeding him enough.

"I've never, never let this child go without food. Accusing me of starving him is so unfair!" Mrs. Toda cried. "You don't know what he is really like. If you really knew what he is truly like, you wouldn't accuse me like you do." Saying thus, she looked at Tamio-chan with tearful eyes full of frustration.

At the next mealtime, Mrs. Toda repeatedly urged Tamio-chan to eat, in front of everyone so they could see and hear her efforts. "Eat. Eat!" But Tamio-chan only ate a tiny amount.

"I can't eat," he said, to which his step-mother fiercely tried to feed him again. But it was no good. Later I learned from the doctor that Tamio-chan had already reached the third level of starvation, where the body begins to devour itself. Tamio-chan's tiny stomach couldn't digest even two spoonfuls of rice gruel. But once the meal was over, he began wandering around the house again, glaring at everyone, and looking for bits of food spilled onto the floor.

CHAPTER FOURTEEN

Shooting Stars Are Alive

The snow and wind stopped for a moment so I took Masahiro's hand, and we went outside to the single pine tree that stood in the crack of a broken rock. As I often did, I picked some pine needles from the tree. Two clusters lay cold in my hand.

I counted the needles out loud, and plucked them out one by one. If the total number of needles was even, that meant my husband was alive and well. If that number was odd, it meant I would never see him again. I played this pine needle game often but never told anyone about it. This was my secret pleasure.

Recently, for two or three days running, I went out to play my little game. Although Masahiro didn't know what I was doing, when I was happy with the results, he would be glad for me and join me in laughing. My son waited patiently again, until I finished my game. On this particular time, I prayed especially hard for my husband, as I dropped the stiff needles on the frozen ground.

The final number was twenty-six. "My husband is alive," I

rejoiced to myself. I carefully picked up the last needle I dropped. "Masahiro-chan, here — look." I gave that needle to Masahiro with a smile on my face. Masahiro looked into my eyes and smiled with me.

Suddenly, a young Korean man, in fluent Japanese, said to me, "*Okusan*, what are you doing?" He must have been silently watching me. He was from the *Hoantai,* the Korean police. I cringed as if I had been caught doing something bad.

He must have come up the hill on official business and began asking me questions about our *dan.* "How many are in your meteorological group?" He didn't seem to care what I had been doing with Masahiro. He asked about the number of people, their gender, ages, and economic background.

Then he began to talk about other things. He told me about himself. It turned out that he had been a Korean draftee in the Japanese air force at one time. I invited him into the house where he met the other women, and he told us about the chaos of the war front. When somebody asked him about our missing men, he sadly shook his head and said he had no idea what happened to the Japanese men.

This Korean *Hoantai* officer's name was Mr. Kim, and after we first met him, he started coming up the snowy road to our little house almost every night, to chat with us. The children looked forward to his visits because he always had candy in his pocket. Mr. Kim had a beautiful voice, and we enjoyed hearing him sing popular Japanese songs, especially sad songs, over and over.

One night, he asked, "Shall I teach you a song no one knows?" And sure enough, Mr. Kim sang a beautiful song no one had ever heard of before. He explained, "When I was in the south, a Japanese soldier in our battalion wrote it and another soldier sang it.

They taught it to me, but both of them were killed in the fighting."

Mr. Kim remembered them and sang it for us in his melancholy voice. Then we all learned to sing that song from memory. That melody flowed over us and soothed our souls. The song had three stanzas and was very simple, yet it had a certain allure that wouldn't let go of us.

In my heart spring forth,
the roses you planted.
Tonight, take a look
at the window where I will wait alone.
They are reflected in the stars, and bloom

from my heart,
your voice wrapped itself around.
Come take a look tonight
on the hill where we promised each other.
The stars are singing gently.

You live in my heart.
To the northern sky you went.
Come take a look tonight.
The stars, in the same sky I saw you off in
The shooting stars are alive

After I learned the song, and until I got safely back to my home in Japan, I sang this song to myself, over and over. Whenever I felt empty, this song appeared on my lips. And it wasn't just me — everyone in our group learned this song, and cherished it.

Mrs. Kimoto, had a particularly lovely voice and would often sing it for us. There were a number of times, I was so moved by her voice that I stopped whatever I was doing—to listen to her sing it.

At the end of December, Mr. Kim suddenly stopped coming. We didn't know why he came to visit us in the first place, and why he suddenly stopped. Until the very end, he was a dear friend to us. There were rumors that he was too friendly with us Japanese, and thus was let go by the *Hoantai*.

Much later, I ran into him at the marketplace in town. He looked so different that I didn't say anything. But then he noticed me, and came over. He said, "It's been awhile…is everyone well? Are your children well?" He was much thinner. After chatting a little, he asked, "How do you manage to stay alive? Even we Koreans are struggling to survive." This conversation happened long after his visits—it was so good to see him again.

CHAPTER FIFTEEN

I Love You Right Now

When the snow stopped, the wind started and the icy air whistled through the cracks into our little house. Strangely, when the wind stopped, a penetrating cold crept into our bodies, making our bones ache. Our lonely house on top of the hill was forgotten by everyone. The only lively conversations heard were the creaks and groans of the wood crying under the weight of the snow.

I layered all the clothes I had on the children, and rarely took them off in the cold. At night, they kept everything on, and lay side by side on the single quilt we had, with my husband's blanket on top. But when the children's feet got cold, and they couldn't sleep. Sakiko and Masahiko cried in turn while Masahiro shivered. I curled myself beneath their feet, and pressed six little feet against my body, holding them against my stomach and my breasts. Little by little their feet warmed and finally—I heard the peaceful sounds of their snoring. But by then my back had turned to ice and my spine ached with the cold.

When the children slept, I couldn't sleep. I waited for morning, and held still to keep their feet warm against my body. Such nights continued for some weeks. When the sun started shining through the windows around noon, I was finally warm enough to sleep for an hour or two. I don't know how I survived that December cold.

Toward the end of December, the *Fuku-dancho* Mrs. Kurashige resigned her position, saying that she couldn't work with *Dancho* Narita. So we had a vote and I was selected. What a cruel bunch of women they were! I complained and objected to the vote results, "Mrs. Kurashige has just one six-year old child, and a twenty-two-year-old sister, Kuniko, who helps her with everything. She's much better suited than I was to do the extra work. Five other women had no children. Two other women had just one child... why force this job on me, the one who with the most children in this group?"

Dancho Narita was pretty much bedridden, so that meant the *fuku-dancho* would have to do all the work; go talk with the other groups, and represent the *dan* at the Association meetings — if it were me, I'd have to go out on the snowy road with Sakiko on my back. But when we had another vote, it was unanimous. Again, I was selected to be *fuku-dancho*.

Maybe they chose me because they thought I was everybody's friend, and never fought with anyone. But I was not, definitely not, everyone's friend! As my husband often used to complain — I was a cold, self-centered woman. It was just that I was very good at putting up a nice facade, and to be honest — I only did that so my kids wouldn't be bullied in my absence.

I had promised myself that until I got back to my home in Japan, I would try to get along with everyone. If I were child-less, I probably wouldn't have been so nice. I would have fought

with everyone, driving them away from me. I resigned myself
to being the *fuku-dancho* and doing all the extra work: representing the *dan* at the Japanese Association meetings, negotiating
with the Korean *Hoantai*, coordinating the food distribution, and
bookkeeping with Mr. Narita.

I grumbled to myself, "If I have to do this job, then give me
back the two rations of rice my family deserves!" But in the end, I
gritted my teeth and said nothing. Perhaps Mrs. Kurashige felt a
little guilty after resigning, because she agreed to help me.

We decided to have a New Year's Eve party on the evening of
December 31st. Each person had to pay in two yen which might
seem like nothing now — but it was really painful for me to pull
out that ten-yen bill. I was glad we did it though. Working together to prepare for the most important Japanese holiday made
us happy. We even managed to make some traditional dishes:
go-mame, *kobu-maki*, and *mitsuke*! And we pounded a tiny amount
of white rice into *mochi* rice cake, for each person. It was a simple
mochi we made without the use of the traditional tools; the wood-
en mallet and the bowl made from a tree stump.

On New Year's Eve everybody received one stick of candy
and the party began. We agreed to have each person take a turn
entertaining everyone else. How bold we women became without the men! Adults and children alike sang songs and recited
poetry. Fifty-two year-old Ms. Oe recited an old poem, "Where
is My Dark-eyed Love?" Even Mrs. Sakiyama, who never smiled,
recited *Sadookesa*, impressing us with her skill. Mrs. Narita sang
"Colorado Moon" in English while her husband lay sick. I sang
this song about my hometown of Nagano:

Komoro naru Kojo no hotori
Kumo shiroku Yushi kanshimu

There was only one person who did not sing. Poor *Dancho* Narita was ill and lay in the corner, covered from head to toe with a blanket. Everyone else, one person after another, stood up and performed a poem or song. As the evening wore on, the performances became more and more melancholy.

Finally, Mrs. Kurashige's younger sister, Kuniko, stood up. She was a beautiful, tall, twenty-year old woman with round breasts and clear eyes. "I want to recite a poem I wrote myself," she said. "Please don't laugh at me, all right?"

Everyone became quiet and all eyes were on Kuniko who stood nervously in the middle of our crowded room. Then she poured out her sad poem:

I want to press my lips to my hand
and say I love you,
I love you right now.

Kuniko was singing about the man she was supposed to marry. They were separated because of the war and no one knew if he was alive. "I love you, I love you right now." Her words touched everyone.

"Please sing it again," Mrs. Kanaya said. We were all moved. There were two, three encores. Everyone listened to Kuniko's poem, tears streaming down their faces but they didn't want her to stop.

"Once more. Once more," everyone cried.

Kuniko didn't try to wipe away her tears and kept singing over and over until finally, her voice gave out and she crumpled to the floor.

Everybody cried and cried. Even the children, who knew nothing clung to their mothers and cried.

CHAPTER SIXTEEN

A Sundial of Ice

In January, permission was given for the opening of a school for the children. There was no paper, pencils or textbooks but the children brimmed with happiness, eager to go down the hill. From our *dan*, three children were selected and the other groups sent children as well. Going to school meant we had to know the time, so the children could be there as expected. Even if anyone had clocks or watches, they were too valuable to use every day.

Dancho Narita saved us. Using his knowledge as a meteorologist, he made a clock for us — a sundial. In front of the house where the sunlight was good, he formed a half circle on the ground using rope. In the middle, on one of the marks he made, he stuck in a stick. That night the sky was clear, and using the stars, *Dancho* Narita figured out where north was and drew an orientation on the half circle.

Then the next day, he made a triangle out of cut branches and, using that as a drafting compass, he miraculously made a sundial. True north was marked with a big branch, while short branches marked north-east, south-east, south-west, and north-west. With that he had sixteen sticks standing up. He got a bucket of water and carefully poured the water over everything so that all the pieces froze in place. "An ice sundial!" The middle stick bent a little and *Dancho* Narita frowned. "Can someone find a straight stick?"

When I asked, "If that stick is crooked, will the time be wrong?"

He replied, "Yes, that crooked stick is going to make the sundial ten minutes off."

"Ten minutes isn't bad," I said to Mrs. Kurashige who stood next to me.

"Will it really work that accurately?" Mrs. Kurashige said, echoing my thoughts.

Dancho Narita was determined to find a better, straight stick but it wasn't easy to find such a stick. So he left the crooked stick in place. *Dancho* Narita taught us how to use it, and everyone, including the children, was delighted to be able to tell time.

His claim that the sundial would be ten minutes off because of that one crooked stick was later proven to be true. When the people from the *Hoantai* came up to visit us on business, we compared it to that one of the officers' watch. There was a fifteen minute difference between that man's watch and the sundial.

Afterwards, *Dancho* Narita said, "A fifteen minute difference shouldn't happen. That man's watch must be five minutes off."

CHAPTER SEVENTEEN

The Sound of Breaking Ice

The nights terrified me, but I had to get up in the middle of the night to break ice for water. When the children's breathing settled into a steady pattern, after my body had warmed their feet, I listened for the eerie sound of ice forming. Eventually, I heard the sound through the windows. I slowly got up, grabbed a bucket with my left hand, a heavy pick with my right, and went outside.

The stars shone with a piercing cold clarity, and I could make out the dark shapes of our two emergency water tanks made of concrete. In the summer, water pooled inside these tanks. Now they contained thick ice. I set down the bucket, and held the heavy pick with both hands to aim it at the center of the ice. I swung the pick with all my strength, so hard my hand vibrated painfully with the shock of impact. I kept hitting the ice until a good-sized chunk broke off, and I tossed it into the bucket. Again, my metal pick hit the hard ice.

Echoes of my pick biting into the ice reverberated back to me from the invisible valley. These sharp sounds frightened me, especially as I worked alone in the cold, inky night. After I filled the bucket half-way, I stretched my aching back and looked at the sky. In the east, the three stars of Orion's Belt sparkled, and below them, a long tail of a falling star streamed down and faded away.

Shortly after we got married, we lived near the Tonegawa, one of the biggest rivers in Japan. Summer evenings, my husband and I liked to walk along the riverbank and admire the reflection of the sky on the smooth surface of that big river. During one walk, we saw a falling star.

I enjoyed asking my husband about the stars, and I remember I asked, "Dear, when falling stars burn up, they become invisible, right?"

My husband said, "That's right."

I asked, "Well, when falling stars disappear, are they...reborn?"

He laughed and said, "Are you asking me a scientific question or a philosophical one?"

"Maybe both," I said.

He explained, "Falling stars are basically air and friction, which we can't see. But their energy still exists. The energy transforms into something else, something alive."

My husband was so kind then...I felt he loved me.

My fascination for falling stars must have come from him. My belief that somehow my husband's survival was connected to falling stars came from that memory. It was my consolation.

When we saw another falling star, I said, "Look. Look. It disappeared." That star's energy was still alive somewhere—in some other form. Perhaps my beliefs were as silly as soap bubbles. But

I clung to them.

I put the bucket of ice quietly inside the room. I didn't want to wake the children with my cold body so I sat beside them for awhile before crawling under the blanket. By morning, about half of this ice melted. If there was any hot water left after our group's meals, I would add that to the bucket of melted ice and use the water to clean the diapers.

When it was Mrs. Kurashige's turn to heat up the water, she gave me extra hot water. Of all the childless women, only Mrs. Sato sometimes put part of her hot water into my bucket. The others seemed to have no sympathy for mothers like me. By getting up in the middle of the night to get ice, I saved myself a trip to the valley river during the day.

I shudder when I imagine what it would have been like if I had gotten sick then. My three children would have grown thin and starved as they waited by my prone body. Any illness for me then would have meant death for my children.

One windy night, I collected the ice in my bucket. But when it melted, I couldn't use it because the water was black and dirty. If there was fresh snow, I was happy. In the morning, there would be nice, clear water in the bucket.

At the beginning, everyone asked me, "Mrs. Fujiwara, why don't you break ice during the day?" I had my reasons. During the day, I noticed that the ice in the tanks melted a little when the sun warmed the top of our hill. The ice was then too soft to break into chunks when I plunged the pick in. The small ice chips I managed to collect melted into worthless small puddles. And anyway, the only bucket that was available during the day was needed by the group to boil water.

When I tried it again in the evening, it still didn't work. The ice wasn't hard enough. The ice broke best in the middle of the night when it got cold enough to freeze. That's why I listened for that sound of ice forming. But even when I did this chore while everyone slept, a couple of the women complained, "Mrs. Fujiwara, you're disturbing our sleep." These two were part of a group of childless women who spent much of their days reading novels they borrowed from the Japanese Association. They whined at having to work in town once or twice a week for pay.

They complained, "We have to do real work in town for the rest of you mothers, so you can get rice rations to feed your children."

Unless a woman has a child, she will not understand the depth of a mother's feelings and how far a mother will go to care for her children.

CHAPTER EIGHTEEN

Smoke from the *Ondoru*

Every night, I comforted my shivering, crying children until they fell asleep in a cold room, then went out into the frigid night to collect ice — while in the very next room, other women and children slept soundly on a warm floor heated by the *ondoru*, the Korean floor heater. I should tell you about this unequal sleeping arrangement and how it came about.

When our men left in November, and then ten people left our *dan* to go north to Anton to join their husbands, our group shrank in size. At the same time, the weather suddenly turned cold. We abandoned three rooms on the north side of our house, and moved into two six-mat rooms on the south side. Next to the kitchen, bath and toilet, there was one six-mat room with an *ondoru* heater, and next to that was our six-*tatami* mat room with no heater.

In this unheated six-mat room, eight families — nineteen people — slept crowded together. In the room with the *ondoru* heater, there were five families — ten people. Why did we divide up the *dan* into two groups, nineteen and ten, into the two same-sized rooms in this strange way? There was a reason.

Those who stayed in the *ondoru* heated room paid for the fuel needed to keep the *ondoru* burning, and therefore it was decided that only the people who paid for the fuel had the right to use the heated room. This was Mrs. Nagasu's idea. I was shocked at her selfishness but couldn't argue with her logic.

On the first day of this new rule, even *Dancho* Narita didn't oppose Mrs. Nagasu. Only the few *dan* members who could afford to pay would have stayed in that room — Mrs. Nagasu, her daughter, and the childless women including pretty Mrs. Sato. Mrs. Nagasu allowed only one exception — Old Woman Oe, because of her age, bad hip and since she was alone. Mrs. Nagasu was determined not to let anyone else have a free ride and sleep in a heated room without paying.

Only grim Mrs. Sakiyama managed to defy Mrs. Nagasu. There was no particular reason that Mrs. Sakiyama should have been able to stay in that room. She had pretty much used up her funds, her two boys were young, and she was pregnant. On moving day, while everyone else packed up their possessions to move into the unheated room, Mrs. Sakiyama planted herself and her children right in the middle of the heated room.

Of course, Mrs. Nagasu didn't like that. "Hey there, Mrs. Sakiyama, please move over to the unheated room," she said.

Mrs. Sakiyama didn't say a word. Night arrived. Mrs. Sakiyama still made no move to go to the other room. Meanwhile the unheated room got crowded with nineteen people and there was no room for any more people to come in to sleep.

When Mrs. Sakiyama saw that, she relaxed and prepared her

boys to go to sleep. Mrs. Nagasu was furious. She almost kicked Mrs. Sakiyama in her rush to stand up. "Mrs. Sakiyama! Do you intend to stay in this room without paying?" she fumed.

Mrs. Sakiyama clutched her two little boys, Ichiro and Jiro, and glared up at Mrs. Nagasu, without saying a word. Mrs. Nagasu kept repeating her refrain. "I'm really shocked. How am I going to sleep with such a selfish person here...really!" She pressed and bullied Mrs. Sakiyama relentlessly but Mrs. Sakiyama didn't yield an inch, or say anything.

Finally, Mrs. Nagasu gave up, saying, "All right, tomorrow morning, please go over to the other room." Of course, Mrs. Sakiyama did not move the next morning. For four months, Mrs. Sakiyama, Ichiro and Jiro used the heated room, free of charge. I understood Mrs. Sakiyama's feelings and if I had her courage, that might have been the only way to handle the situation.

Mrs. Kurashige held her son and tried to creep as close as possible to the door of the *ondoru* room get a little bit of that warmth. If I had a little more money, even though I was afraid of Mrs. Nagasu, I would have joined her group in the heated room to sleep. But I was too much of a coward to stand up to Mrs. Nagasu like Mrs. Sakiyama, and too proud to creep like Mrs. Kurashige.

In January, out of the blue, a letter, arrived for me from Mr. Taya, my husband's old boss. The letter came from Anton, just north of us on the border with China, where he must have escaped to from Shinkyo. The envelope was addressed to me with a note. Inside were two smaller envelopes, two letters. He wanted me to deliver them. One letter was addressed to his wife in Japan, and the other was to his boss, Mr. Sakuhei Fujiwara, the head of the Meteorological Department in Japan, (who also happened to be my husband's uncle).

Mr. Taya must have sent these letters to me since it looked like our *dan* in northern Korea might go home soon. He asked me to take these letters for him. I trembled as I recognized his handwriting and pictured this gentle man writing these words. I wondered if Mr. Taya sent me these letters because he heard something on the radio. Anyway, I carefully put the letters away in my rucksack. Getting Mr. Taya's envelope felt ominous. Did he send me these letters because he was being sent away to a Soviet prison like my husband? Did he fear he would never make it back to Japan?

I remembered Mr. Taya's glasses and imagined them glinting in the Anton sky.

CHAPTER NINETEEN

Cause of Death

The end of January was miserable. As usual, dinner was a tin can of watery soup. The few *daikon* vegetable leaves floating in it were carefully doled out so that each person received an equal portion. I took my family's portion in my metal *hango,* and divided it up into our three tin cans. My two hungry boys watched and waited. Masahiro and Masahiko looked carefully at each other's portions and if there was the slightest of difference, they put up a big ruckus.

After I gulped down my soup, I hurried the boys so I could go wash the cans. My boys were slower than the others, so I always ended up washing our cans in the tub of dirty dishwater everyone else had already used.

"Mrs. Fujiwara, are you ready yet?" Mrs. Mizushima would press me. She was in charge of washing the communal cooking pot after everyone finished washing their own cans. I was the last one, as usual.

"Yes, I'm almost ready," I said and hurried the children to finish. I scolded Masahiko who was still licking his empty can.

By the time it was my turn to wash, the dish water had cooled. I plunged my hands into dirty, cold water. On the side, the communal cooking pot sat, not yet washed. When I was done, I was supposed to pour my dishwater into this pot.

As I washed my cans in the corner of the hallway, I looked outside. The sun was in the far western sky; the red clouds huddled together as if they were cold. The evening sunlight poured through the window glass, while shadows of bare tree branches stretched across the yard.

In front of me a small form moved. I took a good look and saw that it was Tamio-chan crouched near the cooking pot, almost hidden by the shadows. He was running his little finger along the edge of the pot, then sucking his finger. Tamio-chan was just out of sight of his step-mother, Mrs. Toda.

"Tamio-chan, you are going to be scolded by your mother if you do that. Hurry, and go back with the others." I whispered to him. For a moment, he stopped his hand and looked at me. He said, "I don't care." Then stuck his hand back into the pot. The strip of white cloth that was always wrapped around his neck was grimy, and above it, his rough, deformed head stuck out defiantly. His head reminded me of the old stone statues of Jizo that stood out in the Japanese farm fields all year, hard and encrusted with lichen.

"Mrs. Fujiwara, are you done yet?" With her sharp voice, Mrs. Mizushima suddenly appeared. Her baggy dark blue pants stopped when she saw Tamio-chan.

"Oh, Tamio-chan! You are naughty again." Then she called out in a loud voice, "Hey, Mrs. Toda, your Tamio-chan is licking our cooking pot again!" I was annoyed at how Mrs. Mizushima immediately told on Tamio.

Mrs. Toda came from the kitchen shuffling in small steps, her face pale green and her mouth set in a scowl. She scooped up Tamio-chan by the waist and lifted him up as easily as if he were a small bag of rice. I watched her march outside into the darkness with the boy dangling by her side. I glared at Mrs. Mizushima. Everyone in the room turned and looked at her with disdain, accusingly. She tried to deflect everyone's disapproval and sheepishly said to me, "Mrs. Fujiwara, don't you think Mrs. Toda is pretty scary when she gets angry?"

Tamio-chan was taken far enough away so we couldn't see or hear anything. We all suspected Mrs. Toda beat him although we didn't hear him cry. It was an especially quiet night. The moon rose late and the bare branches reflected in the window, yearning and forlorn. I was awake late into the night, listening for the sound of ice. In the six-mat room lit by a single faint light bulb, nineteen people slept in a jumbled arrangement. There was no space between the bodies crammed together in this small room, but even in sleep, each mother staked out her territory and tried to prevent even a small amount of her family's bedding from being used by the others.

Everyone would have slept better if they all stretched out and let themselves move freely, but their bodies were all tense and thin. Even in sleep, no one let down their guard. No rosy cheeks on any of the children, including mine. In the light of that single bulb, my three children's faces looked pale and sickly. Tamio-chan got up and tottered out to the toilet, and returned. As he stumbled by me, he stepped on Sakiko's foot and she immediately started crying. "Tamio-chan, please be careful. The baby is right here." I said.

"Okay," he said, and bowed his head. He went back toward

Mrs. Toda and snuggled back into the bedding next to her. Five minutes hadn't gone by when Tamio-chan got up again and went to the toilet. He returned and got back into bed. Then he immediately began moaning in a strange voice, "Uuuu, uuuu"

First, he whimpered but then gradually he let out loud, anguished groans. First, Mrs. Toda got up—then everyone else woke up—even those sleeping in the heated room. Tamio-chan's eyes rolled up into his skull so that only the whites showed. It was clear he was having a convulsion. Someone had to go out to get the doctor, but no one wanted to go out in the middle of the cold night. Even the *dancho* found it awkward to ask someone to go.

Finally, Mrs. Nagasu and Mrs. Kurashige stood up in the *ondoru* heated room. "We'll go." The two of them ran out into the night, their figures bathed in the moonlight as they rushed to get the doctor. Before long, Dr. Oya from the Japanese Association, arrived. Twice a week, this good doctor climbed our hill to check us, so we knew him well. Dr. Oya looked at Tamio-chan's eyes, and then sadly shook his head.

Right away, he tried to open up Tamio-chan's clothing to give him a camphor solution injection. As the doctor did this, Mrs. Toda tried to hide Tamio-chan's chest by putting a kimono over him.

"I can't give the injection with so much clothing on him, Dr. Oya said. Annoyed, he pushed Mrs. Toda's hands out of the way to give the shot. Tamio-chan's eyes rolled as another convulsion began. Dr. Oya struggled to remove the dirty cloth wrapped around Tamio-chan's neck. It was difficult for him to undo the hard knots so Mrs. Nagasu helped him.

We expected to see Tamio-chan's thin, white neck when the neckerchief was removed. But we all averted our eyes when Mrs.

Nagasu untied the cloth. It was horrible. Blood oozed everywhere. Pus and dark blood congealed all over the boy's neck, and the inside of the dirty cloth shone black with old blood.

"Ah!" The doctor and all of us cried out in horror .

Before, we accepted Mrs. Toda's explanation for Tamio's neckerchief. She told us, "This child has bronchial trouble." We all believed her story and never questioned why his neck was always covered. But now the wounds in front of us told us how terrible a step-mother's wrath could be.

His neck was covered in welts that had been pinched and pinched so often that blood was drawn. The wounds accused us all. And it wasn't just the neck — everywhere — all over his body, there were dark bruises. Dr. Oya looked at Mrs. Toda.

"Are you his mother?"

She turned her face away. Just then, Tamio-chan who lay with eyes closed, suddenly tried to get up. He squirmed his small body but wasn't able to lift his head. His eyes jerked open and, with a clear voice, he said, "Mommy, Mommy".

"Tamio, Tamio," cried Mrs. Toda as she rushed close to her step-son's side. Tamio-chan looked bright-eyed — straight up — at some spot in the dark ceiling and said nothing more. His body became rigid.

"There's nothing more we can do." Dr. Oya placed his stethoscope once more on Tamio-chan's chest and shook his head. Then he looked down on the back of Mrs. Toda's head as she crouched over the boy's body, and waited for her to lift her head.

He watched her with such a frightening look in his eyes. There was no trace of the kindly doctor who came to do the health exams. Mrs. Toda never did raise her head and remained crouched over the body. Dr. Oya wrapped the kimono around Tamio-chan's body which grew cold, and quietly got up.

"*Dancho*, may I speak with you for a moment?" he said. *Dan-cho* Narita stood up. He looked at me for help as he always does and silently asked me to come. I got up and followed the two of them out to the front door. Dr. Oya, spoke softly so the others wouldn't hear. "*Dancho*, are there any other children besides this one who has not had a health exam?"

His voice was low. His question pierced our hearts like a needle. "No, there are no others." *Dancho* Narita lowered his head and said this as if it were an apology.

Dr. Oya's job was to check the health of all Japanese in this town. He remembered that he had never checked Tamio-chan on the days that he visited our group. On Tuesdays and Fridays, when Dr. Oya came around, Mrs. Toda always took Tamio-chan and hid themselves away somewhere. Never once did they have a health exam.

Dr. Oya put on his coat and put his hand on the door.

"*Sensei*, wait just a moment." I wanted to have someone walk him down. As he breathed in the frosty outside air, he said, "Don't bother, I'll get back on my own."

Saying that, he picked up his small black bag and walked out into the night. The moonlight reflected brightly off the worn, shiny shoulders of his coat. The next day, there was a notice from the main office that a death certificate had to be sent back to Japan. As part of my responsibilities as *fuku-dancho*, I went to officially report Tamio-chan's death to the officials at the Japanese Association.

On the way back, I stopped at Dr. Oya's place. Through the courtesy of the Japanese Association, the doctor lived alone in a single room which was very unusual for the refugees then. I was surprised when I opened the newspaper covered sliding door to find the doctor right in front of me. The 'room' was very small, more like a three-mat closet. I started to talk with him about the other night. Then the doctor gently bowed his head, and opened a drawer, and carefully took out a piece of rice paper folded into four. He prepared a simple death certificate for me which he had already filled out:

Death Certificate

Name: Tamiacho Toda   Age: 5

Cause of death: ~~abuse~~ starvation

I certify the death of the individual named above on this 28th day of January the year Showa 21. (1946)

Dr. Akio Oya

I didn't know the reason for the single line crossing out the word 'abuse.' Without saying anything, I looked at the word, then at the doctor. He explained it to me." There is no use in saying that after he's dead. Anyway she doesn't seem like the sort of person who is going to take the death certificate back home."

As he said this, he turned his back on me. He was the epitome of a learned doctor, but to me he seemed cold and unfeeling. Is there such a diagnosis such as "death by abuse"? The other night he had witnessed the existence of this illness, but here he had denied it and had changed it to 'starvation.'

If Tamio-chan hadn't been with this pathetic group of refugees in the first place, he wouldn't have died. He wouldn't have starved, and the abuse might not have happened. But even if he had managed to survive, he probably would have been mentally-deranged. This child would have grown into a twisted adult. A sociopath. In any case, I knew he would not have been happy.

When I got back to our rooms, I saw that Tamio-chan's body was being cleaned in warm water, in preparation for the burial, by the other mothers. Mrs. Toda sat alone in the corner, weeping.

His naked body was even more horrible. Bruises covered more than the parts we saw the previous night. Signs of internal bleeding covered his entire body. Also we realized there were too many bruises to count on his head. The reason his head looked deformed was that there were bruises on top of bruises. His right ear was torn and blood coagulated there.

When Tamio-chan was alive, no one had felt pity for him. Everyone disliked that child. But now, some of us cried out at the sight of the small body, a body which had suffered and died in such misery. Mrs. Nagasu hurled her words at Mrs. Toda who kept crying. "It would have been better if you had just strangled him instead of abusing him like this..." With tears streaming down her face, the rest of Mrs. Nagasu's words drowned out in sobs.

But no matter what anyone said, Mrs. Toda continued to cry alone. She did not eat anything all morning. She just watched what everyone was doing and wept. The winter days darkened quickly so we hurried to bury the corpse before the ground became too frozen to dig. We put Tamio-chan in a small willow trunk and carried him up the snowy road. Halfway up the mountain, there was a small wooden sign: "Japanese Cemetery."

Snow had already been cleared off the row of fresh grave mounds dug by others. But the ground was already so hard, we couldn't dig. By taking turns we finally made a hole deep enough for the willow coffin to go in halfway. Without our men, we couldn't dig any deeper.

The sun disappeared. The dirt and ice we had just dug up blew painfully back against our cheeks with the cold wind. We hurried to cover the coffin and prepared to return. Mrs. Kurashige's younger sister, Kuniko, picked a dried up wild chrysanthemum and placed it on Tamio-chan's grave.

The chrysanthemum made a rustling sound as the wind blew. After we returned to the house, no one spoke and we went to bed in silence. I couldn't sleep with Mrs. Toda's crying near my head. "All of you don't know what kind of child he really was. That's why you said those things." Mrs. Toda said quietly.

If you didn't know about Tamio-chan's birth you would not know the real reason why he died. No one knew whether Tamio-chan's real mother was alive or dead. But I do know clearly that Tamio-chan said, "Mommy, Mommy," when he died. He had never called Mrs. Toda 'Mommy' before. Whenever he talked to his step-mother, he just glared at her face and didn't address her. Who was the 'Mommy' that Tamio-chan called out to when he opened his eyes wide? I suddenly felt chills go up my spine. I knew what he saw. He must have seen his real mother right before he died. Mrs. Toda mistook Tamio-chan's cries. He didn't call her, he called his real mother. Anyway, it didn't matter what I thought.

Outside, a blizzard stormed. The wind blew from the valley and pounded on the shuttered windows. Last night a five-year-old child died right here, right next to all of us. I held my children's feet and covered their faces halfway with the blanket. I couldn't stand the sight of the single light bulb that hung from the ceiling.

PART II

THE TOWN WITH A CHURCH

CHAPTER TWENTY

Below the Hill

Around the tenth of February, we heard some wonderful news through the grapevine. Our men were released from the *gulag* and might soon return to us! I was excited to hear that my husband might have been sent from Heijo to a prison near Enkichi city in Northern Manchuria — somebody said the men there were released on December 31. We were crazy with happiness and prepared for our husbands' return.

Sure enough, on February 12th four Japanese men arrived in our town. But those four men couldn't be considered living human beings. They returned to see their families before they died. When we saw them, we wondered whether returning to us was even moral. We thought, "They should have waited for spring before coming back." Looking back now, I'm ashamed of such terrible thoughts.

From Enkichi, the men began to stagger in. In groups of three and four, they returned — one pathetic group at a time. Most of those men died soon after they arrived, and it became common to see a crowd gathered at the Japanese cemetery, to bury them.

Even worse, these pitiful men from Enkichi brought lice and typhoid with them. Our house was selected to be a crude hospital where these men could be isolated. We were told to move out and go across the valley to another house already selected for us. When we got the order, a couple of us went to take a look at our new home. It was a depressing sight.

There were only two small rooms with a Korean *ondoru* heater. With no glass in the windows, the cold wind made itself at home by blowing right through the shabby house. But the worst was that we couldn't sleep on Japanese *tatami* mats anymore. We would miss that modest reminder of home. Maybe because no one had slept in the two rooms of this house for years; red dirt covered the cold rough floors. There was no way we could live in this place. As the representative of our group, it was up to me to plead with the Korean *Hoantai* officials for a different place we could move to. Of course, that did little good.

We had to figure out how to make this place habitable. There was nothing we could do except obey their order. All of us together cleaned and polished the place. Cleaning was easy, but fixing the house to keep the wind out was much harder. We borrowed a saw from the Japanese Association and cut wood, plugged up the gaps, and fixed the door so that humans could live here. Then we lit the *ondoru*. There used to be a metal door on the stove of the *ondoru*, evidence it had been well built. The smoke from the cooking fire flowed through the *ondoru* heater beneath the floor, warming and drying the rooms before finally flowing outside. Thus the cooking fire from our two meals each day was well used.

Dancho Narita, myself, and a couple of others went back once more up the hill to our old house to finish up the move. After we cleaned up, there was nothing left. We locked the door and went outside. But we forgot something important. Mrs. Kanaya was the one who remembered. She said, "What are we going to do with the sundial?" She was a cute young woman who rarely spoke. "What shall we do, Mr. Narita?"

He said, "Let's just take the sticks — since there's no way we can take the ice." *Dancho* Narita made a rare joke and we all laughed.

The sticks were firmly frozen in place and wouldn't come out. In the end, Mrs. Honda, the strongest of us, got a rock and knocked the sticks out, breaking each one off at the base.

The sundial was marked into sixteen degrees and was left behind at the old house. There was some fuel left from the heated room which we could use for everyone's benefit now. Our new home had just one furnace and the smoke warmed both rooms equally, although the cold still slipped in through all the cracks in the walls.

Despite her insistence on reserving the *ondoru*-heated room for the wealthier members like herself, Mrs. Nagasu became ill with pneumonia. Since she was too ill to walk, several of us carried her to our new home. By the time we got back from the hill, the rooms had warmed up. She couldn't claim the same privilege in our new home. Fuel was expensive, but if we didn't keep the *ondoru* fire going for both rooms, the warmth finally generated would be wasted. The smoke billowed cheerfully and I felt better as I watched the smoke pour out of the crooked little chimney pipe.

From our new home, I looked towards the train station. On the right side, I saw a straight road covered in snow. From the edge of town, the road bent to the left and then joined a road going into the mountains. Even when daylight was almost gone, the Japanese crowded that road with funeral processions. A coffin glittered in the evening sun as it rode on the shoulders of four people. All the men who staggered back from Enkichi were those we knew in Sensen, and that day, of those men who passed away, half were from Manchuria, like my husband. I was amazed that these half-dead men found us.

Around the end of February, two or three relatively healthy groups of men arrived. Unlike the walking cadavers from earlier, these men could actually talk and tell us things. I went to the Japanese Association to try to see if I could find out anything. Old Man Gomi accompanied me. We met a Mr. Moritomi, who said he shared the same room with my husband in the Soviet labor camp. He knew a lot about my husband up to December 31st, but not beyond that date. Still, I was relieved to hear he was alive, at least to the end of December. Mr. Moritomi also told me that Mr. Kimoto and our former *dancho*, Mr. Oe, died. Although I believed the good news about my husband, I chose to not believe the bad news about Mr. Kimoto and Mr. Oe.

He said uncertainly, "I think those men from the Meteorological Station said they were... going to Shinkyo and they took off." That made no sense, that they would go back to Shinkyo in Manchuria. But in the midst of all that chaos, there was nothing else that Mr. Moritomi knew.

I was grateful that my husband was not one of those who collapsed, like decayed logs, after being brought back on litters, only to die a week later. He might be safe and waiting for the spring. I knew how my husband thought. Somehow I guessed that he decided to put off coming back to us. When I saw those men who did came back, even after they recovered — to a somewhat human state — they were beyond hope. They remembered nothing and remained half-dead, I learned how dangerous *hikiage* was.

From Enkichi to here, in a straight line was over 300 miles, but the treacherous Chohaku Mountains, the highest peaks in northern Korea, draped itself between us. The men couldn't possibly climb those icy peaks thousands of feet high. They had to go south to Seishin, go down towards the Japan Sea coast, somehow get down to Kanko, then turn west and cross the mountains in the dead of winter. Those who made it couldn't even remember what roads they had taken — hundreds of frozen miles without any consciousness. They must have gotten on trains at some point, but they couldn't tell us where the trains were.

None of them could even remember who amongst them had succumbed to exhaustion and perished along the way. I prayed that my husband wasn't one of these forgotten dead. I fervently hoped he waited for the warmer spring, but really, it was too painful for me to accept the likelihood that he wouldn't come back at all. Every time a train pulled in, I went into the crowd, and with mixed emotions, searched for the dirty, ragged figure of my husband.

At night, the bitter cold made us feel as if we slept in a stone crypt, not a house. Maybe because of the cold drafts, a number of us became ill and were bedridden. Mrs. Nagasu's pneumonia got no better, *Dancho* Narita's wife also became sick. I felt feverish and sluggish and I worried over Masahiko who developed a nasty cough for several days. Finally, a high fever hit him and he had to stay in bed. Dr. Oya declared, "It's pneumonia." I held Masahiko in the corner of the room, feeling worthless, like piece of rubbish thrown out.

CHAPTER TWENTY-ONE

The Men from the Graveyard

Human emotions are an amazing thing. Just when I thought we were thirty desperate individuals forced to live together, there were suddenly moments when we connected and saved each other. When Masahiko had pneumonia, everyone helped me. A spirit of care grew within our *dan*. We survived day to day depending on that care. Even those who sold everything they had — somehow they managed to survive. But I know that those who still had money, kept it close and tried not to use it.

March was finally upon us and everyone had almost exhausted their funds. Still, we had to buy fuel for the *ondoru* heater. Twice a month, we paid but it was like drawing blood from stone.

At this house, there was a wall between us and our neighbors. Beyond that wall, we had no idea what was going on. I figured out that our house used to be the storage room for the *onpanya* food shop next door. Now that I remember, every night we smelled something from next door, the smell of food which made our mouths water. Our entrances were completely separate and because of that wall, we didn't know what was happening on the other side.

From time to time, we heard voices of customers. But at night, it was quiet — very quiet — perhaps the shop closed early. Once the sun set and the cold night arrived, we tried to keep the warmth inside our room by keeping our bodies still. Talking became our main activity and distraction. Night after night, we talked about food, delicious food. We carefully avoided talking about our husbands, but when something slipped out accidentally — everyone tensed up.

Around the middle of March, after dinner, we huddled together again and tried to forget the cold with idle chatter when we heard a loud commotion coming from the train station. Someone suddenly pounded on our door. "Who is it?" we yelled.

"I'm from the train station. Please come out," a Korean man shouted.

The same thought crossed our minds. Was it news about our husbands? Have they returned? We all stood up so quickly that the children woke up. Mrs. Honda lifted the thick wooden door latch, and we saw a man we didn't know, stamping his feet in the snow.

"I'm sorry...can you lend me some cloth?" The station man was very nervous.

"What? Cloth? We don't have any to spare," Mrs. Honda said pointing to a rag we had stuffed into the crack of the wall in a vain effort to stop the cold.

Mrs. Narita asked, "What do you need cloth for?"

"Just now, a Japanese jumped onto the train tracks and committed suicide," the station man blurted out and slammed the door shut.

We felt awful. It was no use trying to cheer ourselves up with chatter now. We just sat quietly, only our eyes moved. I wondered, "Was it just one person who killed himself?" Suddenly, a vision flitted across my mind. I saw myself with Sakiko on my back, Masahiro holding my right hand, and Masahiko my left. With pale faces, we jumped as a train came hurtling towards us. A shiver went up my spine and my whole body started shaking.

Beginning in March, such visions of death haunted me. In my visions—all four of us—me and my children died together. Sakiko, as a helpless baby, died without any protest. Masahiro looked at me with accusing eyes but silently did as I asked, and joined me. But Masahiko fought to the end, screaming and yelling that he didn't want to die. Such scenarios played over and over in my brain, and at the end of every vision, I found myself in a pool of tears. I'd scold myself, "No. No. I've got to return to reality. What am I going to do if that vision comes true? I've got to stay calm." I forced myself to think about something else—money.

I made plans for the next day and said to myself, "I'm going to go early to the marketplace, buy the left-over dried fish at the cheapest price, find a stalk of green onion and add them to my can, to make some soup. That's going to cost three yen..." That night, I tried to fill my mind with such trivial things as I nodded off and drifted down into a cold dream world where restless sleep was the only refuge.

But the next morning, we learned there was another suicide. Everyone fell into a disagreeable, somber mood. We occupied ourselves with preparations for work. It was unusual that day, for us to have work—someone hired us to do some brick work. While we were getting ready, we heard a strange sound from outside. "Hey…," someone called out in a faint, low voice. We looked at each other and a couple of us peeked outside. We saw nothing. But after a while, we heard something again, definitely a man right outside of our wall. Mrs. Kimoto looked out and started crying, "Ah. Ah. Ah."

Something awful must have happened. We all hurried out-side and then—we saw them—three men, barely alive crawling through the snow. The man in front tried to stand up, holding onto the wall. Another man lay face down in the snow. They had been trying to reach us. A third man, way behind the other two, lay in the snow, as if dead.

The man standing against the wall—Mr. Mizushima? Snow had filled in his glasses which had broken and were tied onto his face, and we couldn't see his eyes. His face was brown and swol-len. His pitiful figure looked like an old rag doll, shining with dirt. We stared at him until we knew for sure it was Mr. Mizushima. I immediately thought, "My husband? My husband?" He wasn't there. Mrs. Honda ran out to the second man face down in the snow and she screamed. Mr. Daichi's daughter, Seiko-chan em-braced the third man splayed out in the snow, and she began cry-ing in loud sobs, "Papa! Papa!"

I ran in the snow, like a demented woman, towards the train station. But the station was empty and no one was there. When I got back, the entire group was in tears, huddled over the men laid out in the snow. Not a single person had dry eyes. The children cried without knowing whether we were rejoicing or grieving.

The three men looked as if they had emerged from the grave-yard. They were so close to death—they couldn't hear us—they couldn't speak—they couldn't stand. Only their eyes wandered, as they searched for a face to focus on. Each of them clutched an old army blanket wrapped around their tattered clothes. The wives struggled to pry their fingers loose.

The men collapsed again after we dragged them to our doorstep. But we couldn't let them in. Strict orders had been issued. We had to prevent the spread of the deadly "Enkichi fever" (typhus), notify the Japanese Association, and take these men immediately to the makeshift hospital on the hill, the building which used to be our old home. We were afraid, but one by one, we put the three men on a litter, and hauled them up the hill. Sick men already filled the sunnier south room. We put our three men together in the eight-mat room. Dr. Oya came to examine them. Over the next days, all of their clothing was stripped off and burned because they were infested with lice. Seiko-chan and her mother were horrified at Mr. Daichi's emaciated condition. He remained in the hospital room while Mr. Mizushima and Mr. Honda were put into a special bath. The wives brought their own spare kimonos and pants and put them on their husbands. Leaning on their wives, Mr. Honda and Mr. Mizushima—staggered back to our house.

After they came back, they remained bedridden for days and days. We all waited anxiously for the moments when the two men woke up to eat, and pestered them with questions about our own husbands. But the two men only spoke a few garbled words. No one could understand most of what they said. All we could make out was, "Mr. Kimoto died. Mr. Oe died."

When Mrs. Kimoto heard this news, I was shocked at how this simple-hearted woman reacted. Her normally kind face distorted into one of terrible anger—what must it feel like to learn of her husband's death and to know she would never see him again? She must have loved her husband deeply. Old Woman Oe refused to believe that her brother, our former *dancho*, was dead and said, "No. No, that can't be true…" and clung to hope.

We stopped talking to the men. "Asking them questions like this won't do anyone any good. Let's wait until their minds heal."

A week later, I finally heard from Mr. Mizushima that my husband was released from the *gulag* but had come down with typhus, and was put in the Eighth Route Army Hospital, run by the Chinese. Mr. Mizushima was the strongest of the three, and his memory eventually came back. He peered at me though his broken glasses, and told me that at the end of January, he was let out of the Soviet military hospital and went to see the former Meteorological Station Director in Enkichi, and there he heard that my husband was hospitalized.

"Was my husband's condition good? Was it bad?" That was all I wanted to know.

But he couldn't tell me. They had been separated in the *gulag* and Mr. Mizushima could only give me second-hand information. I had read somewhere in a newspaper that if a Japanese contracted typhoid, there was an eighty percent chance he would die. To hear that he had contracted that frightening disease, and moreover, that he was put in the hands of the Chinese, in their Eight Route Army Hospital, I despaired.

Before they burned everything, I saw in the clothes of these three men—the filthy rags were covered with so much lice and lice eggs that the seams weren't visible. Even in the hats and button holes, countless lice squirmed. I was tortured when I imagined my husband covered with this lice, lying sick and alone in the Chinese hospital.

Mr. Daichi's condition deteriorated. When I went to visit him at the top of the hill, he finally recognized me but only mumbled, "...Fujiwara...bring...hot water." When they were in the *gulag* together, I guessed and hoped that my healthier husband may have brought him hot water.

Mr. Daichi strained his eyes to look at Seiko-chan's tear-stained face and his baby daughter, and he said in a fading voice, "I wanted to see you two so badly." His gaunt face had no trace of the gentle, friendly spirit I knew five months earlier.

It was the second night, after Mr. Daichi's condition worsened, I was woken by Mrs. Daichi. "Mrs. Fujiwara, my husband isn't going to make it," she whispered to me. "Can you call the doctor?" Then she ran back up the hill to the hospital. It was a freezing cold night.

The cold penetrated into my bones. Dr. Oya woke up immediately. "It's no use, *Okusan*. It would do no good for me to go up there," he said and he wouldn't even stand up.

"But you don't know unless you come, whether he's really going to die or not," I pleaded.

"I am a doctor. There is no hope for that man. There's no point in my going and wasting our precious medicine..." He stopped talking.

I couldn't convince him to come no matter what I said. I ran back along the cold, night road back up the hill, angry and blinded by tears. I said to no one in particular, "He's heartless, he's inhuman!" When I got back to the hospital, Mr. Daichi had already breathed his last.

His wife was in a stupor, her eyes locked on his face. When I came into the room, she came out of her trance and began to cry.

Mr. Daichi's dead face was smooth, with no trace of terrible suffering I saw earlier. As I listened to Mrs. Daichi cry, I felt horrible. I asked, "Mrs. Daichi, are you going to stay here?"

She said, "Please, Mrs. Fujiwara, please go home and tell Seiko-chan...she loved her father so much. I'd rather be alone here. I want to stay close to my husband until morning, then..." Her words dwindled into sobs.

CHAPTER TWENTY-TWO

A Potato with Teeth Marks

We woke early to pick up Mr. Daichi's corpse from the hospital, to begin our funeral and the procession up the hill to the cemetery. I was shocked when we saw his body. In one night, his appearance completely changed. He was dressed in an immaculate wool business suit, and a white cloth covered his face. Alone with her husband's corpse all night, Mrs. Daichi managed to undress him, clean him, and dress him in that new suit. He looked very fine now. I wondered, "How did she manage to keep this suit in the little baggage they carried from Manchuria?" If she had sold it, there would have been enough money to feed Seiko-chan and her baby for a month or two.

When we imagined of how she must have felt as she prepared her husband's body, we cried. If I were in her place, could I have done the same? We placed his body in a wooden coffin. In the afternoon, we put the coffin on an oxcart. The snow slightly softened by then, and the cart wheels made spongy sounds as we went up the hill to the cemetery.

Since the time Mrs. Toda's step-son, Tamio-chan, died, the

graveyard had changed. There were several new, large mounds of dirt lined up. Finally, we selected a spot, brushed away the snow, and dug a hole. The soil was softer now than it was at Tamio-chan's burial. The end of March was close. The thought crossed my mind, "Will we still be here in north Korea next spring?"

At the afternoon *dancho* meeting at the Japanese Association, I criticized Dr. Oya for not coming to see Mr. Daichi before he died. I said, "Even if a person is sick beyond hope, he deserves to have the doctor come." I knew I expressed what we all felt. It was also a lecture to the central Japanese Association people. Everyone's head was bowed and no one spoke. Then I got very nervous and stopped.

Deep down, I knew there was nothing any of us could do in our miserable situation. It probably didn't make sense to put all the blame on Dr. Oya. As the rice rations got cut back, more and more children became sick. Their stomachs couldn't digest the rough mixture we fed them instead of rice. Mrs. Honda's little son, Ken-chan, became very thin, weak and caught pneumonia. In just a matter of minutes, his fever spiked and he stopped breathing. Why did death come so easily? It was terrible to see Mrs. Honda, usually so strong, huddled over Ken-chan's corpse, while her husband still lay sick. We didn't know if she would ever recover, but we prepared a small coffin to carry her son up to the Japanese cemetery. Another small grave to join the many already there.

April arrived but no sign of spring yet. Rumors of the *hikiage* came and went, swirling like the wind. We all wondered, "When will we begin the journey home?" We went up into the mountains to buy cheap wood and bring it back. There was a small hamlet about two kilometers away, with the Ogawa River running through the middle. From there we climbed the mountains, to pick up wood scattered on the snowy ground and carry the pieces on our backs down the mountain. Around noon, the snow melted and our feet broke through the crunchy surface and sank into the spongy ground. Pieces of ice slipped into our shoes when we pulled our feet out from the mud. Then the ice melted in our shoes, and the cold pierced the soles of our feet.

The snow on the forest floor was thin where the sunlight had penetrated the trees. I smelled it—spring was close. I stopped to rest for a moment after I tied a bundle of the fire wood, and hoisted it onto my back before the climb back down. I glanced toward Sensen—it looked farther away than I expected. The town was hazy, the outlines of the buildings were unclear. This moisture in the air was a harbinger of spring in the valley. Only the church steeple stood out. "If those church bells rang, this whole scene would glimmer," I thought and ignored the branches poking into my back as I climbed back down the hill. When I got home, I was relieved to find my three children safe and sound.

Masahiko's pneumonia didn't seem to have slowed him down at all. He was lively as ever after recovering. He was also as hungry as ever, and always pestered me for something to eat. Today, after the wood gathering was finished, the *dan* decided to boil potatoes as an afternoon treat. After the *dan* bought and cooked the potatoes, we made a small mountain of the tubers. Instead of trying to divide the motley roots into to equal portions, we let thirty people draw for chances to choose their own potatoes.

I paid for four potato servings, so I received four chances. Once I got our potatoes, I divided them up into three small equal portions for me and the boys. Masahiro ate his potatoes slowly and with care. But Masahiko gobbled his up quickly, with gusto. As always, he then wanted some of mine. I scolded him to behave, but he didn't listen. He kept tormenting me and finally, I gave up and let Masahiko have the rest of my potatoes. Exasperated, I said, "Masahiko-chan, this is all there is. Don't give Mommy such a hard time." Masahiko finally settled down after he had my potatoes in his hands. I almost started to cry as I watched him eat so voraciously.

Suddenly, Masahiro, who had been quietly watching me and Masahiko said, "Mommy. I'll give you my potato. You can't nurse the baby if you're hungry." He handed me his half-eaten potato, one with his teeth marks still in it.

Masahiro's face was so earnest...my sad heart ached. I couldn't help but cry out. My son, who was starving himself, understood my predicament and tried to help me. I was so happy to witness this child's goodness, I started crying. Mrs. Daichi and Mrs. Kurashige turned to see why I was sobbing. Worried, they came over to me. " What's wrong, Mrs. Fujiwara?" they asked.

"It's nothing," I said and wiped my tears. I carefully tucked away that beautiful memory of Masahiro's kindness deep into my heart.

Meanwhile, his little brother, Masahiko, who had finished his potato, laughed innocently, and crowed, "Mommy's crying. Mommy's crying."

CHAPTER TWENTY-THREE

A Marriage Proposal

The snow melted in patches, and revealed the dead, flattened remnants of the previous year's grass. Between their stringy brown roots, tiny green shoots emerged. The children excitedly anticipated the arrival of spring. As the ice retreated, pale evidence of spring rose up to take its place. The boys' hair I had cut in the autumn — close to the roots — now almost reached their shoulders. Our clothes were soiled and tattered from constant wear, and we were embarrassed as we looked at each other. But our survival through the winter gave each of us a new confidence and hope.

In April, two new people joined our group. They didn't come from the prisons in Enkichi. Mrs. Kanaya and Mrs. Sakiyama gave birth. For Mrs. Kanaya, this was her first child. For Mrs. Sakiyama, this was her third baby, a girl after her two boys, Ichiro and Jiro. The babies were born ten days apart in our simple birthing area. We had set aside a third of one room by hanging large *furoshiki* squares and mats as curtains. We waited outside the curtain as a mid-wife, from another *dan,* helped with the births. Loud, healthy cries cheered us as the midwife washed the newborns in the warm water we provided in buckets. Both babies were healthy.

Afterwards, the birthing room was put away and it was as if nothing had happened there. Life soon returned to the usual pattern of waking up, sleeping, and looking for food. To supplement our meager diet, one day we bought a big *daikon* root from a handsome young Chinese man who came around to our house to sell us vegetables. One Japanese *kan* (about eight pounds), of *daikon* cost seven *yen*. We chopped the *daikon* into small pieces, and mixed it into the rice gruel. The young vegetable seller was not married and he was the one who actually proposed to Mrs. Daichi's daughter, Seiko-chan.

Seiko-chan had just turned fourteen. The heartache of losing her father made her beauty even deeper. Once, someone at a Japanese Association meeting said to me, "Your *dan* has the beautiful girl, right?"

I said, "Is she tall?" I guessed she was referring to Kuniko, Mrs. Kurashige's younger sister.

"No, she's a cute girl who's still thirteen or fourteen."

"You must be talking about Seiko-chan," I said. Not only was she beautiful, Seiko-chan was also kind and unaffected.

Often, when I was having a hard time with the children, she gave me a hand. Seiko-chan was the one who took care of her baby sister so her mother could rest. But we worried about her. When spring finally arrived, she looked so thin and pale, her skin seemed transparent. Mrs. Daichi fretted over her and said, "Oh, dear — she's at that age, she needs to eat more."

He proposed in the middle of April. One day around noon, the Chinese vegetable seller came to our place. He was dressed in clean clothes, and Mrs. Kimoto, who was good at speaking Chinese, went out to talk with him. I remember Mrs. Kimoto said, "Today, he's not here to sell us his vegetables. He wants to discuss a very important matter." Then the two of them stepped outside to talk.

Mrs. Kimoto returned with an unusually serious face. She went straight to Mrs. Daichi, and said, "*Okusan* (Ma'am), the vegetable seller asked for the hand of your daughter, Seiko-chan — in marriage." Mrs. Daichi frowned. "That man? What?" Mrs. Daichi looked with fear at Mrs. Kimoto. The vegetable seller quietly appeared at the front door. His handsome, sincere face looked very nervous while Seiko-chan, when she heard the proposal, stiffened and hid behind her mother.

"Mrs. Kimoto, would you please decline his proposal?" Mrs. Daichi said very coolly and turned a hundred and eighty degrees to face the wall, picked up her sleeping baby and began to cry softly. After a while, Mrs. Kimoto returned.

"I'm so sorry, Mrs. Daichi," Mrs. Kimoto apologized as if she were responsible, and placed her hands on the floor.

Mrs. Daichi didn't say anything and kept crying. "He asked me to speak to you," Mrs. Kimoto said as if to atone for her part in the drama.

Mrs. Daichi turned her face away as if no one was in the room, and said nothing. Mrs. Daichi and Mrs. Kimoto, both widows now, must have felt the pain of their grief again with this mention of marriage. The silence of the women filled the room.

That morning, I felt itchy and restless. We hadn't bathed for over two weeks. In order to escape the silence and the stale air in the damp room, I took the three children and went to the bath in town. The willow trees were in bloom and the distant mountains were surrounded in mist. Clouds, creamy and soft, floated through the valley, naturally losing strength as they collected near the base of the mountains, and a gentle, warm rain fell. Now that the harsh winter had faded, I thought of northern Manchuria, where my husband was. Was a warm spring rain falling there, too? If my husband's grave was on a mountain top, then the rain would be very cold.

When we got back from our bath, Mrs. Daichi was still in the same position — holding her baby in silence — while Seiko-chan's face shone white as paper in the dark room. Tears glistened off of tips of her long lashes which made her eyes look even more luminous. It pained me to see her crouched next to her mother, as if it was her fault for causing her mother this anguish.

The children ran about in room in excitement, raising a cloud of dust. From time to time, Mrs. Nagasu, who was still ill with pneumonia, woke up and weakly scolded the children. "Please stop making so much noise," she wheezed painfully.

CHAPTER TWENTY-FOUR

The White Cross

Church bells rang gracefully across the May sky. Along with the sound of the church bells, the breeze carried the smell of budding plants to every corner of the town. A group of well-dressed Koreans gathered at the church — amongst them a man in a white robe laced with deep, dark blue trim, and a woman with a bright red skirt. The sound of the Sunday church bells rang out gently in the calm spring air.

I stood there casually watching the people. Masahiro had a fever since morning and so I asked Mrs. Kurashige to go in my place to the weekly Japanese Association meeting in the afternoon. *Dancho* Narita hadn't attended the meetings for a long time. He was still not well and even if he got up, soon he'd have to lie down again. So Mrs. Kurashige and I had taken over all the diplomatic matters for our *dan*.

"Mommy."

I heard Masahiro's voice from his bed.

"What's wrong, Masahiro-chan?"

"My throat hurts." Masahiro didn't want me to leave his side. Unlike his little brother, he was usually not so clingy. Even when he had a cold he patiently lay alone in his bedding. It was strange that day, that he spoke in such a sad, needy way. In the afternoon, his fever rose. He complained that his throat hurt and it was difficult to breathe. "Perhaps it's just a cold," I thought. "But remember how bad Masahiko's cold became?" So this time, I decided to stay by Masahiro instead of performing my *fuku-dancho* duty. When the sun set, his fever suddenly shot up higher. He was so hot, steam rose off of the wet cloth I placed on his head.

"It must be pneumonia," I said.

Mrs. Toda went to fetch Dr. Oya but he wasn't there. Apparently he was gone to tend to three patients who were near death and couldn't get away. Masahiro breathed heavily through his mouth and nose, and I heard a rattling sound from the back of his throat.

"Something is wrong," Mrs. Toda said.

We asked Mrs. Daichi to listen. She said she could hear that rattling sound as well. I worried that Masahiro had caught that frightening contagious disease, diphtheria. Mrs. Daichi tried to reassure me and said, "Mrs. Fujiwara, it's all right. It couldn't possibly be that disease spreading here."

If it was pneumonia, for Masahiro that was a serious, grave situation. But if it was diphtheria...I couldn't just sit there. Noticing my agitation, Mrs. Toda ran again to get Dr. Oya but he still wasn't there. That night there was no wind at all, and in the hazy moonlight, several large dark shadows loomed. The water I pulled up from the well was icy cold. A halo glowed around the moon as it rose higher while I went back and forth between the well and the house to rinse the cloth.

Masahiro started twisting his body uncomfortably. His face was red, his eyes bloodshot and his body convulsed with the difficulty of breathing. Watching him was torture. Suddenly, Masahiro sat up and trembled.

"What is it?" I cried and stopped wringing out the wet hand cloth. Dark, foul smelling blood and pus gushed out of his nose.

"Oh!" I held Masahiro in my arms and whispered for help, "Hurry, go get Dr. Oya!"

Mrs. Toda had been by my side, watching Masahiro. She went running. I waited and listened for their footsteps, "Are they back yet, are they back yet?" I only heard one pair of feet instead of two return.

Mrs. Toda gasped, "Dr. Oya was there but he didn't come. He told me that it must be diphtheria. He said we might as well give up. I begged and begged him to come but he said that as long as we didn't have the diphtheria serum there was nothing he could do. He said it costs about one thousand yen for a diphtheria injection. "

I thought about going to the doctor myself to beg him one more time, but then when I thought about what happened with Mrs. Daichi's husband, I knew there would be no use in going to Dr. Oya. I asked Mrs. Toda and Mrs. Daichi to watch the children, and I rushed in to town to find another doctor. But I didn't know the layout of the town. I knew where one small hospital was, but they didn't have anyone on night duty. I knocked on their door, but no one woke up.

I returned home and waited anxiously for dawn to break. The question, "How am I going to find one thousand yen for the serum?" tormented me all night. I only had about a hundred yen left in my wallet. I used up the one thousand yen hidden in the corn husks. The only thing I had left was the Longines watch, still hidden in the bar of soap. I despaired, "How much would I get if I sold that watch to a local watch dealer?" The other day, Mrs. Toda sold her wrist watch for two hundred yen. From that I guessed I would, at the most, get about two or three hundred yen. There was nothing else I could sell. Even if I were to borrow that money, there were no Japanese who had that much cash.

"One thousand yen. One thousand yen — how...how am I going to make that?" Such thoughts raced through my mind as I held Masahiro and agonized while everyone else slept through the night. I made my plan: the first thing I could do when dawn broke was to go to Old Man Gomi and his wife to borrow some money, then I would collect as much money as I could from my *dan*, and sell the watch. Could I collect one thousand yen with all that? It didn't seem possible...but as I looked at poor Masahiro's anguished face, blood streamed down his face, and I suddenly saw the Japanese cemetery.

"Damn," I cried fighting off the horrible vision. I became frantic and knew that somehow I was going to have to overcome that premonition. Morning finally arrived. I left Masahiro and ran to Old Man Gomi's place. He came out in his usual manner, shoulders narrowed and back bent. His wife also came out. I blurted out my case.

He said, "That is too bad. What can we do? We don't have much money. " The old man paced back and forth in the narrow hallway, blinking his eyes helplessly. I wanted him to lend me two hundred yen — even just one hundred yen. I lowered myself like a miserable street beggar. "Please even a hundred or two hundred yen..." I swallowed my pride, and pleaded and begged. The old couple looked at each other helplessly.

They didn't say anything but I realized from the look on their faces. "It's no good!" I said to myself. My head almost burst with feelings of worry, shame and frustration—but in the end, they couldn't help me. I didn't bother to say anything else to the old couple, and rudely left. I didn't even try the Japanese Association. Next was the watch shop. The night before, I had melted the soap to get the watch out. I clutched it now to my chest and ran into the store.

The store owner was startled when I came rushing in a panic. When I demanded five hundred yen, he didn't even look at my watch. He turned me down, saying, "Right now even the best watches go for around three hundred yen. A pocket watch like yours would much cheaper than that."

These days the town was full of watches. More and more desperate Japanese from Manchuria sold their watches to anyone who would buy.

"So how much can I sell this for?" I asked.

"Well, at the most, it would be two hundred and fifty yen." The shopkeeper said this without enthusiasm and tried to go slip in to his back room. I had to somehow get five hundred yen for this watch. But at the next shop they also offered only two hundred and fifty yen.

"I must not panic. If I panic, I will lose. I must sell this Longine for five hundred yen." Saying this mantra to myself, I went into a third watch shop, but suddenly felt I had to see Masahiro who was still at the house. When I got back I saw that Mrs. Toda had wiped more blood from Masahiro's nose.

Her face white with fear, she said, "Mrs. Fujiwara, unless a doctor sees him soon..." I asked Mrs. Toda to help me lift Masahiro. His body limp across my back felt like a burning fire ball as

I ran to the biggest hospital in the town. There was no one in the waiting room. I gave Mrs. Toda the watch and asked her to raise the money. I prayed that somehow she would be able to do it. We were taken into the examination room. The doctor looked at Masahiro's throat, left the room and came back with another doctor. The two doctors examined Masahiro in turn.

"It is diphtheria," they said. Those words were a death sentence.

The doctor saw the look on my face and said, "I am so sorry to say this, but we have no diphtheria serum here. Hurry and take him to the Salvation Hospital. They may have some there."

"Do you know how much the serum will cost?" I asked a small female doctor who stood nearby.

"Probably about a thousand yen." she said as she looked with pity at Masahiro.

I ran into the street with the doctor's directions to the Salvation Hospital. When I crossed the bridge I saw the tall red-brick tower of the church above the other buildings. The Salvation Hospital was next to the church. A large white cross stood above a big wooden placard with the English words, "Salvation Hospital."

"This hospital must be run by the church," I told myself.

Inside it felt like a different world. I went through the front gate, across a beautiful lawn, and noticed the green leaves of the willow trees in sharp contrast to the white building. Right away they took me and my son into an examination room. On the table, there were Japanese and German medical books lined up. A young Korean doctor sat behind the desk. He looked up at me with kind eyes as I walked in.

"What seems to be the matter?" he said as he looked at Masahiro who was taken off of my back. I told him what had happened. He listened carefully and then said, "Let's take a look," and took out his stethoscope.

"Yes, it's diphtheria and it is quite advanced. I can see the white spots in the back of his throat." He spoke calmly as if he were lecturing me and the assistant who stood nearby.

"Prepare the serum right away for the injection," he ordered the assistant and then busily cleared the area.

"Excuse me, doctor, how much will the injection cost?"

The doctor turned around and looked at my face searchingly. I saw his face soften from a look of concentration to one of compassion. I held onto Masahiro and broke down crying.

I said, "I am sorry, I do not have a thousand yen. My friend, Mrs. Toda is trying to collect as much money as she can and will come here later...but there will not be close to one thousand yen. But please help my child, please help him..."

I could no longer look at the doctor's face. It was as if a veil fell over my eyes. I only saw the doctor's white coat reflected inside a prism of tears. The white coat came closer. "*Okusan*, we are ready for the injection. Please turn your child this way."

The doctor's voice rang through my head like a sharp bell. He understood my situation. I did as I was told. My tears flowed as he promptly gave the injection. Without any change in his manner, the doctor quietly finished and then said, "He is all right now, *Okusan*."

"Thank you very much," I blurted out, but all I could do was cry.

"Excuse me, Mrs. Fujiwara," the door opened a sliver, and Mrs. Toda peeped in. She had waited until the injection was done. I looked at her and knew right away that she hadn't been able to raise the money. I went into the hallway with her.

"Mrs. Fujiwara, I'm sorry. I just couldn't get more than three hundred yen together. And no matter where I went they wouldn't offer more than two hundred and fifty yen for the watch. So I brought it back with me."

"Thank you, Mrs. Toda. I'm surprised you were able to find us here."

"Yes, the female doctor at the other hospital told me."

I took the watch and the three hundred yen and went to the examination room. I decided to tell the young doctor everything. First, I would have to apologize.

"I am sorry, Doctor. I don't have my money ready. I know I am wrong to ask a favor of you after you've already given the injection." Then I explained everything to him and the doctor listened in silence.

"Madam, who said anything about paying a thousand yen?" he asked me in a gentle tone.

I thought, "That was true, I had determined for myself that the price was a thousand yen."

I said, "I'm sorry. The people at the other hospital said..."

The doctor interrupted me saying, "I haven't written any bill yet." The doctor smiled very gently as he said this. "Let me see the two hundred and fifty yen watch." He took the Longines watch from my hand and placed it on top of the sheet of paper lying on the table.

He said, "Well, it really is a Longines watch."

The doctor looked at me. "This used to be your husband's?"

"Yes, it was. He had it since before we were married."

"Pardon me, but can I ask what your husband was doing?"

"He used to work at the meteorological station in Manchuria."

"He was a scientist, wasn't he?" he said.

I didn't answer his question. The doctor took the Longines and placed it next to his ear. As he listened to its second hand, he went deep into thought. The examination room was so quiet I heard that second hand echo.

Finally, he said, "I will accept this watch as the thousand yen payment."

As he declared this plainly, he said something very quickly in Korean to the accountant who was sitting in the corner of the office. The accountant didn't seem to agree with the doctor and he opened his eyes wide in disbelief. "I will cover the bill." This time the Korean doctor spoke very clearly in Japanese. The accountant still didn't seem to agree completely. The assistant stood up and explained the situation to the accountant. I was just in a daze. But I felt I mustn't take advantage of this man.

So I got up, "You are doing too much. Please take this three hundred yen."

The doctor shook his head and motioned me back. When it appeared that everything was settled, he returned to his seat and instructed me, "Tomorrow, please come here again." Then he motioned with his eyes to the assistant to let the next patient in.

As I stood up to go, he said in a quiet voice, "Don't lose hope, Madam. Keep up your spirits until you return to Japan."

Mrs. Toda waited in the hallway. We walked out together through the front door. As we walked by, I thought of the American missionaries who built this red-brick tower so many years ago—the church spire seemed to soar before my eyes. The bells that rang out joyously every Sunday gleamed in their black paint, and were now silent. I turned back once more to look at the Salvation Hospital sign, and quietly lowered my head in front of the white cross. Now I began to have faith that Masahiro would live and get better. I started to go across the same bridge I had earlier crossed in a desperate panic. Halfway, I stopped and looked down on the spring waters which flowed beneath the bridge. The river was an opaque blue-green, like the leaves of the willows dragging along the sides. From both grassy green banks of the river, Korean women did their wash. Their robes reflected beautifully in the river, the white images shimmered and danced, and made the river stand still.

CHAPTER TWENTY FIVE

The Element of Love

Masahiro, once he received the injection for diphtheria, was finally able to sleep on the third day. When everyone back at the house first learned that Masahiro had diphtheria, some reacted badly. Mrs. Kurashige blanched, clutched her son, and without a word, moved out from the room we shared, and went to the next room. No one else moved. Mrs. Kurashige was so callous in her behavior that everyone glared at her reproachfully. I felt awkward and said to Mrs. Daichi who remained nearby, "Please, Mrs. Daichi, it would be terrible if Masahiro's illness spread to you so don't hesitate to move out, too."

But she held onto Seiko-chan and the baby, and didn't move. "I couldn't do such a thing. Don't worry about me. Please take care of little Masahiro-chan. We'll watch Masahiko and Sakiko-chan, for you."

I made a little isolated spot in the corner of the room. I lay down with Masahiro. I hadn't been able to sleep for the past three days, but still couldn't rest until the fifth day, when Masahiro was able to smile. Then I slept like the dead for the next whole day. Willow leaves and the white cross drifted in and out of my dreams.

Beginning in April, our *dan* decided to hold a formal meeting once a week. In these meetings we discussed various things. That Saturday night, Masahiro completely recovered. Mr. Narita began the meeting with announcements and then a discussion about future plans on how to get back to Japan. But we were all aware that his wife, Mrs. Narita, said nothing. Usually, she was very talkative. Everyone couldn't help but notice her silence and wondered what was going on.

Something was up. Sure enough, at the end of the meeting, she spoke up. "I witnessed something terrible in our group recently that I just cannot remain silent about." She spoke about the night Masahiro was sick with diphtheria. She criticized Mrs. Kurashige and the way she fled from our room. A number of the other women voiced agreement with her. Mrs. Kurashige was silent, then finally spoke, "But I wanted to save my little boy, my son..." and she broke down.

Everyone's anger abated and they fell silent. I understood how angry Mrs. Narita felt. But I also understood how Mrs. Kurashige felt. The unfortunate reality of terrible things happening one after another.

I interjected, "I feel like I imposed on everyone with this illness. I especially have to give my thanks to Mrs. Toda who worked so hard for me." After her step-son, Tamio-chan's death, Mrs. Toda hardly spoke with anyone. There were even days when she remained in bed all day, not even washing her face. But as spring approached, she seemed to regain her strength, and began to speak. When we went to a far mountain together to gather firewood, I learned about her true nature. As we walked along the two kilometer road, we talked. I realized that Mrs. Toda was not the sort of woman that I had imagined her to be.

She said, "Mrs. Fujiwara, do you still think that I am that horrible woman who killed Tamio?"

"No, I don't." I said. "I remember when Mrs. Nagasu yelled at you and you said that no one really knows Tamio-chan. Since then I thought that there must be a deeper reason for what happened."

"Really, Mrs. Fujiwara? You are so kind to think that way." Mrs. Toda's face lit up in a way that had never done before. "Mrs. Fujiwara, love is such an essential element for people, the absence of it can be tragic."

"An essential element?" I asked.

"Listen—Say there are two people. It doesn't matter whether they are men or women. Anyway, there are two people. If there isn't that element of love, some potential of love between the two people, no matter how hard they try, they will never be able to love each other. I think that love is defined by certain conditions from the time one is born. There are people who cannot love— even their own children. For them, that element of love didn't exist from the beginning.

"That was what happened between Tamio and me. The element of love was missing. When I first saw him, I was repulsed by that unattractive child. Tamio must have felt the same way—repulsion toward me.

"He glared at me so hard as to bore holes into my face. I tried and tried so hard to love Tamio that first year. But it was no good. As those cold eyes of that child glared at me, I realized that all my efforts didn't make one bit of difference. You see, Mrs. Fujiwara, after it became clear that there was no element of love between us, the harder I tried to hide that fact, the more suffering it caused both of us.

"I was so frustrated that—for the first time in my life—I hit a child. But Tamio did not give in at all when I did that. Instead, his animosity grew even stronger. And so that abuse kept escalating until you saw what happened. I know what you would probably say. That love between two people can be learned. No, no, I thought so hard about that. I tried to create that love, but it was no good."

When I saw how much Mrs. Toda suffered, I felt truly sorry for her. I said, "I don't know what I would do if I had a child like Tamio-chan. I would probably either be a hypocrite and pretend to love him or...do what you did. "

"Wait, Mrs. Fujiwara. Are you saying that—do what you did—means kill him? That is not what I meant at all. I didn't think that you, of all people, thought that way. He is dead now so I will tell you exactly what I think.

"Even though that child was only five, he was clever. He knew how to upset our entire *dan*. He was a truly frightening, evil child...that child. If he had lived, what sort of an adult would he have become? I admit I am the one who killed him. It wasn't anyone else. I tried to use violence and force to control his evil spirit. From his head to his feet, the blood..."

"Please, Mrs. Toda, please stop," I said. "I understand now how you feel. Tamio died because...maybe we are a people maimed by war—a war that spawned monsters—men, women and children. That is the most important cause. And I understand clearly what you mean by the essential element of love. I apologize for criticizing you when I didn't really understand how you suffered so deeply."

I looked at Mrs. Toda's face, a face flooded with relief. She had said everything she wanted to say. After this, Mrs. Toda became a close friend. She was alone now, and free. She often looked after my children. She was especially fond of Sakiko and often held her for me.

I even lightly said to her once, "If I die, I want you to bring Sakiko to my family."

"Oh, yes. That would be my pleasure," she said.

"But...," I mumbled.

She said, "I know. You are afraid that I might treat her as I treated Tamio. Don't worry. I love this child. Right, Sakiko, chan?" she said to the baby. It was such a moment of joy and happiness.

After I began to trust Mrs. Toda, Masahiro became ill with diphtheria. I thanked Mrs. Toda from the bottom of my heart for helping me. "And I have to thank everyone who contributed money to help Masahiro," I said to her.

"But you don't need to do that since I returned the money I collected to everyone." Mrs. Toda said this with a nod of her head.

"No, you are wrong. I have to thank people for at least their gesture of kindness, when we all have such hardship."

"Well, Mrs. Fujiwara, you are a more noble person than I am. I remember when I asked everyone to contribute. I said to myself, that person...she makes me mad. She has lots of money but she only gave a stingy 20 yen. That woman..."

I quickly raised my hand to her lips and stopped her. "Don't say such things. If you start talking about how much each person gave, it's only going to create bad feelings. I don't want to have those thoughts when I am with that person. Isn't that right? Just tell me who contributed." I said.

"Well, in that case. Everyone, every single person contributed," she said sharply, still angry.

"Everyone contributed? Is that so?" I said. I felt my chest tighten. I was so happy to be part of this *dan*, this miserable group of desperate women.

CHAPTER TWENTY-SIX

Fighting the Spring Wind

When I think about it now, I don't know whether May 15th was a day to celebrate, or a day to mourn. At first, we were happy to hear that the Japanese Association released us from our assigned *dan*. On the one hand, we no longer had to follow their rules for where we lived, worked or bought our food. But on the other hand, we would no longer receive their daily rice rations of two *go* (a little over a cup) per person that they gave us through the winter. I thought about it all night. The problem was this: how was I going to feed my children? By morning I still hadn't come up with a solution. That evening, the town was full of Japanese looking for work, red-eyed with desperation.

I had to do something, so I walked with everyone around town, but most of us returned empty-handed and with heavy feet. In ten days, our *dan* would be formally disbanded. We would all have to fend for ourselves. Rice cost forty-five yen for one *sho* (about 7 cups). Corn was fifteen yen for one *sho*. I calculated that the four of us would have to have at least twenty yen a day to survive. I asked myself, "How can I earn twenty yen a day?"

Before the week was out, the women who were childless or had older children, found jobs one by one. Many of them got hired as maids, and often the employers provided food, too. Women with small children had the hardest time finding work. On top of that, we were the ones who used up money the fastest. The women worst off in our group were Mrs. Daichi with her baby, Mrs. Sakiyama with her two boys — Ichiro and Jiro, and her newborn — and myself. With Sakiko on my back, I went to find work in a desperate mood, but as soon as any prospective employers saw my baby, they turned me away.

Ten days passed quickly, the group divided up the remaining food amongst the members, and our formal *dan* pretty much disappeared. We were each left to our own devices. No more rations, no more communal meals. Each family cooked their own food in a *hango* hung over a small fire. The differences between rich and poor became very apparent. Some ate white rice while some ate only corn. But the worst part of this change was that we still had to live side by side, and try to ignore these differences.

At first, I imitated the others and sold cigarettes at the train station. I bought a cigarette for four *yen* and sold it for five *yen*. If I didn't sell twenty of them, my family starved. To be honest, at that time, I didn't have even one *yen* left. On the first day, I managed to sell five cigarettes.

I went through my rucksack to find something to sell. The shirt I made for my husband was exchanged for two *sho* of dried corn. I sold my husband's pants for twenty-five *yen*. If I crushed the corn kernels and soaked them over night, they would get soft. Mixed in my *hango,* I made a gruel which turned into a glue-like paste. After it sat for a while, the thick lump popped out of the *hango* in one piece. Then I cut it into slabs, added salt—and we ate it. That's all.

After a while, I figured out how to add wild plants, especially goosefoot weed. While I was out, Masahiro went out and gathered the tall, spindly weeds growing everywhere. That became our main food. Right before I lay down exhausted every night, I put away my *hango*, and nursed Sakiko. But my breasts stopped producing milk—and Sakiko cried. I scraped the gruel left on the sides of my *hango* with a spoon and fed that to Sakiko while I swallowed a few bits.

"Mommy, I want more," Masahiko incessantly whined.

While I knew that a three-year old boy could not be satisfied with such puny meals twice a day, I scolded him, "Masahiko-chan, please don't worry me. Mommy doesn't have any money now. That's why I can't give you more food. Understand? Be patient just a little longer and we'll get to Grandma's house. Then you can eat lots and lots of white rice."

I told the children this same lie, over and over but Masahiko no longer accepted my stories. Finally, I said, "Look at your big brother." Masahiro was quiet, watching the two of us argue. Masahiko finally gave up, and stuck his fingers into the *hango* to find any remaining specks of food.

Then Masahiro noticed something across the room and his eyes shone. Over in another corner, people ate bowls full of white rice. Sometimes, they even put an egg on their rice. I shifted my body to try to block his view, and Masahiro then craned his neck to look around me. When he caught my angry look, my poor son adverted his eyes as if he had done something bad. The word— 'inhumane'—comes to mind. Inhumane refers to moments like this. That person who ate a simple meal—that person had no idea how much suffering was caused.

There cannot be a greater torture in this world for children, than that of starving while watching others eat. I used to cry every night as I thought about this. But I stopped crying when I decided, "This is war. This is our war to survive." I grabbed the *hango* that Masahiko was still licking and took it out to wash at the well.

The warm spring air tickled my face as I faced the wind. I pulled up my long hair so tight it hurt, and tied it into a knot.

CHAPTER TWENTY-SEVEN

Teacher of Soap Sales

Mrs. Daichi usually slept next to us, and I noticed she was gone early one morning. I asked Seiko-chan, "Where did your mother go?"

"She wrapped something up in a *furoshiki* cloth and went out," she said.

I thought, "She must have gone out to sell something. Do I have anything else I could sell?" But I had already looked through my rucksack. Mrs. Daichi came back with her *furoshiki* wrapped around something heavy. When she unwrapped it, I saw she had blocks of — soap.

"Mrs. Daichi, are you going to sell soap?"

As she sorted and wrapped ten bars of soap, she turned to me. "I'm going to start a soap business today. And I sold my last kimono to buy this."

"Can you really make money with soap?" I said uncertainly.

"I think this is better than selling cigarettes. I buy the soap for eight *yen* a piece, then sell for ten. I'll make two *yen* if I sell one."

"That's true but...," I pictured myself going door to door trying to sell soap.

Mrs. Daichi snapped, "Mrs. Fujiwara, I'll bet you don't like the idea. This isn't something you can do anyway. A privileged lady like you can't do this."

"What? Me, a privileged lady?" I was hurt.

"That's right. In order to do this, you need street smarts. When my father failed in his business, I had to quit girls' high school after just two years, get married at nineteen, and have my baby, Seiko when I was just twenty."

Seiko blushed when she heard her mother.

Mrs. Daichi continued, "It was really tough. My husband worked at a delivery company, and only got forty *yen* a month. He tried to save money by having half of a ten *sen* fried potato croquette for dinner, and then saved the rest for lunch the next day. Somehow we managed to get by, but one day he got hurt and lost his job. What do you think I did? This is what I did."

Mrs. Daichi pointed at the soap. "Fate led me that way. We were at the end of our rope back then, and now here's our second time to be at the end of the rope."

She looked at me. "All right, Mrs. Fujiwara, don't just sit there being impressed. If you want, why don't you come with me and learn to sell soap door-to-door? Back when I started, I had a soap sales teacher. She was a nasty, stingy old woman but she taught me. Now I'm going to be your teacher. I'll bet you don't even have one *sen* now. If you don't completely change right now, your family is doomed. Your problem is, you're always trying to be on everyone's good side. You're a brownnoser. "

I was shocked. "What? You accuse me of being—a brownnoser?"

"It won't do any good for you to get mad. I know your true nature. You're really much tougher than you appear — but you try to hide it from people. You've been brought up to be a lady. But that's no good now. You're finished unless you're willing to put yourself out there."

I couldn't say anything. She was right.

Mrs. Daichi became my teacher — I was her student. I went with her out to town. She instructed me, "Mrs. Fujiwara, don't carry more than ten bars of soap. When you sell out, go home to get more. If you carry more than that, they won't feel sorry for you. The most important thing is to make them feel sorry for you — they must feel pity. Once you do that, you can lead the customer into thinking something like, 'I guess I'll buy something from her.' I can't explain it in just words. Buying a bar of soap is nothing to most people, but still there's a hesitation to reach into the wallet. If we put ourselves in the head of the customer, we can understand her and mold her actions."

She showed me her hands. "And you've got to always keep your hands and face clean. In that respect, you're good. Always keep your baby on your back, and keep the baby's hands and face clean, too. Nobody likes to get near a dirty person. You've got to let them know you're clean."

We walked along the mountain road near town, and stopped before a grand house. She said, "See this stone gate? Don't go to a house with this kind of a gate. You'll get run off like a stray dog. Rich people despise beggars and door-to-door salesmen. Go for the middle-class households as much as possible. Keep your eyes and ears open — you want a place with elderly people. If there's an old person holding a baby, that's the best. It's not good for two of us to walk together but I'll go with you today to teach you.

It's your first day, but it's been fourteen, fifteen years since I did this."

We came to another a nice house with a stone gate. "Mrs. Fujiwara, let's try this house. As I said, we probably won't sell anything to rich people like this." We went around to the kitchen door and knocked. An old lady came out but she didn't understand us. Mrs. Daichi explained in pantomime, and the old lady went back inside. A couple of children came out to take a peek at us, then a tall, younger man came out.

"Soap? We don't want any," he said as he looked at us with contempt. We felt his coldness and went back out through the fine stone gate. I was impressed at Mrs. Daichi's confidence.

She said, "See? Just as I told you. Don't go to rich houses. Sometimes there are exceptions but it would take all day to find that one exception."

I followed my wonderful teacher and we went towards the town. She said, "Also, I remember…people who are poor are no good either. Sometimes they even threw buckets of water at me!" Mrs. Daichi's memories of those hard times and humiliations many years ago came flooding back, and she laughed out loud.

CHAPTER TWENTY-EIGHT

The Couple Who Lived on Bickering

The water well area got lively with chatter when we all washed our tired feet at the end of the day. After our feet were clean, we gathered around to talk about—food. Everyone had something to say about food—a favorite recipe or a memorable meal. Sometimes the discussions got very animated. But usually, things quieted down after we ate, and got ready to go to sleep. But there was one couple who kept talking after everyone else was quiet—*Dancho* Narita and his wife.

You wouldn't guess this about them from *Dancho* Narita's sickly constitution, and the fact that these two didn't talk much with the rest of us. This couple spent hours talking, or rather, bickering with each other every night. And the nature of their exchanges were never calm. Their conversations went like this.

Mrs. Narita would begin, "Why did you only help Hisako-chan with her homework? Why didn't you help our son, Daikyo, with his?"

"I did help him," *Dancho* Narita said.

As she lay down, she said, "No, you didn't. You don't care about your own son. After the Japanese school closed in June, parents are responsible for their education. Didn't you know that?"

"Yes, so I did help," he said.

"You teach other people's kids with much more care than you do for your own child," she said.

"I teach everyone the same way," he said.

"That's a lie. On top of that, you don't really care about your family. When we left Shinkyo, you were the only one who forgot to bring a water bottle and a *hango*," she added.

He shot back. "If you want to talk about somebody's bad points, there's plenty to criticize. Who was the silly woman who made such a fuss bringing Manchurian treasury bills worth less than toilet paper?"

"If we had brought one more kimono, we could have lived for another month off of it," she said.

Dancho Narita did not give up. "What did you say? It was the husbands who had to carry all of the women's kimonos to the train station," he said

Neither did she. She said, "If you had run home before the train left, you could have brought them. Who was the one just standing around? Other men grabbed government hand carts and had gone back and forth two or three times during the time you just stood around," she said.

"If you like that sort of conniving man, you could have married one. I'm not the kind who machinates and schemes."

"That's a lot of baloney you say to cover up your own lack of courage. What do you think is better? Who is better off?" she persisted.

"You can complain all you want after the fact. If you had a

man you could order around, you would have had him get a one hundred thousand *yen* bankbook for you," he said.

"There you go again—changing the subject. You're a man who never thinks about his responsibilities," she said.

"If I thought about all the responsibilities you wanted me to, I'd be dead by now," he said.

"So you'd die and leave us, would you? And not care about Daikyo and me," she said.

"I never said that," he said.

"Yes, you did. Just now," she said.

And they went on and on like this every night. If I recorded all the conversations between that man and woman over the course of a year, the words probably wouldn't fit in hundreds of volumes of books. Those two went on like this every night until about one a.m. Only after they exhausted themselves would they finally stop talking and go to sleep. The rest of us listened to their fights in the dark. We didn't tell them to shut up—but we didn't enjoy it either—we'd just go to sleep.

Dancho Narita never lost his temper with anyone else but he didn't smile either. He was angry with his wife all the time. Half bedridden, he got up but went back to bed every day, looking especially thinner these days.

Sometimes in the bathroom, I noticed scribbles written on the old magazine papers we used for toilet paper. There were tiny symbols written in the white spaces between the lines of text that had faded red. The pencil marks were new and they were scientific terms so I thought it must be *Dancho* Narita. I told myself, "I must ask him about these notes."

One night, I noticed him walking around outside and I asked, "*Dancho* Narita, why did you write the words, fiddlehead fern and duck, on the old magazine papers?"

"What? Ferns and ducks?" *Dancho* Narita's cheeks puffed out and his eyebrows scrunched up. "What do you mean, ferns and ducks?"

I said, "Fiddlehead fern is what I call the integral sign and duck is what I say for the differential symbol."

"Oh. That. Mrs. Fujiwara, you're pretty good at figuring out what I wrote," he said. "I was trying to calculate the errors."

I said, "Errors in what?"

"Errors in calculating the constant year," he said. "I'm trying to calculate it as much as I can."

I said, "That's impressive that you're doing that without any of your books."

He said, "Yes, I'm doing the best I can." *Dancho* Narita stopped talking and looked at me. "*Okusan,* you just called the integral sign a fiddlehead fern. Why did you do that?"

I laughed. "Oh, that's from when my husband and I had just gotten married. I saw my husband writing something and I asked him, 'What's this fiddlehead fern?'"

Then my husband said, "What? Fiddlehead fern? Oh, I get it. Yes, you're right, the symbol does look like a fiddlehead fern." He was very tickled and amused. "What about this symbol?" he said and wrote the differential symbol."

I said, "That's a duck."

"A duck? Yes, that's a duck," he said. My husband and I had a good laugh over that. That's when I started calling integral signs 'fiddlehead ferns' — and differential symbols 'ducks'."

As I remembered that time, I laughed harder than I had in a long time. But *Dancho* Narita didn't laugh, not even a smile. He just frowned in concentration and said, "Very interesting. Integral signs are fiddlehead ferns, and differential symbols are ducks. Fascinating."

Dancho Narita was the scientific sort, the kind of man who didn't have a sense of humor. Sometimes, I thought he would die never having laughed in his life. Once, in the middle of winter around January, I took Masahiko out to pee and—probably because it was so cold—I noticed his penis was small and shriveled up. As I helped him go to the bathroom, his piss streamed out sideways.

When I mentioned this back in the house to the other mothers, *Dancho* Narita, who overhead me said, "Ladies, don't worry. When I went to the public bath in town, there was a naked man who came in with a tiny one, and he had three fine boys with him. Don't worry. He'll be fine."

When we heard this, we burst out laughing. We kept thinking about what he said, and couldn't stop giggling. Soon our laughter turned into howls, and silly Mrs. Kimoto laughed so hard, she fell to the ground, out of breath, and tears streamed down her face. *Dancho* Narita just looked at us women, his face set in a frown. He didn't understand why we thought it was so funny.

I must say though that *Dancho* Narita has some amazing talents. In bookkeeping, he always calculated every item to the smallest *sen* and *ren* in his reports. He also had an internal clock. Whenever anyone was late coming home from work in the evenings, he always noticed, and sent two people out to find out where she was. Without looking at any watch, he'd say, "It's around six-thirty. Mrs. Sato is late. Please go out and see where she is." Before we had the sundial he made, we were amazed by *Dancho* Narita's sense of time. His ability was not something to be sneezed at. Everyone was convinced he could tell perfect time, just as a few people had perfect pitch.

But he wasn't very good with people. Mrs. Sakiyama's baby often cried at night when she couldn't nurse. *Dancho* Narita, without any empathy to her situation, would say, "Mrs. Sakiyama, we can't sleep when your baby cries."

Grim Mrs. Sakiyama beautifully shot back, "The sound of the two of you arguing is much more annoying for those of us trying to sleep."

Not surprisingly, Mrs. Narita then leaped to her husband's defense, and said, "Mrs. Sakiyama, you have an obligation as a mother to raise your baby so it doesn't cry. It seems to me that you're always sleeping and ignoring your baby."

Mrs. Sakiyama said, "You're right. I'm sorry about that, but why do I then have an obligation to have to listen to the two of you bickering every night?" Mrs. Sakiyama went to the corner of the room and glared at Mrs. Narita with tired, sagging eyes.

The Narita couple, together with their child, Daikyo-chan, were also quite the sight. The three of them at mealtimes with an upside-down trunk for a table, were quite amusing. Mrs. Narita scolded her son, "Daikyo, your chopsticks are five centimeters too high. Your knees are twenty-five degrees off to the left." Every time his mother corrected him, poor Daikyo obediently changed his sitting position and the way he held his chopsticks. The open can of corn gruel was evidence of this family's poverty but she was determined to maintain their standards.

I must admit the rest of us whispered to each other and make wisecracks about Mrs. Narita. "That woman only knows how to criticize everyone else. With the defeat of Japan, men and women are equal now. So it looks like women like that can be politicians now."

"Yeah, she should be a politician. Women who become politicians, lawyers, and such are all going to be like Mrs. Narita. I'm sure of it."

We nasty women would gossip like this under our breaths. But if there was even one night where the Naritas didn't bicker for some reason, and it was quiet—we missed it.

CHAPTER TWENTY-NINE

I'm Just a Beggar

The business tips I learned from Mrs. Daichi were pretty much on the nose, and my soap business picked up. But it wasn't always true that people who lived in houses with stone gates didn't become good customers. One day, I met a middle-aged woman in such a house, and after she bought some soap, she gave me leftover food. Since that time, I always carried an extra bag hanging off my arm. That way, I was ready to collect any *miso* paste, leftover rice or other food that the lady of the house might give me. When I brought this food home, my boys would greet me, round-eyed with happiness.

We relished the *miso* and rice — especially the *miso* soup I made. If I was lucky with a wealthy household, I'd wait about three days before approaching another stone-gated house. That seemed to be the limit. I'd go over to the side door of such a house, and with a humble voice, I'd call politely out, "*Gomenkudasi*, excuse me."

Sometimes a Japanese woman came out saying, "Yes?" She

was the live-in maid for the house. She'd come out and stare at me with contempt and say, "What do you want?" I'd show her the soap, and then as if she were the master of the house, she'd arrogantly say, in informal Japanese, "I don't want any of that junk."

At first, when I was turned down like this, I timidly ran away in shame. But eventually, I learned to talk back. I ignored the maid's disdain and demanded, "Where's the mistress of the house?" When I did that, the Japanese woman would be a little shocked. Then I'd switch back to my pitiful role, and say in very pathetic voice, "Please go fetch her. I need her help."

Sometimes the maid would then try to drive me away saying, "No. No, we don't need any soap." But if I bowed low, got more teary eyed, and cried harder, I'd finally succeed and she'd go get her mistress. These Japanese maids had it easy. I'd often see them and envy them.

It was worse when I ran into other Japanese doing the same thing I did: sell (or beg) door to door. I really, really hated that. I couldn't stand it. Even if we knew each other, we averted our eyes, pretended not to know each other, and ran to the next corner and escaped.

The end of June was soon upon us and the cheerful sound of the *shamisen* (the Japanese guitar) resonated throughout the town from early in the morning. Japanese women dressed in red kimonos, danced on the street corners, their faces painted white, accompanied by the *shamisen* music. They were hawkers for an amateur Japanese theatre troupe organized by the Hosaka *dan*. In the evenings, they made a living by collecting entrance fees from the townspeople, and entertained them with plays and dance performances. There were rumors that they raised a thousand yen in one night. In the early evening, their six and seven-year old girls painted their faces white, put on red lipstick, and flicked their red kimonos as they walked by the houses to lure customers. The girls were showy and attracted attention.

I really hated running into this group. If I saw them in the distance, I'd avoid them. But once I ran into them in the middle of a bridge. To get to that part of town across the river, there was only this bridge. It was too much trouble to take the side streets so I had to go on. As I crossed, I saw Mrs. Nagasu right in front of me. She didn't notice me as she watched the musicians intently. As they finished a set and moved to another spot, she went up to them and borrowed their *shamisen*. I saw her straighten her shoulders and play it, with a catchy rhythm, *ton-chika-chin, ton-chika-chin*. I was astounded. The theatre troup people were also surprised.

With warmer weather here, Mrs. Nagasu heard rumors about the *hikiage* and complained, "If I stay in bed in any longer, I'm going to croak." That was why she was in town. Soon, she was hired as a star performer in their theatre!

* * *

I found other ways to feed the children. I woke up earlier than everyone else and went out to the vegetable market. The marketplace was wet with morning dew and still asleep. Like a mouse, I ran all over the big marketplace to pick up vegetable scraps off the ground. A stalk of green onion. An ugly *daikon* root. A potato someone threw away. I threw them into my rope basket and rushed home. If I didn't get them before they shriveled up, they would get thrown away. Too early didn't work. Too late didn't work.

Sometimes I felt like dying as I waited to go into the

marketplace at dawn, with my rope basket. One morning I overslept. I ran but heard the sound of the sellers' doors opening before I got there. When I went in the vegetable market, the windows were all already open. I stopped and looked around me but there was nothing. It was too late — the children would be hungry that night. When I turned to go home, a man kicked a half-rotten *daikon* root that had been by his foot. It hurtled toward me like a sport ball. I missed catching it and it hit me on my left knee. That man thought that was hilarious, and he whooped out loud towards the red sky.

Humiliated, my face hot with anger, I bent over and picked up that dirty *daikon* off the ground. I ran from the vegetable market as if I were running from a crime scene. That man's laughter followed me — it seemed forever — down the street. When I washed the battered vegetable under the water pump, green and white emerged and it looked completely different. Then I chopped it into small pieces, put it into the *hango* and made soup. "Hey, here's a nice piece," I'd say and the children's happy voices made me feel better. "I'm not a thief. I'm not a thief," I'd say to console myself as I went every morning to scrounge for food.

* * *

When the wooden wall that separated us from the *onpan* food shop next door was taken down, we suddenly became friends with the old Korean couple, Mr. and Mrs Park, who ran the shop. I called him Old Man Park. They were very fine people who did a lot for us. Corn that cost fifteen *yen* at the marketplace; they would sell us for eleven *yen*. They even found work for us. One morning when it was raining, I went to see them and asked, "Can you lend me an umbrella? An old, torn one would be fine."

Park said, "Are you going to sell that soap in this rain?"

as she lent me the umbrella. "By the way, there's some indoor work I wanted to tell you about. I forgot all about it until now."

"What?" I held my breath and got closer to her.

"It's knitting socks. Would you like to try it?"

"Yes, I'll do anything."

The couple introduced me to the job, and I started making socks. They gave me ten *yen* for every pair. After sundown, under a dim light bulb, I'd knit until about one in the morning. In three days, I knitted a pair. My income grew by ten *yen*, but because I didn't get much sleep, I sometimes got dizzy in the bright morning sunshine. Still, I pushed myself because if I didn't earn at least twenty-five yen a day, the four of us would starve.

One morning, I went up the mountain road, avoiding the sun as much as possible—to get to a house with a stone gate—in the hopes of finding some food. When I went there about a week earlier, they gave me white rice. This day, I was especially tired. Halfway up the hill, I was blinded by the bright sunlight and my eyes suddenly felt like they were on fire. I stopped and tried to shake myself awake, then kept walking. But I got dizzy again and almost fell over. I grabbed the railing by the side of the road then I heard a young man's voice behind me, "Lady, are you all right?" On, no. A Korean man up to no good.

"I'm fine," I said and turned around to see well-dressed man trying to avoid something with one hand. Bright circles of light danced around his hand and face. Someone was playing with a mirror in a house window nearby. Oh, he looks harmless, I thought with relief.

"Lady, what are you selling?" he said.

"Oh. Soap and cigarettes."

"My house is just right over there. Will you come with me?"

From outside the gate, the young man yelled for someone. A pretty young girl — maybe his sister — came out dressed in a light green dress that suited her well.

He said, "Why don't you rest here for a moment?" His sister took care of me while he went into the house. In the window, there was a sewing machine with a colored blouse half-sewn.

I asked, "Do you use a sewing machine?"

"Lady, do you also know how to sew? How about Western sewing?" she said.

"Oh, I know a little," I said.

That's how I got to know the Lee family. I sewed the younger sister's dress, and in return for my work, they gave me a generous amount of money. After they paid me, I went to town, happy with a full purse.

In town I saw a barefoot Japanese woman who staggered and almost fell over. Her face was soiled, her hair a mess and she wore torn ragged clothes. She was filthy and as she wobbled down the street, her hands grasped at something invisible. Then I recognized her. She was a fellow refugee from the *dan* next door at the Sensen Agricultural School a year ago. She was an attractive, proper woman back then. I couldn't stand to get any closer. "Look. Look at her. You're going to end up like her," I said to myself.

CHAPTER THIRTY

Trembling Hands and Lips

Selling soap required capital. In order to have an inventory of soap at eight *yen*, I had to have eight *yen* cash on hand. Eventually, I ran out of money. There was no more capital at all. When I could no longer buy soap to sell, I resolved to carry out my plan—a plan of last resort.

In our town surrounded by mountains, there was still snow left in the shady spots of the streets. The willow blossoms on the banks bloomed, but the wind off of the river was still chilly. I went out without telling the other women anything.

Masahiko held my right hand. Sakiko was on my back as usual, and I left Masahiro back at the house. Using the map I had when I sold soap, I looked for a house. Sakiko was quiet, and made no sound at all. That was because she no longer had the strength to even cry. She hadn't nursed at all. Her young life couldn't last much longer on what I fed her—watery soup with pieces of *daikon*. Day after day, her high fever continued so I took her to see

Dr. Oya, but there was nothing he could do. Even if he wanted to, he didn't have any milk or medicine to give me. Somehow, someway, I had to find something to feed her. I was determined to get some *miso* or just one *go* of milk — anything to give her some nourishment.

"Don't go to rich houses with big stone gates." That's what Mrs. Daichi taught me when I started selling soap. But I found myself standing in front of the stone gates of such a house. They seemed to have so much. "Please. Please, give me even the burnt rice left on the bottom of your pan," I thought to myself.

I rang the doorbell. The concrete walls stood forbiddingly but lovely lace curtains hung in the windows, and promised life inside was comfortable and safe. This was clearly a very nice home. I waited and waited — but there was no sound.

I pushed the doorbell again. But there was still no answer. There must be someone looking out of one the windows facing the street. I pressed the doorbell again. Masahiko looked at me with earnest eyes. He believed that I would get food for us, and waited patiently. His trusting eyes drove me on and his belief in me gave me the strength to swallow my pride and — beg. I pressed the doorbell again. Still no answer.

I turned away from that house and said to my son, "I'm sure Mommy can get a rice ball somewhere. All right?" My eyes filled with tears. Do I have to do this in order to live? For a moment, I thought I cannot go on. Maybe we should...? No. No. When I see my children patiently waiting, no matter what, I can't let them down. I overcame any hesitation I had as I went to another house, another more modest one that was separated from town, across a muddy creek. This house was near the market, on a shortcut street I sometime took.

"Excuse me," I called out. Inside the gate was a yard. A woman wearing a white dress (traditional Korean clothing) came out. When I saw her, I couldn't speak.

"Please…please, give me something," I wanted to plead. Oh, yes. I should be able to say that. 'Please, give me something.' But the words disappeared in my throat.

The woman shook her hand, and gestured for me not to say anything. She spoke softly. "I feel sorry for you Japanese. But if I give you something, I'll be shunned by my people. The reason we've suffered is because of the Japanese. We Koreans all hate you."

She paused. "But that's not really your fault. You aren't to blame…I'm going to throw away some things in the street…you come and pick them up right away," she said.

"Thank you. Thank you," I said and bowed over and over. I went out into the street and waited.

The woman brought out a *pakachi*, (a traditional Korean container), packed with food — a lot of rice, Korean pickles and *miso*. She set it in a bush in front of me and, without looking back, quickly went back into her house.

"Thank you. Thank you," I whispered. With trembling hands, I picked up the food from her *pakachi* and wrapped it with my *furoshiki*. It was the first time in days — no, months, that I had touched white rice.

I tried to keep my voice calm as I spoke to Masahiko. "Let's go home. Let's go home where your brother is waiting and have dinner." But my lips trembled and the words didn't come out right.

CHAPTER THIRTY-ONE

A Mad Woman

The days were just getting warm when Mrs. Mizushima, who worked as a maid, didn't come home after sundown. A group of us split up and went out to look for her, asking around the dark town late into the night—but we didn't find her. What happened to her? In the morning, she finally came back but something was wrong—she had gone mad.

What we figured out was that she heard that the Japanese would begin the *hikiage*, and so she went to find her husband who worked on a farm. Apparently, she wandered out into the countryside, couldn't find him, and finally came back in the morning. This was very strange because during that time, we all heard these *dema* rumors almost everyday from all sorts of places. They said, "The *hikiage* will begin soon!" But we learned to ignore most of these rumors since they weren't true. Why did Mrs. Mizushima choose to believe the *hikiage* rumor this time? She wandered all night, got covered in dirt, and lost her *zori* sandals. When she got back to our house with a loud bang of the door, she collapsed and then slept as if she were dead.

"How strange," we thought and looked at each other. But we were horrified when she woke up three hours later. She bolted upright with her eyes wide open, and stared straight ahead. Then she stood up, walked around the room two or three times, picked up Mrs. Sato's glass bottle, and smashed it on the floor.

"Ha, ha, ha," she bellowed like a man. It was truly frightening to see her stand there and laugh like a demon, with pieces of broken glass all around her. Her face was ghastly pale, her eyes wild and shining — Mrs. Mizushima had truly lost her mind.

We tried to restrain her and calm her down before she broke any more glass, but she got even wilder, and we couldn't hold her any longer. We needed a man's help. But we had only three men in our group. *Dancho* Narita was sick in bed and too weak to do anything. Her husband, Mr. Mizushima, was away at a distant farm where he worked. Mr. Honda was the only man we could reach. As soon as one of the women found him at the print shop where he worked, he came running home. It took Mr Honda all his strength to calm her down but she still screamed, "I want water."

Mr. Honda managed to drag her outside to the well. But when we tried to help, she glared at us and bolted — quick as a rabbit — and slipped out of our grasp. She disappeared back into town. We sent one person right away to find Mr. Mizushima out at the farm while the rest of us split up again to search for her.

Things weren't the same after that. Poor Mr. Mizushima's life became hell as he struggled to take care of his crazy wife. He couldn't work anymore because he had to watch his wife all day. Although she calmed down with him around, often she still tried to run away.

But the worst was when she started babbling nonstop. She started bringing up all sorts of past grievances. There was nothing we could do except listen. She started ranting and yelling, and the targets of her rage were all of us. What a lot of things that woman knew! She brought up all sorts of things from the past, about our lives back in Manchuria, in Shinkyo. Almost everyone was stung by her vicious tirades. The things she said…made us gasp and silently beseech, "Oh, no. Please. Not that."

She said things like: "Mrs. Fujiwara, hey, you—you look so kind but you're such a phony—who do you think you are? You stick your nose up in the air—you brag you're the wife of a *kacho* (manager). So what?

"Shit. You just got here from Japan. You brainless idiot. It's your fault that Mr. Sasaki got depressed and died. You stopped Miss Kimura and Mr. Sasaki in the middle of the night and wouldn't let them marry. Who do you think you are, ignoring the feelings of the young people? What the hell…"

Let me tell you, this was the *least* of what she said. She said much, much worse things about other people, things I can't bring myself to mention here. Still, she wasn't this horrible all the time. There were times when she was in a better mood and satisfied just to make a fool of herself. She'd put a spoon in her mouth, hang a cup off of the handle, and prance around the room in circles. The children laughed with delight, and that spurred her to act even more foolish.

Even her eating habits changed. She didn't eat for two days, then suddenly ate an enormous amount. I was really impressed by how poor Mr. Mizushima looked after his wife, even in the midst of this tragedy. Many days he went without food because he couldn't earn any more money to buy anything. She didn't care anymore about her looks, and her hair flew loose every which way. No matter how many times her hair was tied, she'd take it all out.

She liked to dance. She suddenly started dancing in the middle of town—people pointed at her, laughed and called her, "Crazy Japanese woman." Then for awhile she was obsessed with water. For days on end she did 'laundry' at the well. But it wasn't really laundry—she just made a lot of noise all day at the well, playing with the water like a child. Then Mr. Mizushima would get all wet wringing her kimono dry to hang it up. As soon as he did that, this woman grabbed the kimono and got it all wet again. "I like this well," she chirped and splashed all over the place.

That was tolerable but when she started spitting over and over into our water supply—we couldn't ignore that. We asked Mr. Mizushima to come and keep her away from our well. He dragged her off, but she escaped his hold and ran back to the water hole. Perched on top of the well wall, she let her rear end droop into the hole, and 'scrubbed' herself. All the while, she laughed maniacally. Someone called out, "Mr. Mizushima, this is terrible. Your wife is on the edge of the well!"

Mr. Mizushima fumed behind his glasses, "I hope that bitch falls in and dies. I can't go home with a woman like that...I'll have to tell people—look what I got in Manchuria." But he still went to the well and pulled her off the edge. Then he grabbed her hair and yelled, "Don't you dare go to the well!"

I was amazed this woman listened to her husband, at least some of the time, but he couldn't let her out of his sight. Because he couldn't go to work, he had no money to buy food, and the poor man couldn't eat. He got weaker, even staggered from lack of food. There were days where he only drank water. He finally sold a kimono so he could buy some food. We watched and worried, "What is he going to do? What a test of his marital devotion!"

He still felt responsible for her and every night, to keep her from wandering away, he tied her arm to his arm before going to sleep. He even kept his glasses tied onto his head at night, in case he had to chase after his crazy wife.

CHAPTER THIRTY-TWO

The Molested Doll

There's a Japanese saying—*kiyu sureba tsuzu*, 'When you're at your wit's end, a solution will appear.' We frantically thought every day of how to survive. The soap business wasn't going as well as before. All the Japanese refugees tried to make money in different ways, and it wasn't easy. Most failed. One evening after Mrs. Kurashige's sister, Kuniko, came back from her job working for the Soviet military dormitory, she came up with a wonderful idea—"How about we try to make and sell dolls?" Everyone knew that pretty Mrs. Sato had experience making dolls, so we decided this was a marvelous idea.

The first thing we had to do was get cloth. Mrs. Sato said it had to be good quality, beautiful cloth. But our plans came to a standstill when we couldn't figure out how to do this. "It's no use after all." Another failed scheme.

But the next day, during the evening meal, Mrs. Daichi whispered to me, "Mrs. Fujiwara, do you want to go with me to get cloth for making dolls?"

I whispered back, "Where are we going? Who's going to give us cloth?"

"I thought about it all night and figured out a way. I want to go to this place and ask," she said.

"Where is that?"

"I'll tell you after we go out," she said. Mrs. Daichi took more care than usual in washing her hands, feet and smoothing her hair. Then she put her baby on her back.

"Mrs. Daichi, where are you going?" someone asked.

"I'm just going out with Mrs. Fujiwara for a little fresh air," she said.

"Is that so...?" a couple of the other women watched us with curiosity as we went out.

"Those women are such busy-bodies. Always poking their noses in other people's business," Mrs. Daichi snapped as we headed out.

"Mrs. Daichi, where are we going?" I asked.

"I intend to go to see the Soviet military people."

"What! Are you serious?"

"Of course. Let's ask them. If we ask and they turn us down, it can't be helped. We haven't lost anything. But I have a feeling this will work. I thought about going by myself but I feel better with two of us, so I invited you, Mrs. Fujiwara—Don't be so nervous. We've got to be confident but at the same time, they need to feel sorry for us," Mrs. Daichi said as she reached over and fixed Sakiko's kimono. We were two poor Japanese women with babies on our backs.

Perhaps because I was nervous, I was distracted. As we walked by the river, I noticed something green growing along the dam. Grasses stuck in the dam? No, it wasn't that. Were they water weeds? No, not that either. "I wonder where it's flowing?" I asked.

"What?" she said.

"The river," I said.

"I have no idea. What a funny woman you are," she said.

"Probably the East China Sea," I said to myself as we crossed the bridge.

In front of us was a large gate with strange Russian letters written across the top. The yard was quiet and no one was around. There was an open entrance on the other side of the thick grass.

"*Gomenkudasai,* excuse us," we called out together. I felt the nerves in my back prickle against Sakiko's body. There was no answer.

"I wonder if no one is here...," said Mrs. Daichi. "*Gomenkudasi,*" she said louder.

Footsteps from deep in the building were followed by the appearance of a Korean translator. As we nervously explained our mission to the translator, four or five large Soviet soldiers came lumbering out. We became frantic and explained ourselves again.

We said, "We want to make dolls and sell them. Please give us any scraps of cloth you have."

The translator must have been good. The faces of the Soviet soldiers lit up and they gestured for us to come inside. We looked at each other with fear. We've come this far. We can't back out now. We took off our *zori* sandals, lined them up neatly at the entrance, and followed the soldiers.

They took us down the stairs to a basement room. They opened a door into a large storage room and turned on the light. My heart beat wildly against the straps holding Sakiko. We were astounded to see mountains of various colored cloth stacked high.

"Take what you want," they said.

We grabbed as much as we could hold and went outside.

"Is that all you want?" the translator said.

We found a treasure beyond our wildest dreams and were so excited we couldn't speak and just nodded our thanks. We rushed through the gates of the building. Unsure of our good fortune, we ran to the middle of the bridge where we stopped to catch our breath. We looked back to the other side of the row of willow trees, and saw the red-brick building shimmering, as if nothing had happened.

When we got back to our house, the others were astounded at our success and looked at us round-eyed. We pulled out the cloths to show them, as if we had found a great treasure.

"With this much cloth, we'll be able to make a lot of dolls. Right, Mrs. Sato?" I said.

"Yes, we'll be able to make a lot. And there are many colors." Mrs. Sato's eyes gleamed as she inspected the fabric.

Then Mrs. Nagasu butted in, "*Yokatta*, this is very fortunate. Everybody start making dolls right away."

I was annoyed at Mrs. Nagasu's bossiness and couldn't help but retort, "What do you mean everybody, Mrs. Nagasu? This cloth is ours. If you want to make dolls, you should go and get cloth yourself. We can't just give you this cloth."

Mrs. Nagasu was mortified and turned away.

"You're a selfish bitch, aren't you?" she said.

"What did you say? You're the one who is selfish. In fact, you're the worst," I said.

"Since when was I selfish?" she shot back.

"Do you remember what you did this winter?" (How could I forget how she hogged the room with the heater and tried to force Mrs. Sakiyama and her boys out.) The tension rose between Mrs. Nagasu and me — until Mrs. Kurashige jumped in between us.

With Mrs. Sato as our coach, we began making dolls. When she was in girls' high school, Mrs. Sato had won first prize in her class making Western dolls. Anyway, Mrs. Sato herself had a pretty face like a doll's — a cute nose and small, round rosy lips. She said, "The secret to making a good doll is the face. The face is the most important. Who's good at drawing?"

No one would admit to be good at drawing. But we practiced with brush paint and eventually made doll-like faces. I made two dolls in a day. Compared to taking three days to knit only one pair of socks for ten yen, selling a doll for ten yen was much better. The dolls sold. We went door-to-door, found houses with children and let them hold the dolls. Then of course, the children didn't want to let go of the dolls, and the parents would be forced to buy them. A regular doll was ten yen. A well-made doll was fifteen yen. Mrs. Sato's dolls were twenty yen. That's how we decided on the prices.

But competitors soon appeared from the other *dan* and they cut into our market. Under Mrs. Sato's guidance we changed our designs and kept our quality high. We made high-end dolls. After our successful sales, we splurged and made *miso* soup with bits of fish, green onions, and corn gruel.

My boys cried, "Mommy, this is real *miso* soup , isn't it?" They would see the little bits of fish and say, "Hey, look. Here's a fish head. Look." And pick them out and put them in their mouths very carefully as if they hadn't had any decent food for years. The children made me cry whether we had food or not.

One night, I made two dolls which I thought were particularly lifelike. I decided to sell one for fifteen yen, the other one for twenty. The next morning, I went to town—full of confidence I could sell them. As I walked a little nervously, two Soviet soldiers approached from the other side. They noticed the dolls in my arms and they stopped.

"Here's my chance," I thought—suddenly one of the soldiers grabbed one of my dolls and started laughing. Before I could say anything, he pulled out a big pencil from his pocket, pulled up the doll's dress and drew in nasty things. "Damn! A pervert," I thought, and ran with the doll that hadn't been hurt yet.

The Soviet soldiers chased after me yelling, "Hey! Hey!"

"Oh, no," I said as the two tall men quickly caught up to me, as I clutched my poor remaining doll.

A big hand grabbed my shoulder. "Madam," he said and with his other hand, he thrust three bills into my face. Thirty *yen*!

"Oh...That's what they want," I said with relief. I didn't have to run. I showed him the doll I still clutched to my chest but he shook his hand, "I don't want that one." He held up the doll he already had, and walked into town laughing and happy.

CHAPTER THIRTY-THREE

Black Gloves for Gennadi

Compared to the previous year, our feelings towards the Soviets completely changed. It seemed so long ago we were terrified of them. When they invaded Manchuria, we ran for our lives because the authorities told us Russian soldiers raped and killed Japanese women. Now, here in Korea, the Soviets hired many of the Japanese women as maids. Kuniko, Mrs. Kurashige's younger sister, worked for them. She did kitchen work, I think. Everyday, she left early and came back early evening. I think the Soviets liked this tall, young Japanese woman. Kuniko was intelligent and generous, compared to her older sister.

Sometimes, they give her a hard loaf of delicious black bread to take home. From time to time, a tall Soviet soldier who knew Kuniko came to visit us. "*Zuraschii,*" he always said as he stuck his head into our window. He made us laugh. He always arrived with a loaf of their black bread, and our children jumped and screamed in delight when he tossed the loaf around like a toy ball before giving it to us.

Then slowly, he would bend his tall frame and step inside our little home, and he said compliments that sounded like, "*Japon-ski*" *and* "*Madamu Harashu.*" Then he entertained us with stories using a lot of funny hand gestures and facial expressions. He talked about how he fought with the Germans, and how great Stalin was.

"How do you say *Zuraschii* in Japanese?" he asked one day. Mrs. Kimoto, who was proud of her knowledge of foreign languages (but also a little careless), thought he asked, "How do you say *zuroosu* in Japanese?" (*Zuroosu* is another foreign word which means women's underwear, I think, and I don't know why Mrs. Kimoto thought this Soviet soldier would ask about such a thing.) With all earnestness, Mrs. Kimoto taught him how to say: sa-ru-ma-ta, which means 'underpants' in Japanese.

Then the following day when a group of friendly Soviet soldiers came to visit, several of them stuck their heads in our window and said with thick Russian accents, "*Saru matta. Saru matta!*"

At first, we were puzzled when we heard them say, "*Saru matta*" (which in Japanese sounds like—'monkey is waiting'). "What are the Soviets trying to say?" we all wondered. Suddenly, Mrs. Kimoto explained that she taught one of the Russian soldiers how to say 'underpants' in Japanese—*sarumata*. Then I realized they were trying to be kind and use the Japanese word for their Russian greeting '*zuraschii*' — not '*zuroosu*' which is what Mrs. Kimoto thought he was asking about. When we finally figured out where the misunderstanding came from, we thought this was hilarious. Encouraged by our mirth, the Russians greeted us even more enthusiastically in loud voices, "Monkey is waiting! Monkey is waiting!" We had such a good laugh with them.

When we learned that one of our Soviet friends, a handsome fellow named Gennadi, was going home to Russia, Kuniko, who was especially fond of this soldier, stopped her night work of doll making, and instead worked late for three nights in a row to knit a pair of black gloves for him. What a lot of effort Kuniko put into making those gloves!

On the warm day he was scheduled to leave, Gennadi came by our house wearing Kuniko's black gloves on his hands. We were touched by his sincere appreciation, and so we all decided to go to the train station to see him off.

Once he got on the train, Gennadi yelled, "*Dosvi danya*," to us and waved his black gloved hands. Kuniko stood tall, and her big eyes filled with tears as she waved at him. We kept waving as he waved both of his black hands back at us — as the train drew away, he got smaller and smaller until we couldn't see his black gloves anymore. I suspect she had strong feelings for that soldier.

I was sad because I envied Gennadi going back home. I wondered what Kuniko felt that day.

CHAPTER THIRTY-FOUR

Food Shop Assistant

In July, a sudden heat wave engulfed our town—further inflaming the Japanese already feverish with talk of the *hikiage*. Every day at the Japanese Association office, the *dancho* and *fuku-dancho* of every *dan* gathered together around a big map of Korea to make plans. As *fuku-dancho*, I attended those meetings since *Dancho* Narita was usually too ill.

All the Japanese were eager to join in the *hikiage* but we all worried—how would we get home, and how were we going to pay for our journey? We worked for anyone who would pay us, even if it wasn't much, and saved money for the journey. I worked very hard—every day I made dolls until one or two in the morning—then woke up at five the next morning to sell soap. No wonder my body gave out.

One night, in the beginning of July, I suddenly couldn't see the end of my needle as I worked on a doll and thought, "Oh, no. I've got night blindness." I tried to keep sewing but kept piercing my finger, so that I bled. That's it. I can't work anymore. If I can't work, my children and I will starve, much less have any money to get home.

Every day at the meetings, they announced the deaths of more and more Japanese and I wondered if we might be next. Things looked very bad but I didn't expect our end to come so soon. Hopelessness seemed to surround us.

At night, the air was still cold and the smell of damp earth was sharp. We heard sounds of the *onpan* food shop next door. "They must be closing shop early and getting ready for tomorrow," I thought. The owner, Old Man Park's, rough voice came through the wall. When he was in a good mood, he sang, "...I'm a sixteen year old Manchurian girl. Spring is coming and snow is melting..."

His singing made me laugh, not just because of the incongruous words but because he sang out of tune. Then I suddenly thought, "Why don't I ask Old Man Park if I can work for him as an assistant in the *onpan* shop?" I raised my head — what a good idea — the *onpan* shop was just on the other side of that wall.

He'll probably be against the idea of hiring a shop assistant, but I kept this precious idea in my breast and waited for the next day. The next morning, I went to see Old Man Park, and pleaded my case with him in tears, to which he responded, "In such a tiny shop, how could two people work?" He shook his grey beard and resisted my request.

But I persisted. "I don't want any salary. Just give me the tips. We're neighbors anyway. Let me help you in the evenings for a couple of hours." I nagged him mercilessly.

Finally, the kind old man relented. "All right. All right. You can help me."

I talked with Mrs. Toda and we decided to go together. Of

course, Old Man Park frowned when the two of us showed up when he just expected me. But he quickly changed his expression back to his usual smile and said, "Is it the two of you?"

Why did I bring Mrs. Toda with me? Despite the horrible death of her step-child, I sensed she had a special talent with people. I remembered that she had once said her parents ran an inn, and that she was used to dealing with customers, even as a child. That's why I asked her to come with me. Using the cloth we got from the Soviets, I carefully made a top and pants for work.

As I had hoped, Mrs. Toda was very good at dealing with customers. She smiled and chatted with every customer. The *onpan* shop seemed brighter and more cheerful. After two or three days, it was clear — the *onpan* shop had more customers and sold more food thanks to our presence. Old Man Park was delighted.

A lot of the customers were Korean men — young, brainy types. If we smiled and flattered the customers, and pleased them, then when they left, they left tips. The shop closed at eight, cleanup took thirty minutes, so it was a good job. I noticed when these Koreans tipped in front of women, they tipped discretely so that others could not see the tip. So I figured out how to earn generous tips — thank the customers profusely, no matter how much they actually paid.

The young man's face beamed when I praised him. "I'm sorry to take so much from you as a tip," I apologized. It was actually just a five *yen* tip but I'd thank him as if it were twenty. Then the next time he came, he gave me a ten *yen* tip. This work was a lot more profitable than making dolls. It only took ten minutes to get from the shop back to my house.

Once, after work, I turned the corner of the wall and almost ran into someone in the dark. I was frightened but it was only

Dancho Narita — gazing at the stars — dressed in his shorts in the warm evening. His bare legs were as thin as a child's, and he looked very sad and lonely.

One night, someone in the group said let's calculate how much we've earned. It turned out that Mrs. Toda and I earned the most money by working at this *onpan* shop next door.

By the meeting at the end of July, I recall feeling more optimistic I survived somehow by bouncing between these jobs — selling soap, doll making, and being a waitress at the *onpan* shop — but in the end, I still hadn't saved much money for the *hikiage*.

Dr. Oya still came to our house do his regular health checkup. I constantly worried about my children and asked the doctor to check Masahiro. He pressed his finger into Masahiro's distended stomach — it reminded me of a frog's pale swollen belly — and turned my son's head.

"What do you think, doctor?" I asked. I told him that Masahiro had diarrhea recently.

Dr. Oya shot back, "What do you mean, what do I think? It's all the same. It's no use giving you the name of a disease." He was no longer a kindly doctor — he had a hateful expression all the time now. I knew he meant my son was suffering from malnutrition. The doctor was surly towards everyone by that time, and I felt his hostility grow.

This doctor's family were all back in Japan, in Tokyo, and he probably didn't know if they survived the war. Dr. Oya no longer knew what he was doing here in Korea — he said, "It doesn't matter if there is a doctor here or not. It's inevitable, people who are going to die, will die."

We knew that all too well.

CHAPTER THIRTY-FIVE

Two Lives Versus One Life

Mrs. Sakiyama was the grim type who didn't talk much, and she mostly kept to herself — unless she was cornered like she was by Mrs. Nagasu in the *ondoru* heated room. Mrs. Sakiyama was busy caring for her two boys, six year-old Ichiro and four year-old Jiro, and now she had the new baby. She went to her job at the flour mill everyday — with the baby strapped on her back — and came home late, covered in white flour. Her baby didn't cry much anymore. Even after she cleaned off the flour, Mrs. Sakiyama's pallor contrasted with the dark circles under her eyes. She scolded Ichiro constantly, and hardly talked with the other women in the group. Her eyes, deep in their sockets, sometimes shot out looks like plumes of flames. If she happened to look at me, I felt a chill in my bones. She wasn't afraid of anyone, but she also never fought with anyone. She broke the rules of the *dan* all the time, and she didn't seem to care what anyone thought.

After that showdown in the *ondoru* room in the winter, even

Mrs. Nagasu stayed out of her way and never confronted her again. Everyone was so afraid of her that no one reprimanded her any more. Some time ago, Mrs. Sakiyama had run out of money and sold her only blanket. She and her two boys slept on the bare floor.

Once, she suddenly spoke to me in her harsh tone. "Mrs. Fujiwara, when can we go home?"

I couldn't help but apologize, "Well, the Japanese Association hasn't made up its mind…"

She interrupted me saying, "I want to go home soon, don't you? The Association is a bunch of idiots, aren't they?" She then turned around and turned her back on me. Mrs. Sakiyama and I couldn't get beyond this cold, distant relationship. Every day, we saw each other in the same room without so much as a simple greeting of "good morning" or even "good night."

Mrs. Sakiyama's baby didn't grow any bigger than when she was first born. The tiny baby's color was very bad and only when she nursed did the child let out a feeble cry.

I saw she struggled to breast feed. "*Okusan*, I guess you're having trouble nursing," I once said sympathetically.

"Yeah. It's always been that way with me. I used cow milk to raise Ichiro and Jiro," she said.

"So you don't have enough breast milk."

She said, "Yeah. But there's nothing I can do about it."

I tried to help. "How about giving her some soup?" I said.

Mrs. Sakiyama jerked up, glared at me and loudly said, "It's no good anyway. What's the use of letting her live a little longer?"

"But…," I stammered.

She fumed. "Mrs. Fujiwara. Two lives or one life. What is

more important to you?"

"They're all precious. The lives of two children, and the life of a baby," I said.

"Well, if you have the luxury to believe that, you can do what you like," she said and went back to her children.

I knew what was going to happen to that baby that night. Just like a gentle breeze that waned with the arrival of dawn, the baby was dead the next morning. Mrs. Sakiyama put the tiny corpse in a small wooden box and got ready to go to the graveyard. She didn't shed a single tear as we all watched her. "What a heartless woman," we thought.

Everyone was horrified at her lack of feeling. But simple-hearted Mrs. Kimoto didn't want Mrs. Sakiyama to be alone. She went with Mrs. Sakiyama up to the cemetery and told us a story in a hushed voice after they got back.

Mrs. Kimoto said, "Mrs. Sakiyama headed to the cemetery saying, 'let me go ahead of you' and wouldn't let me walk beside her. After we buried her baby, she stood alone at the grave for a moment. Even though, I was some distance away, I don't think she knew I could hear her. You see, the wind blew her words right toward me. Well, what do you think she said? She said, 'Yoshiko, please forgive me. Please forgive Mommy. Yoshiko, please forgive Mommy.' That's what she said! Then she wiped away a single tear and turned toward me with a look as if she didn't care and said, 'Let's go home.'"

Mrs. Daichi's angry voice suddenly shot out from across the room. "Mrs. Kimoto, stop it." She frowned at Mrs. Kimoto.

CHAPTER THIRTY-SIX

The *Hikiage* Plan

A big map of Korea spread before us. A thick red pencil mark ran across the middle of the map, to show the location of the 38th Parallel, dividing the peninsula into North and South Korea. Crowded around the map, about twenty men and women looked at it with anxious faces. Mr. Tanaka, from the Japanese Association, explained the *hikiage* plan to get us home in Japan. He used a long match stick as a pointer as he spoke. Mrs. Kurashige and I listened carefully.

"If we can get as far as Shinmaku by train, then we can walk following the same direction as the tracks to get to the Kaijo refugee camp. We know there's about thirty-four miles between these two towns by train, so walking along the roads — let's see, there's probably at least forty-four miles," he said.

Mr. Tanaka lay the match stick against the map's distance scale to measure, then laid his match stick along the route to calculate the distance. "If we try to reach the Kaijo camp by going west from Shinmaku, we'll run into mountains so that's no good. If we go round east, it's over fifteen miles to Shinkei. From here we can go south, and it's another fifteen miles to Shihenri. Then from here, if we go south through the mountains it's almost twenty-eight miles to reach the Kaijo camp — so that means there's about sixty miles in all that we'll have to walk." Sixty miles.

"Excuse me, Mr. Tanaka, isn't that like walking almost in a complete circle?" Mr. Tokushima of the Miyamoto group spoke up.

"According to the information we have, this is the safest route," said Mr. Tanaka.

"Whose information is that?"

"It comes from people in Heijo."

"From what I've heard it's better to go straight south from Sharin to Kaishu," said Mr. Tokushima.

"Who said that? Was it someone reliable?" asked Mr. Tanaka.

Mr. Tokushima had a bald spot in the middle of his head — that reminded me of the mythical *kappa* in Japanese picture books, a magical part-man, part-turtle creature. He was at the *dancho* meetings everyday, at the request of their former *dancho's* wife. Finally, he abruptly said, "Our group will take a different route."

"If that's the case, don't bother to come to our meetings," I thought. All he did was argue and complain anyway.

The Japanese Association Central Committee had these daily meetings because they wanted everyone in Sensen to travel together along the safest route. But 'Kappa Man' didn't make any effort to contribute or cooperate with the other refugees. He only cared about his *dan*.

(There were a lot reasons, I started calling Mr. Tokushima,

'Kappa Man' — even now I can't bring myself to use his real name. It brings up such bad memories. You'll understand if you read further on.)

Once, at one of the meetings, he had the gall to actually say to me and Mrs. Kurashige, "We don't want to work with a poor group of beggars like your *dan*."

Of course, he said that because his Miyamoto *dan* was rich. They used military cars to bring their luggage which they stored somewhere. Compared to the other groups, they didn't seem to have suffered at all.

Mr. Yamagishi, the elderly *kaicho*, head of the Central Committee, furrowed his brow and said, "Today, the Japanese Association can only confirm the information Mr. Tanaka has just given you — we will go south. This is definite."

With that, the afternoon's two-hour meeting ended.

Suddenly, on July 15th, a group of Japanese set out from Sensen to go south. When everyone heard about this, people quit their jobs and focused their attention on getting ready to go south. I went with Mrs. Kurashige to the Japanese Association office every day to hear the latest information. There were dreadful stories flying everywhere — refugees walking for days along roads lined with the corpses of Japanese. They also said that the elderly and the young were sure to die on this difficult route. This is some of what I heard in those days.

I had no choice but to focus on what I could do. The most worrisome information was that it would cost a thousand yen a person to go home. Money to pay the guides, to pay for ox-carts, and for food. Altogether, a thousand yen per person. I was in despair.

Somehow I had to find a way home without spending so

much money. I figured, the best way would be to follow a rich group. I decided on the Miyamoto *dan,* the richest group led by Kappa Man. When that *dan* starts moving, we'll follow right behind.

Everyone in my *dan* had pretty much stopped working and spent the days talking and worrying about the hikiage. We had to be ready to leave at any moment, so we prepared food, mainly dried soybeans for *daizu.* During our preparations, from time to time, Mrs. Mizushima appeared, not comprehending what we were doing. She was still crazy so she couldn't do anything useful to help us. She ran back and forth between the well and our house, sometimes forcing herself into the middle of our work. Because of her antics, it took a long time to make everyone's food supplies.

Her poor husband, Mr. Mizushima, was exasperated from trying to control her. "I'm going to dump this woman in the mountains," he threatened. Everyone worked feverishly to prepare *daizu* — roasting and drying the soybeans for the hard journey ahead. But this mad woman suddenly appeared the middle of all of our work, and declared, "I'm going to *hikiage* first." Then she grabbed the soybeans we had just prepared and ran towards the well. Mr. Mizushima darted after her, tackled her, dragged her back and forced her to sit in the corner of the room. Suddenly, she said, "My head hurts," and went to sleep. She didn't wake up for two days straight.

"Is she OK? Maybe she hit her head on the well?" Mrs. Kimoto worried.

Mr. Mizushima said, "She's crazy anyway. She can't get any worse." But he worried and tried to wake her, "Hey, hey. Get up."

But she didn't wake up until two days later when she sat up

and quietly said, "I'm so hungry," and looked puzzled at every-one's faces. She quietly asked, "What happened?" Mrs. Mizushi-ma had returned to her normal self, the woman she used to be. I don't know why she suddenly got better. At first, we weren't sure if she would start raving again, but after she learned what had happened to her, she sat quietly in the corner.

She said to her husband, over and over in a timid voice, "I am so sorry." I guess her mental illness was cured by the talk about *hikiage*. I don't understand why she went mad, or why she got well—the medical reasons behind her recovery. In any case, we were all very happy she came back.

CHAPTER THIRTY-SEVEN

How I Made Three Hundred Yen

After the *hikiage* meeting with the Japanese Association, Mrs. Kurashige and I went home and explained the map to the waiting *dan* members, using an old newspaper and piece of charcoal. It had been a long time since our group had gotten together like this. We excitedly talked about the *hikiage* and what we would do.

I presented my idea, "A poor *dan* like ours can't pay for the guides and such so we should follow another group. In my opinion, that's the best strategy for us." Everyone agreed.

We decided I would approach the Miyamoto *dan* with our plan, and we also talked about how we would take care of ourselves during the difficult journey. We mapped out our strategy: we needed to help our sick leader, *Dancho* Narita. Who will look after the little ones? Who will take responsibility and stay with each person? I would carry Masahiko. Mrs. Toda, after losing Tamio-chan had no children and she agreed to carry Sakiko. Mrs. Sato, our pretty doll-making teacher agreed to help with my bag since she also had no children. Masahiro could walk on his own. Everything was decided—or at least I thought so.

The *fuku-dancho* of the Miyamoto group, Kappa Man, made a disagreeable face when I made my request. "Your poor group is going to make things difficult for us."

I kept my temper in check, "But you won't mind if we follow your *dan* like a stray dog, would you?"

"That's up to you," he scoffed.

"All right. Will you please just let us know when your group will leave?" I asked.

Kappa Man didn't answer at all at first. "All right. I will let you know," he finally said grudgingly. "Why do you want to stick to us so much anyway?"

"Your *dan* has plenty of money and you've already researched the route," I said. "I'll bet that you've already hired your guides," I flattered him.

"So you're saying your group can't do that? I get it. We'll let you come, and follow us like a street mongrel," he said.

I bit my tongue. Kappa Man was shorter than me, so I looked right down on his head—I was really tempted to slap his shiny, bald spot right there. I should have followed my gut reaction. His *dan* left early and tricked us. Earlier, he told me in a seemingly thoughtful manner, "We'll leave in about five days, so get yourselves ready." Then, that very night his group slipped out on a late night train!

When I heard the next morning at the Central Committee meeting that the Miyamoto *dan* snuck out early, I turned to Mrs. Kurashige next to me and said, "It's my fault—I thought that *kappa* was human."

Anyway, the *dan* with money were the ones who left first. Every day, more of them got on the trains to Heijo. We watched them with burning envy, and everyone's nerves were frayed with each day. Dr. Oya got angry and yelled at Old Man Yamagishi, "Are you telling me I have to stay here to the end to look after the sick?"

Old Man Yamagishi tried to calm him down. "It's the same for me, Dr. Oya. Someone's got to stay here to tie up loose ends. Please, we've got to be a little more patient." At the Japanese Association office, Old Man Yamagishi was the last man to remain. His thankless job was to calm the remaining Japanese who buzzed around him like angry flies. A very bad tendency among the Japanese became clear to me. Everybody started thinking—"I don't care about anyone else, I just want to get out of this town as soon as I can."

It was awful to see everyone's selfishness and greed come oozing out, including my own. To raise money, the Japanese refugees sold possessions, clothing and valuables that had been hidden until then. As the market got flooded, prices for anything the Japanese sold dropped. But at the same time, the prices for supplies rose. I also sold the few things I had as the last days approached.

I knew that pretty Mrs. Sato had three lovely silk kimonos. I advanced on her in a dark corner with my plan, and said, "They say we can't take any silk kimonos with us. We've got to get rid of them now…the prices are dropping fast. They say a five hundred *yen* kimono won't even fetch three hundred now."

Mrs. Sato had already been thinking about this. "I guess it's no good holding onto my fine clothes. I'm going to keep one kimono and sell the other two."

Cold-blooded, I planted the seeds of my scheme. "Mrs. Sato,

where are you going to sell those two kimono?"

"Where? I have no idea," she said, her doll-like face frowned.

"Do you want me to sell it for you? I know a rich family. I'll take it over there and ask them," I volunteered. Mrs. Sato sadly brought out her futon, cut the seams where they had been hidden, and gratefully handed the two kimonos to me.

I took them to the house with the stone gate, the one with the sewing machine where I was friendly with the young girl. I told them my sad story with tears in my eyes to squeeze out the greatest amount of pity—and got them to buy the kimono for eight hundred *yen*. And then, as if it were completely natural, I turned right around and said to Mrs. Sato, "Isn't this wonderful? I managed to sell your kimono for six hundred *yen*," and said nothing about the two hundred *yen* I slipped in my pocket. Out of the six hundred I handed her, she gave me a hundred *yen* for my trouble. I didn't think of myself as a low-life cheat when I kept the money that should have gone to Mrs. Sato. I convinced myself that—I rightfully earned that three hundred *yen*, including the two hundred *yen* I didn't tell her about. But when I looked at Mrs. Sato's pretty face, I felt terribly guilty.

CHAPTER THIRTY-EIGHT

Our *Dan* Divides

Early in the morning on July 28th, I noticed Mrs Kurashige and Mrs. Nagasu with their heads close together, whispering in the room next door. These two women then began whispering with the others, and made sure not to let me hear. But I had my suspicions. Around noon, this group of secretive women moved their discussion outside into the yard. One by one, more members of our *dan* were called outside. I had had enough. I knew what they were up to—I couldn't just stand by and do nothing.

"Mrs. Kurashige, please—I want to have a word with you," I said from inside the house.

But instead of Mrs. Kurashige, I heard Mrs. Nagasu's harsh voice. "If you want to say something, you're the one who should come out here."

"All right," I said, and steeled myself—thinking, "Today I'm not going to hold back. I'm going to say everything I think." I went outside. Mrs. Kurashige, Mrs. Nagasu, Mrs. Honda, Old Woman Oe, Mrs. Kanaya, Mrs. Kimoto, and Mrs. Mizushima all stood outside – all women who were childless or had only one child. The most able-bodied of our *dan*.

"Mrs. Kurashige, I want to say something to you," I said. "If you really want to leave our *dan* now, why don't you be honest and say so to my face, instead of whispering behind my back?"

I continued. "I understand how those of you who are strong and have fewer children want to leave the rest of us behind. We're really not officially a *dan* anyway. All of the Japanese are independent now. But Mrs. Kurashige…," here I wanted to make my point, "Please don't sneak around, and talk the others into going with you and Mrs. Nagasu instead of staying with *Dancho* Narita and me. We should be open and let each member decide for herself."

"We're not talking anyone into anything," said Mrs. Nagasu with a smirk.

"Shut up, I'm not talking with you," I said. "I'm talking with Mrs. Kurashige, who used to be *fuku-dancho* and worked with me for this *dan*."

Mrs. Kurashige looked embarrassed and wouldn't look me in the eye.

I said, "Mrs. Kurashige, maybe it's no use for me to say anything now but – all those times you went with me to the Japanese Association meetings – were you just doing that for your own son and no one else? All that time, were you just thinking of yourself? You must be very proud of yourself," I said as I faced everyone there.

I continued, "If you really want to leave us, please do it right. As long as there's still some semblance of a *dan* here, have the decency to go in and tell *Dancho* Narita (who is sick in bed), that you intend to desert us." My voice grew high-pitched with nervousness.

I pressed Mrs. Kurashige who stood there silent with her head bowed down. "Hurry up and desert us. Leave us with your head high," I yelled. From inside the house, no one spoke. The children seemed to understand the crisis and remained silent. When I came back inside, no one raised their face to look at me. I didn't want to stay in this cold, ugly place any longer than I had to. I didn't want to say another word with anyone as our *dan* broke in half.

The train they chose was leaving late, in the middle of that night. Until the time for their departure, we stayed apart in the two rooms of the small house, without saying a word to each other — there was no conversation at all for two, three hours. This was a painful, excruciating silence. All I heard was Mrs. Mizushima talking softly to her husband in the corner of our room. She was trying to convince her husband, as he cleaned his glasses, that they should leave with Mrs. Kurashige and Mrs. Nagasu.

It finally came time for them to leave. The people in the other room began moving. Mrs. Mizushima said, "Dear, hurry, let's go." Then, finally in a loud voice, she started begging and pleading with her husband who remained silent. Suddenly, Mr. Mizushima raised his hand and slapped her across the face with a loud smack.

My beloved *dan* crumbled before my very eyes. These people, these women — we helped each other survive through so much suffering, pain and death for the past year — how could they abandon us like this? Without any tears, without any kind words, they left us. They didn't look back, and those of us left behind saw them off without any friendly words or hope.

Only Mrs. Kurashige finally looked back to me and said farewell but I didn't answer her. As we heard their train leaving, I sat still and grimly told myself, "I'll show them. We'll survive the *hikiage*." Twelve people abandoned our *dan*. Twelve people who believed they couldn't survive with us. Now there were only eighteen people left in my *dan* and I was responsible. After our *dan* fell apart on the 28th, I was terrified that our group would break up again, so even though it was late that night, I ran out to talk with Old Man Yamagishi who was still at the Japanese Association office. I said to him, "Of all the Japanese left in Sensen, you are the only person I trust anymore. Please tell me what you think I should do."

Old Man Yamagishi felt sorry for me. "You're not the only one, Mrs. Fujiwara. Everyone is suffering—everything is falling apart. The only thing I can say to you is that in the end, fate will determine what happens. If you get to Heijo, but get trapped in the refugee mob there for ten days, that might be the end. You might die there. Even if you get to Shinmaku safely by train, beyond that...," he couldn't say more.

"You're saying that beyond that, it's up to fate," I said.

"That's right. I can't tell you what to do. All I can say is, when you make your decision, take action. When you make your decision, that's when you're most confident," he said.

I made my decision. Old Man Yamagishi's information indicated our plight was not going to get any better. I decided we would leave on the 30th. When I told the others of my decision, everyone was relieved and began preparations. I got rid of everything. I'd have to throw everything away anyway so, other than some food in our *hango*, and a few extra clothes for the children, I let go of everything. I sold our blanket, our futon, and other things. With this I made two hundred *yen*. We cleaned up our kitchen. Finally, I went next door to say good-bye to Old Man

Park and his wife at the *onpan* shop.

When I told them the news, they said, "Is that so? Well, well. Please come see us again, Mrs. Fujiwara."

I thought, "The hell, I will. I hope I never step foot inside this miserable hole again." I went around the wall back to our house. As I looked back, I saw them peeking through the bean vines. They looked lonely.

We decided to leave the morning of the 30th. Mrs. Narita, Mrs. Daichi, Mrs. Sakiyama, and I all had our burdens. We were the most unfortunate of the *dan*. A sick husband, young children... how would we survive? We held each other's hands and cried, 'We've got to help each other." For the first time, I saw tears in Mrs. Sakiyama's eyes.

"We're a pretty pathetic bunch to be helping one another," I said.

Pretty Mrs. Sato with no children could carry more things. Mrs. Toda no longer had the burden of caring for her poor step-son Tamio-chan. These two women were alone now, so they were better off than me. Mr. and Mrs. Mizushima also didn't have children so they were all right.

I felt better knowing that there was still one man in our group we could count on. I bowed my head and said, "Mr. Mizushima, thank you. It means a lot to me that you stayed with us," I felt truly grateful.

He wore his usual scowl but he wiped his glasses and said, "But I didn't do anything—I'm just doing what I want to do."

While we nervously waited at the platform for our train on the 30th, someone handed us a scrawled note—a message from the Japanese Association office—it said, "Do not, under any circumstances, depart today."

What did this note mean? I left the children with someone and ran to the office. Old Man Yanagishi waited for me.

"Why can't we go?" I gasped.

"At Heijo station, there's a terrible situation. A huge crowd of Japanese refugees are stuck there and can't move. It's chaos down there," he said. "If you go now, you'll end up getting caught in that desperate horde at the station and die. Wait a little and leave after we know what is going on, down the train line from there."

"Where did you get this information?"

"A trustworthy man who just came in the train that arrived."

I didn't know what to say.

Old Man Yanagishi wouldn't lie. We still had three days until our train tickets expired. Reluctantly, I decided we would wait. Everyone, still trembling with excitement and fear, went back to the house we thought we had left for good. We felt like intruders in our own empty home, but stayed there on the 30th and the 31st. Our former home had nothing left inside—no sign of our life here—we were done here. I felt our will to live ebb away with each minute. Nothing seemed to matter anymore. Dying here or dying in Heijo—it would all be the same. Without waiting for more news from Old Man Yanagishi, I decided we had to leave on the first of August.

As we stood on the train platform once again and waited for our train early in the morning, a cold wind hit our faces. "We're going to ride the train," I said to Masahiro who was holding my right hand, Masahiko held my left, and Sakiko was on my back.

Around my neck hung a bag with two weeks of food—the strap of the heavy bag bit into my neck. I turned my eyes to the northern sky and thought about how far we had to go—and how we survived thus far. "Dear, if you are still alive, please pray that the four of us reach home safely," I asked my husband. At the same time, in my heart, I knew this might be my farewell message.

We got on the train, stood near the wall of the open car and looked back to Sensen. Above the thick green canopy of trees, only the church steeple was visible. It bravely stood straight up and saw us off.

The train whistle blew. Mrs. Daichi began to sob with Seiko-chan clinging to her arm. The train passed the Japanese graveyard where our dead would be forgotten. I wasn't sad. I wasn't happy. When I looked back one more time at the town of Sensen, the train whistle blew a note higher and — our car plunged into the dark tunnel.

There would always be light at the other end. In that light, I could let myself die. If I'm going to die anyway, I wanted to die even one step closer to home. On the other side of this tunnel.

PART III

THE VOICE OF BEELZEBUB

CHAPTER THIRTY-NINE

The Content of the Letters

The train reached Heijo in the afternoon and — as Old Man Yamagishi had warned me — the station was packed with throngs of dejected men, women and children, their eyes empty of hope. People had already waited for who knows how many days, sitting anywhere there was space, on the ground, in the dirt. I managed to find space for the four of us under the roof of a storage shed. We sat there for two days and chewed *daizu*.

There didn't seem to be anyone leading this teeming horde. Two or three men ran about frantically, trying to coordinate the trains. Finally on the afternoon of the third day, we were told we could get on a covered freight train to Shinmaku.

But before we could get on, ragged Japanese soldiers inspected everyone's possessions. Everyone knew better than to object to these desperate soldier's demands. Even with the surrender of Japan, these men still clung to the remnants of the military hierarchy. They repeatedly shouted, "Do not to keep any

papers with any writing, any information, on them." (I suppose
they didn't want information to fall into the hands of the vic-
tors.) While I stood in line, I took out the two letters Mr. Taya,
my husband's boss back in Manchuria, had entrusted to me. One
was to his boss in Japan, my husband's uncle, Sakuhei Fujiwara,
who was head of the Meteorological Department in Japan. The
other letter was to Mr. Taya's wife in Japan.

I had only one choice—before they were confiscated by these
soldiers—I decided to read Mr. Taya's letters, try to memorize
them, and then recite them to my uncle and Mrs. Taya, if and
when I got back to Japan. First, I ripped open the envelope hastily
written in pencil to his boss, Dr. Sakue Fujiwara, and read quickly.

> Dear Dr. Fujiwara,
> I trust that this letter has reached you. I am at a criti-
> cal juncture in my life and must make important decisions
> which will determine my fate and that of many others.
> From the chaos of Shinkyo, I've made it down to the town
> of Anton, on the border with northern Korea. There are still
> many things I have to do.

Kind Mr. Taya was thinking of his staff—my husband and the
men who worked for him in Manchuria.

> Who is going to take care of the families of these dead
> men, and how are they going to get home? When I think
> about the women and children, my heart aches.
> I only have one favor to ask of you. Please look after
> them, the families of my men, if and when they reach home.
> It is not likely that the two of us will meet again, but
> there is still that chance. I will pray for your health.

I knew that if my husband's uncle read this letter, he would have cried. The other letter from Mr. Taya to his wife was three pages long.

> *Dear Setsuko,*
>
> *I feel danger close to me and I'm writing you in haste as the messenger waits to deliver it.*
>
> *What can I write? We've been separated for such a long time, ever since this war started. Now, perhaps we are at the most sorrowful moment in our lives. The first thing that comes to my mind are our three children. If I die, I know your life will be arduous. You will have to endure many dark moments. But remember that you will be their only parent, you must be strong and raise the children with the heart of a lioness.*
>
> *Our three children are like iron, earth, and water – and each child has the strengths and weaknesses of that element. No matter how terrible your situation becomes, please don't forget to take care of each of our children's spirit, their precious unique...*

Something sharp suddenly hit my head. A soldier waved a stick and shouted at me, "Hey, bitch! What are you doing? Why haven't you torn up your letters yet? It's because of stupid women like you that Japan lost the war. Why are you dawdling? Hurry up and throw those papers away! How can you call yourself a Japanese woman?"

That soldier had an ugly, chestnut-shaped head—his eyes gleamed with exhaustion and hatred as he roared at me. I've seen this type of bully before many times. When I was in Manchuria, and had to attend air-raid drills, they'd bellow and rant at me, "Hey, over there, stupid woman, what do you think you're doing?" The harsh voice was the same, only the place and time were different. I answered him with a tip of my nose and got rid of the letters.

The train arrived. When I looked at the head of the line of people—I suddenly saw people I recognized. "Well, what do you know," I thought.

There they were—the women who deserted us on the 28th. The ones who abandoned us back in Sensen—all lined up right in front of me. I saw Mrs. Kimoto recognize me, turn around and tell the rest of her group. They looked at me sheepishly.

I gloated. "See, I told you so."

CHAPTER FORTY

Struggle in the Red Mud

As soon as we got on the train, my head began to spin. The floor of the freight car was covered with a thick layer of horse shit that almost made me throw up. People were packed in, there was no place to sit so everyone was forced to stand in this putrid, sticky mess. The children clung to me, terrified — and I couldn't breathe. After the train started moving, it began to rain and water poured in through holes in the roof, like small mountain waterfalls. The boys and I stood in this hell for who knows how long.

When we reached the next stop, Shinmaku, I couldn't tell how many hours had passed. All I remember is that the children's voices begging for water had died away, and we were finally able to get our feet out of this filthy muck. They slid open the train doors into a pitch darkness where a violent rain lashed us — so dark I couldn't even see my own children's faces.

"Shh!" A man's gruff voice appeared from somewhere. "We are going to walk through a dangerous area all night. Don't carry too much stuff. Stay close to the person in front of you and don't get lost. Walk fast — We're going to start now!" That voice was so deep, it cut right through the wind and rain. He snarled, "We'll leave you behind if you separate from the line. Stay close. — If you lose the person in front of you, you're finished!" That low-pitched, rough voice seemed to rise straight from the underworld.

"Who's speaking?" I wondered.

This frightening voice was the only thing that led this mass of desperate people. Here, I threw away about half of what I had brought — all of the canned food and much of the *daizu*. Somebody lit a lantern that emitted a dim light. Immediately, the eerie voice shot out, "Put that out!" The light went out.

I felt the mass of wet bodies before me begin to move. In my right arm, I half-carried Masahiko. With my left hand, I gripped Masahiro's hand. Sakiko was tied onto my back and the rucksack hung around my neck. I followed the horde.

I stumbled over cans, bags and bundles people had thrown away while the wind and rain pelted my face, undoing the hair so that it flew into my eyes. I threw myself headlong into the crowd to try to keep up as we scurried through the back streets of the town.

Suddenly, I remembered, "I haven't nursed my baby. It's been six or seven hours since we left Heijo. Poor Sakiko!" But there was no room for compassion. All I could do was to tell myself, "Don't fall behind. Don't fall behind," as I pulled the boys with me in the dark.

Eventually, we left the town and went into a mountain dirt road which narrowed — forcing everyone into a thin line. As everyone passed us, the children and I fell to the tail-end of this miserable parade — but I felt something chase us from the inky-blackness behind us, ready to consume a desperate woman with her three children. From time to time, I turned around to look but all I heard was the storm howling, "Run. Run. If we don't run, we'll be killed." I walked with my heart dead — with only the image of the 38th Parallel burned into my mind.

When I remember that time now, I don't know what or who I thought was chasing us — but I was terrified. All of the fear that had been hiding in my subconscious for so long transformed into that man's voice — the voice of Beelzebub. This was what I felt back then, and all I could do was drive myself forward with the words, "If I don't run, I'm going to die." Over and over.

Masahiro started crying behind me, "Mommy, I can't walk. I can't walk." There was no room for comforting poor Masahiro — I had to take care of his younger brother and sister. Every ten steps, I half-carried Masahiko, the next ten steps, I dragged him. The rain drenched Sakiko on my back, the bag hanging on my neck, and all my clothes. As the fabric became water-logged, everything grew heavier and heavier. Water streamed down my back to my pants which almost fell off. Each time the rucksack hit the ground and dragged in the mud, my neck felt as if it were being sliced.

All I could do was, tell myself, "'Follow — follow that shadow in front." My brain was empty save for the thought — we will die if we get left behind.

I was desperate for my boys to keep moving, and began to scream with the harshest language I could summon, "Masahiro, what are you doing, you lazy pig! Masahiko, if you cry, you're going to be left behind!" For the first time in my life, I used rough men's language — words in a tyrannical tone I normally never used. Like most proper Japanese women, I was raised to speak softly and gently. But now, without thinking, a male fury spewed terrible, hurtful words out of my mouth, like a sharp whip to drive the children.

The muddy road grew steep and we struggled up two steps, only to slide back down one step. I hit Masahiko's rear end with as much strength as I could and his cries of pain were torn into bits by the wind. Masahiro was also victim to all my terrible words but he stumbled and staggered behind me so as to avoid my blows.

When we finally reached the top of the ridge, dawn was creeping into the grey sky and I saw the narrow road we had just climbed was bordered by bald mountain sides, a land devoid of trees but thick with grass. I had managed to not get lost in the dark because the road was deeper than the surrounding hillsides.

In the growing daylight, I was horrified to see ourselves. The boys looked terrible. During the night, the red mud had covered them from head to toe—slimy clay plastered their shirts, their pants, everywhere—only their eyes shone white. Are there no more tears? The boys lurched and wobbled like drunks. Masahiko lost both of his shoes in the mud and now walked barefoot. He rubbed his face with his dirty hand, getting the red mud into his eyes, and cried. "Mommy. Mommy, I can't see."

"You, idiot," I screamed and kicked him as he fell. But I was encouraged that he still had the strength to get back up. Weaving back and forth, one step...two steps...then he would fall again into the mud. If it looked like he couldn't get up, I grabbed his left arm and dragged him. Go forward. Go forward. We moved step by step, but the bottom of his soaked pants dragged on the ground, pulling him down. I was amazed this child still had the will to stand up...stand up—again and again. Once in a while I felt the pressure of his hand in mine lighten.

Meanwhile, Masahiro's cries lessened as he saw my desperate efforts — did he empathize with me or simply give up? He became silent and followed. If he fell behind, I turned around and yelled, "Idiot, you want to die there?" He then rushed to catch up and looked at me with anguished eyes.

The rain let up a little and the thin fog in front of us blew away with the wind which came up from the valley below. In the distance, on a hill, tiny figures moved about. "Hey, Masahiko, Masahiro — look over there. Everyone is there. Everyone is there," I yelled in encouragement.

As we got closer, I saw that people covered in mud lay on the ground like corpses, with their bags still on their backs. I looked for people I knew, but didn't see anyone. That didn't surprise me since we had all stumbled about in the red slime, in the dark for hours — there were no *dan*, no individuals, no identities anymore.

When I fell over with Sakiko still on my back and tried to catch my breath, a voice called out, "Mrs. Fujiwara!" It was Mrs. Sato who managed to still look prim despite the muck. She held a blue and white umbrella to keep the rain off! "I'm so glad. Everyone's over there," she said and grabbed my arm. I was barely able to get up with her help and we went to another spot where I collapsed. But in a few minutes, I had to get up to get ready for the next part.

I got the remaining *daizu* from the bag around my neck, put the dry soybeans into Masahiro and Masahiko's hands, and put some in my mouth to chew. The hard beans made my teeth ache and tasted like chalk. The boys just clutched their *daizu* and cried, "I'm cold. I'm cold" and didn't eat. I got Sakiko off my back and tried to nurse her. No milk. I spit some of the *daizu* I had chewed into my hand, and pushed the mush into her small mouth.

She tried to suck it, and cried, "Ahh." The poor baby was hungry after having not eaten for more than ten hours. And I hadn't been able to change her diaper. Her fever and diarrhea started again earlier that day, and I didn't know if she would survive the night, getting drenched in this rain. But she was surprisingly strong. She tried — again and again — to eat the crushed *daizu* mixed with my spittle. The sight of her thin, little body reverberated into the hard masculine spirit that had grown inside me, and although I shouldn't have cried — I did.

People had thrown away wet, soaked bags, unopened rucksacks, and clothes. I grabbed somebody's undershirt and used it as a diaper for Sakiko. I took off Masahiko and Masahiro's pants and — using my teeth — I tore the bottoms off to make them into shorts. I did the same with my pants. Even if it was just a little, I tried to lighten our load. I kept a bottle of water, a *hango*, and a little bit of food in the rucksack but threw away everything else.

The rain started up again. People began moving but I thought, "I can't move. I don't have the strength to move." My children were the same. I looked carefully at Sakiko's face before I put her on my back. Her face was emaciated and small, her eyes half-open in a stupor. I took out my red rope and tied it firmly around my hips. "When the end comes, I can use this red rope to strangle my children and myself" I told myself.

A huge mountain loomed in front of me. I said to myself, "The road heads toward that mountain. Those forbidding mountains. I'm not strong enough to climb them. But if I'm going to die anyway, I'll go further to where we can all die." I forced myself to stand up.

"Mommy, I can't walk," cried Masahiko as he stood up barefoot.

"Idiot. Go ahead and die, you little idiot." I slapped him across his face. In this brutal way, I steeled myself to keep going…forward…forward toward the 38th Parallel.

A voice suddenly said, "Masahiko, come with me." Mrs. Sato's hand extended to him.

"Leave that no-good kid," I said but she ignored me. Mrs. Sato held Masahiko's hand in her left hand, had a big bag on her back and in her right hand, she held the blue and white umbrella. At the last rest stop, she had even changed into fresh clothes that matched the color of her umbrella. Even in this miserable place, Mrs. Satao managed to look proper. I was grateful to see that Mrs. Daichi's daughter, Seiko-chan, took hold of Masahiro's hand. I was freed from pulling my boys.

CHAPTER FORTY-ONE

Before Freezing to Death

The road into the mountains wound its way into a valley between other mountains and turned into a narrow, shriveled trail. Eventually, even the trail disappeared. We followed the shadows, which swirled like a beautiful obi, on and on to the horizon.

The red mud on the trail refused to let go off our feet once we stepped in it. Sometimes we sank in the muck up to our knees. In the distance, Mrs. Sato's blue and white umbrella wavered and I followed, so grateful to those who took my boys. If I had to drag my boys as I had done through the night, I couldn't have gone one step further. We would have sunk into the earth, and died. Everyone went ahead of me and disappeared into the rain while I fell behind and was left alone on the trail. Somehow, I kept moving, only driven by the knowledge that my two boys were alive up ahead.

The rocks closed in from both sides. If I could get through this place, I sensed that there would something up ahead. But what I found up ahead was a woman who had lost her mind.

"Ah...oh...My little boy died..he died," she wailed. A single woman sat in the mud along the side of the trail—the white face of the dead baby sharp against her dark clothes. I recognized her. She was from the Osaka *dan*.

'What happened?"I asked. As I neared, she stood up.

"My boy died…he's dead," she moaned. She showed me the lifeless baby in the crook of her arm. With her other hand she waved his little arm, moved his legs, and looked to the sky, pleading.

I said, "There's nothing you can do for your dead child. Please stop. You've got to get a hold of yourself. Otherwise, you're going to die here, too." I talked to her in a cold, brusque manner, as if her child was just a dead puppy. "Hurry and bury him, and we'll leave," I ordered her.

I took the dead baby from her arms. The corpse was cold and had begun to stiffen—he must have been dead for hours. I took the small body to a spot away from the trail, dug a shallow grave with my hands, and covered him with wet dirt. I went back to the woman and pulled her hand sharply to stand up and said, "You've got to run away. You've got to run away." And pushed her forward.

When we climbed to the spot where we could see the peak right in front of us, the woman suddenly stopped. "I want to die with my son…die together with him…," she cried and ran back down the hill. I could no longer care about her. I had to go forward if I was going to survive. I walked downhill, then uphill again. My head hurt so much it was numb. I lost all feeling below my waist. After I walked for half the day, I finally caught up to the other Japanese resting.

From the top of that hill, I saw a real road—a beautiful road. And moreover, I saw farms dotting the land around the road. I searched for my children as I got nearer to the people in the distance, and saw them just as they got ready to leave, as if they were running away from me.

"Wait!" I cried but they didn't hear me and they kept moving. I knew it was them. That was Mrs. Sato's blue and white umbrella and from beneath the umbrella, a small standing figure appeared. I was filled with joy and as I got nearer I recognized them. The pathetic figures of Masahiko and Masahiro stood alone after the umbrella had moved away with the others.

But I was shocked when I got close enough to see Masahiko. His bare legs below his shorts were purple-blue and his blue lips trembled so much he couldn't speak. Cold rain dripped from both of his shivering hands crossed in front of his chest.

Then I heard Masahiro's weak trembling voice. "Mommy, Masahiko says he's cold." Masahiro's whole body shook violently as he said this. Even in this pitiable state, my older son felt responsible for his younger brother. He was right. Masahiko was indeed in very bad shape — he looked about to die.

"Masahiko, be strong. Mommy's here," I said grabbing him and lifting him in my arms.

I looked around through the rain and saw a grass-thatched cottage roof glistening in the distance. I no longer cared what the Koreans would do to us and rushed toward that cottage. I crossed a road where a woman and her child were crying over a prone man.

I recognized them. "Oh, *Dancho* Narita," I said. *Dancho* Narita's eyes were closed but I saw he was still alive. At the sound of my voice, he feebly moved a hand. I scolded his wife, "What are you doing? You've got to warm him right away, otherwise he's going to die."

I left them there as I ran to the cottage with Masahiko in my arms. Next to the cottage there was an animal stall. I went into the stall and dropped Sakiko in the hay, ran to the cottage with Masahiko, and pounded on the door. "Please have a fire for us," I prayed.

An elderly Korean woman came out and saw Masahiko. With a worried face, she gestured for me to use the hot water sitting on a stove, "Take as much as you need." I got a bucket of the hot water in one hand, and took my son with the other and went back to the animal stall. I stripped Masahiko, dipped a diaper in the hot water, wrung the cloth out and began vigorously rubbing Masahiko's body with it. From his feet to his hands—from his hands to his feet—I rubbed. As I rubbed, I saw his heart beat beneath the thin skin of his chest. He's alive. I rubbed harder with the hot cloth. His lips began to turn pink, then he spoke. His first words were, "Is big brother all right?"

I had completely forgotten about Masahiro. When I turned around, I saw that he had fallen asleep in the hay, still in his wet clothes. His skin had grown grey, and he didn't look alive. It took me longer for me to revive Masahiro using the same method I used for his little brother. I was like a mad woman between the two boys—I took off their clothes, rubbed them raw, fed them hot water with a handful of the *daizu*. Once I knew they were safe, I finally let them fall asleep in the hay.

Sakiko was in better shape. The cloth hat I had put on her head must have kept some of the rain off and my body had shielded her from the cold. The Naritas joined us in this animal stall. Mrs. Narita helplessly sat about while *Dancho* Narita's breathing got worse and worse. Dusk settled in, the rain started again, and the storm grew more violent.

I closed my eyes to try to sleep but sharp pains shot into my chilled body. Inside my brain, the storm still raged. In any case, within an hour, I was up again because the owner of the stall told me — with gestures and words — that we couldn't stay there.

CHAPTER FORTY-TWO

The Bald Head of Kappa Man

As I sat in the straw, I rubbed my aching head and despaired. "What am I going to do?" Then I heard the rumble of wooden wheels. When I looked outside in the rain, I saw an ox-driven cart with about a dozen Japanese refugees on board.

"Oh, yes. There's ox carts. I must use my money to hire a cart for the children," I thought and ran out to find farm houses with ox carts. I finally found one house with an ox cart available. I made arrangements to hire the cart and driver, but they asked for a thousand yen to take us to the town of Shinkei. There was no way I could pay this by myself so I went back out to the road to find someone to share the cart with. Who should I run into but someone I knew – Kappa Man!

"Mr. Tokushima, what a lucky coincidence," I said, trying to sound cheerful. "If there are people in your group who want to ride a cart, why don't we go together? I've found a cart and heard it's a thousand yen to Shinkei."

"A thousand yen for a cart to Shinkei? We can't afford such

an expensive ride. Everyone in our group is walking," said Kappa Man with shrug and left me.

I approached other people on the road and finally found a group of about ten people to share a ride with. Then I ran back to the animal stall, fed the children raw eggs I had bought at one of the farm houses, and ate one myself.

After we gulped down the eggs, I turned to the Narita family still huddled in our animal stall. "Mrs. Narita, what are you going to do?" I asked her. Her husband looked very bad.

"Mrs. Fujiwara, don't wait for us. I'm going to stay here and see my husband off to the next world," she said calmly. "Then my son and I will go." She held her husband's pale head in her lap.

I got closer to them to say my farewell. "*Dancho* Narita?" I said, but his half-open eyes didn't move toward me, and he said nothing.

"Why did this good man who struggled with us for a year, this scholar who loved the starry summer nights, have to end his life in a miserable animal stall on this dark, rainy night?" I wanted to send him off with the vision of that warm summer night and a clear sky full of bright stars. But here there was nothing I could do for him. I said, "Please take care," and left him with silent words of prayer, as I went out into the rain with my children.

We sat on the end of the ox cart, facing outwards, with me in the middle. I wrapped my left arm around Masahiko, my right arm around Masahiro, Sakiko on my back, and covered our heads with a single quilted fabric, a *furoshiki zabuton* I had found on the road. I was glad I had this piece of cloth to huddle under as the ox cart started with a lurch. I sighed with relief. Maybe we had avoided the worst danger. With hope bubbling in my heart, I was determined to survive the night.

When we left the hamlet, we approached three other ox carts. I suddenly realized the Miyamoto *dan* was on those carts. In the last cart, a cigarette butt flared as a man breathed its smoke in. I recognized the face. Kappa Man. I couldn't help myself, I was so angry. "You tricked me!" I yelled at that glowing cigarette.

He knew at once it was me. "What? You say, I tricked you? How rude. I can do whatever I want." He dropped his cigarette off the side, as our two carts came nearer.

With my rough man's language, I shot back, "You always do whatever the hell you want, don't you? – bastard!"

"What are you saying? You beggar! You bitch! " Kappa Man was hopping mad now.

Our cart passed his cart, but before his voice died away, I screamed with everything I had, "You stupid Kappa Man!"

The carts moved with a jerk, and our yelling fight ended as his cart moved ahead. He called me a beggar woman. I was so angry, so enraged I ground my teeth.

When the cart steadied again, the boys almost fell asleep but I was so afraid – afraid they would fall off into the blackness below to be crushed or die – I tried to hold onto them with both arms but couldn't. "If you fall asleep, you'll die. If you fall asleep, you'll die," I screamed but my words weren't enough.

I pulled and slapped the boys to wake them up. By the time my voice gave out, the cart stopped with a jolt. The Korean *Hoan-tai* police ordered the carts to go no further. "It's too dangerous to keep going in this dark," they said.

We got off the cart and sat down on the ground and waited for dawn. The rain died down and the *furoshiki zabuton* on our heads helped so the children didn't get as cold as before. I took off their clothes, wrung them out and vigorously rubbed their bodies red. Masahiko cried, "That hurts, that hurts."

We didn't have a change of clothes so I put the wet clothes back on them and held them close in the dark. Something glimmered   in front of me. When I looked closely, I saw that right in front of us was the bald head of Kappa Man! His shiny bald spot reflected light towards me as he lay down to go to sleep. That bald head right in front of me.

I looked at my hand. Even in the dark, I could see my nails were black with dirt. I thought, "It would feel so wonderful to see bright red blood dripping from the long scratches I could make on that bastard's skull." All night, I glared at that bald circle on his head.

CHAPTER FORTY-THREE

Two Thousand Yen Promissory Note

The next morning, August 5th, the sun grew hotter as it climbed into the clear sky and quickly dried our wet clothes. But now, as we sat on the back of the cart, we suffered from the blazing heat instead of bitter cold. The merciless, burning orb started beating down on our heads. But at least this time, we could relax because we wouldn't fall in the dark and die. I put my arms around the boys so they wouldn't slip, and told them to go ahead and sleep.

The cart lurched back and forth rhythmically as the oxen steadily plodded forward. Behind us, the surface of the road shimmered, like a mirage. We passed farm fields, small houses, then crossed a river around three in the afternoon to reach our first destination—the town of Shinkei.

No one looked up when we arrived because, under the hot sun, everyone had fallen asleep—women slept holding babies who dozed with their mouths open next to their mother's nipples.

We got off and I paid the ox cart driver. Now all I had left was the hundred yen note I sewed into Masahiro's rucksack and a few coins. I was out of money and we still hadn't gone even a third of the way—I knew I had to make more money somehow.

All through the previous night while we rode the ox cart, I schemed and concocted an idea. This was my plan: first, find my group. That wasn't difficult. I found Mrs. Sato's open umbrella right away. Beneath it, she was asleep, her muddy head tilted back. Mrs. Daichi, Seiko-chan and her baby sister were nearby, too, fast asleep. Before I did anything, I had to get some food and sleep—I had been up for two whole days since leaving Heijo. I bought three small melons for ten yen from a street vendor—and the children and I gobbled them up. For the first time since leaving Shinmaku, I tasted something that reminded me of real food. After nibbling on some *daizu* to fill my stomach, I lay Sakiko down under Mrs. Sato's umbrella and curled up next to her to fall into a deep, two day's worth of sleep.

In my dreams, a storm still raged. I struggled and tried to go forward in the wind and rain, yet I couldn't move, not even one step. Something chased me but I couldn't see what it was. Mixed in with the storm, I heard a distant melody, something familiar from somewhere. From that music, a creature jumped out and tried to hold me down. In the mud, in the rain, I couldn't move. I kept thinking, 'If only the music would stop, I could move forward.'

I said to myself, "I know that music. I should know who is playing that music. That piano music that gripped my chest." A figure wrapped in black tried to tell me something. All these sounds swirled in my head painfully. I felt like I had slept for a long time but didn't feel rested. When I woke up my head still ached. Deep inside my brain, it felt like there was a deep wound, a lesion that throbbed with pain. The sun had gone down to the west, so I must have slept for two or three hours. Some of the others also woke up but Mrs. Sato still slept. Her pretty, pale, round face was covered with mud and looked comical, especially with the dried red mud on the end of her cute nose. When I tried to wipe that mud off her nose, she moved in her sleep. I waited for her to wake—I was ready with my plan.

I sat so that when she woke up, she would immediately see me. She finally opened her eyes and saw me. "Oh, Mrs. Fujiwara, I'm so glad…where's Masahiko-chan?" she said. As I expected, she felt guilty about leaving Masahiko behind.

I put on a sweet face and said, "Thank you for asking. Oh, he's sleeping over there—like a little piglet," I said. Masahiko was sleeping with his mouth open. The weeds near his mouth moved in and out with his breath. After I politely thanked Mrs. Sato for the previous day, I said in a small voice, "There's something I need to talk with you about—in private."

I pulled her up and we went to sit under an apple tree. I said, "Mrs. Sato, I have a favor to ask of you. Can you lend me five hundred yen?"

"What? Five hundred yen. I don't have that kind of money." She drew back when she realized what I was after.

"Mrs. Sato, I'm not going to lie. I know exactly how much you have," I said. "Remember, I sold your kimonos for you. You have the luxury of carrying that blue and white umbrella and another kimono. Look at me and my miserable condition. One pair of shorts and one torn blouse. And my three children are almost dead."

I said, "It is your decision which will decide whether we live or die. I'm asking you again—please lend me five hundred yen."

"To tell you the truth, I only have seven hundred yen," she said.

"Yes, I know and I want you to lend me five hundred of that," I said.

"But I don't feel safe for the rest of the trip with just two hundred yen...is there no way? How about three hundred?" she asked.

"No. I've got to have five hundred to get to the Kaijo refugee camp. I've got to put the children on a ox cart. There is still over forty miles from here to the Kaijo camp, much of that over mountains. There's no way they can walk that distance. Please, Mrs. Sato."

"That's impossible," she said curtly and her face hardened.

I made my move. "Impossible? All right, if that's what you say, I won't take one *sen* from you. But if Masahiko or Sakiko dies, I will hold you responsible for the rest of my life and I will follow you forever. If I die, I'll become a ghost and haunt you. If I live, I swear I'll chase you down to every corner and crack in this world.

"Back in Sensen, you held Masahiko and you bragged that you would carry him across the 38th Parallel. Yet, I know you left Masahiko half-dead in the rain — I saw you run off with your umbrella. I'm going to tell everyone about your callousness. I'll tell everyone about you — how you abandoned little Masahiko in the cold rain. He almost died."

I deftly switched tactics and softly said, "Please, Mrs. Sato, don't force me to become this monster, this horrible woman. Lend me the five hundred yen. I'll return two thousand yen to you after I get home. And I'll give you the best kimono I have at home. We'll made a proper contract and I'll borrow the money from you. If you want me to return ten thousand yen to you, that's what we'll write on the contract — Please, Mrs. Sato — There's only one of you and four of us."

Then I flung myself to the ground and broke down crying. The tart smell of a rotten apple on the ground drifted into my nose as I put my face to the earth.

She did as I had hoped.

"Mrs. Fujiwara, I am sorry about yesterday," she said. "It was terrible of me to do that. I'll make out somehow. I'll lend you the five hundred yen."

I got a pencil and a piece of paper under that apple tree, and for the first time in my life, I wrote out a promissory note.

> I (Tei Fujiwara) promise to pay two thousand yen in Japanese money to Yoshiko Sato when I return to Japan,
>
> August 5, ~~Showa year~~
>
>> Signed by:
>>
>> Yoshiko Sato and
>> Tei Fujiwara
>> Under the apple tree.
>> Shinkei.

I signed my name but crossed out the year *Showa* next to August 5th because *Showa* was the name of the year under our current Emperor Hirohito. I didn't know what had happened in Tokyo. Was Hirohito still our emperor? Did we still use *Showa* for the year? Had he been banished by the Americans? Was it a new era, *Daishin,* for Japan? If Japan had changed to a new era from last year, it would be year 2. If the *Daishin* era started this year, it would be year 1. I didn't know what the Americans had decided on the fate of our emperor and Japan, so I left the year blank.

I succeeded. I counted the five hundred yen I got from Mrs. Sato. When I turned to see the children, Mrs. Daichi looked at me. "Nothing is going to defeat you," she seemed to say to the bully I had become. I glared back at her but felt like she was able to see everything inside me. I looked away first. I smiled and said to myself, "I don't care what anyone thinks. Now that I've got five hundred yen, I can hire an ox cart to take the children."

CHAPTER FORTY-FOUR

We Reach Shihenri

A full moon shone brightly that night and the insects cried in protest. The oxen bellowed softly as they pulled our cart, their black shadows sharp against the white road. Step by step, we went south. I walked alongside the cart. Earlier in the evening, I put Masahiro and Masahiko on this cart from Shinkei. All the way, I scolded the boys, ""If you go to sleep, you'll fall off the cart. If you go to sleep, you'll fall," partly to keep myself awake as I walked along the flat road which seemed to go on forever.

The ox cart was full of men and women nodding asleep — so many that people almost spilled out. I was the only one who walked — to save as much money as I could.

At dawn, the cart stopped at a small hamlet to rest. I didn't know when we would start again so I decided to sit under the cart so I'd wake if they moved. I put my thin quilt on the children and sat next to them to sleep. Around my arm, I tied a rope from the cart to be sure they wouldn't leave without me. I tried to sleep this way but the oxen would sometimes shift their bodies, which made the cart move and jerked me awake.

Early the next morning, the sun crept up in the sky, and slowly dried the dew off of me. The ox cart jolted each time the oxen shook off their sleep as we began another day's march. The sun blazed, and people and oxen alike, grew sluggish in the heat. The cheap straw sandals I bought in Shinkei for four yen didn't even last one night. They hurt my feet so much, I threw them away and decided to walk barefoot. But if I stepped on a rock, the pain shot up my leg and made my head ache. I was so tired, I hung onto the cart, and half-dragged, half-walked alongside. (At least my two boys slept well the previous night and they were alert the next day. I was grateful for that.) I was tired but my mood was good.

We reached Shihenri in the afternoon. Tents were set up in a small town surrounded by apple trees. The Korean *Hoantai* Police were in charge of the Japanese refugees. I took Sakiko off my back to nurse her but my breasts still yielded nothing. My poor baby still had strength to suck hard enough to make my nipples hurt. I had to give her something to eat...I went to a farm and bought two small, yellow melons.

I broke the melons open, dipped a piece of the fruit in some water and let the juice trickle into Sakiko's mouth. She smacked her lips hungrily and drank. I was impressed, "This child still has the strength to live." For the four of us, was this good news? Since leaving Heijo, Mrs. Sakiyama's words haunted me. "Mrs. Fujiwara, who is more important? One child or two children?"

I no longer had the strength to say, "One child or two children, they're all precious." I now understood what she tried to say to me — that I might have to sacrifice Sakiko in order to let Masahiko and Masahiro live. But when I watched Sakiko eagerly suck the melon piece, I didn't have the heart to even think of sacrificing this baby. I decided — if I have to give up on Sakiko, then we would all die together.

A Korean man from the *Hoantai* security force saw me. "Are you bringing three children by yourself?" he said incredulously.

"Yes," I said meekly.

"Do you know anyone?" he demanded.

"No," I said.

He shook his head, "Huh, what a pity." Then he brought over a dusky-skinned Japanese man with a tattered, colored shirt.

He ordered this man, "Take care of this woman and children. Take care of them until you reach the camp at Kaijo. All right?" He bullied the dark-skinned Japanese man, shook his stick about, and then laughed. The dusky man understood him but just glared at me with resentment.

The Korean *Hoantai* man suddenly remembered something and forgot about me and my children. He went off somewhere. Of course, I didn't expect anything from this stranger. More importantly, I needed something to eat so I stood up, a little unsteady.

CHAPTER FORTY-FIVE

Rest in the Grass

The night we left Shihenri, a huge gale came through. Several roofs were blown off the farm houses, and it rained so hard water flowed into my collar, ran in rivulets around my breasts and down my body. Finally, the storm was so bad the oxen couldn't go on any further.

Hopeless, I went to a nearby farm house with the children. The first house turned us away, saying they didn't have any room. At the second house, an elderly Korean woman came out wearing a white knit hat and looked at us in the light of her candle, from top to bottom. She went back inside and brought out a young man who could speak Japanese. He said, "Mother feels sorry for you but our house is too small…if you want, you can sleep in the animal shed. We just put new hay in there so it'll be warm. But the *Hoantai* will yell at us so be sure to leave early."

I said nothing but bowed my thanks over and over. The animal shed was full of fresh hay. First, I stripped Sakiko and lay her in the dried grass. I did the same with Masahiro and Masahiko and propped up their heads with the grass as they lay stark naked. I wrung out their wet clothes and hung them to dry over a little of the warmth left in the *ondoru* stove. I wondered, "Where are we?" I was so tired, I didn't know which way was east or west. No others were with us. But I was happy that we could sleep quietly here for one night. So I lay myself down next to the children and buried myself in the sweet hay. I blew out the candle and warmed myself a little in the thin straws of grass. But my body prickled with pain and I couldn't sleep. Perhaps the cows were annoyed by their house guests—their heavy bodies shifted restlessly around from time to time—and every time they moved, the vibrations went through the floor of the stall to my body.

The smell of the fresh hay together with the sound of my children's breathing engulfed me. I wrapped my arms around my chest. "How much longer are we going to have to struggle to get to the 38th Parallel?" I had no idea. I miserably thought, my body might collapse and we wouldn't make it. I tossed and turned in my sleep, and finally got up and opened the door the owners showed me for the toilet outside. During the night, the storm had passed and it was clear now. I faced outside, and suddenly—a brilliant falling star fell on the other side of the mountain.

Whenever I saw a falling star, I thought of my husband. "Was he still alive?" Hot tears stung the tear ducts of my eyes. I closed the door quickly and buried myself back in the dry grass. Since we left Heijo, I hadn't had any leeway to think of him. Tonight, my mind relaxed and fleeting images of him found their way in. But I forced myself away from such hopeless thoughts and instead calculated the expenses for our journey. "How much more would I need for the rest of the way? Have we even gone halfway?"

In the morning, from here and there, bedraggled Japanese refugees appeared. Before our cart left, I bought a couple of potatoes, and cooked them in my *hango*. We blew on them as we ate to cool them quickly. The ox cart started with a jolt. I felt guilty but leaned my body against the back of the cart, and tried to take a little weight off my bare feet.

In one of the hamlets we passed, I bought another melon which we devoured. At the next rest stop, I bought potatoes again and boiled them. My money lasted longer than I expected.

Suddenly, the ox cart came upon a big river and followed it. "This is going to be terrible when we cross this water," I thought as I followed. But when the cart went into the river, it wasn't as deep as I expected and the children didn't get wet although my legs were soaked.

I saw several big mountains ahead but instead of fear, I felt happiness because getting closer to those mountains meant we were closer to the 38th Parallel. But my joy was short-lived. Another storm roared in from the west and the rain started again, this time a downpour. All through the night of August 7th, a storm kept us company. We were soaked but slept in our wet clothes on the wooden floor of an elementary school. At the thought of having to walk on like this the next day, I wanted to quietly die.

On the morning of August 8th, when we got back on the road, I was shocked at how close the mountains were. The road was narrower, I realized. We went over ridges, one after another. When we crossed a fast-running river, I tied the boys to the cart and crouched over the back to keep them from being washed away.

In the hot summer sun, my clothes dried right away. After we crossed another river, the cart climbed a steep hill, so steep, the children almost rolled off the back. I desperately pushed the boys back in as I scampered behind the cart. "Hold onto the cart or you'll fall off," I screamed as I followed close behind.

We crossed several rivers and mountains. Finally we crossed three small streams in a row. Here we ran into a large group of Japanese resting. Our ox cart ride ended here and I paid four hundred yen to the driver under a tree. My spirits sank. "There would be no way to borrow any more money. I'll have to make the children walk and somehow reach the 38th Parallel."

I heard, "If we can get across the 38th Parallel, American soldiers will help us. If we can get there, we'll be saved." That refrain repeated itself over and over in my mind.

I sat the children down under a tree, to talk to them. They looked at me, expectantly as I said, "I don't have any more money to put you boys on an ox cart. No more ox cart. Masahiro, look over there." I pointed to the mountains. "Masahiko, see over there? Tomorrow we've got to get over that big mountain. If we don't cross that mountain, we can't get to Grandma's house.

Masahiro asked, "Mommy, is Grandma's house there?" The boys looked hopeful.

"No. No, Grandma's house is still far, far away. We have to cross ten, a hundred of those mountains. Tomorrow, you boys have to be strong. If you die on these mountains...see, look over there...see on that tree, that scary bird? That big black bird will come and eat you up. So you can't die yet. Do you understand, children?"

Then I lay them down in the grass, side by side. "All right, go to sleep now."

The moon hid behind that mountain. That night, there were no shadows in the black night. I couldn't help but feel that this

would be the last time, the last time the four of us would lie together to sleep, to peacefully rest in the grass with our ragged
little quilt. I told myself, "I must throw away this quilt tomorrow." I knew I had to save my strength for the journey ahead.
Such thoughts drifted through my mind as I went to sleep.

CHAPTER FORTY-SIX

The Agony of Crossing the River

It must have been the morning of August 9th. At a hamlet, the refugees gathered into small clusters — with no greetings or recognition — almost all of us were strangers to each other. This mass of humanity had no semblance of order or plan. No one led us. Like a headless monster, this horde of about five hundred people awoke, milled about, and began creeping up the road. In this chaos, only one person stood out — a white-haired man with a resolute expression on his face.

After about an hour, this white-haired man shouted orders, and three or four ox carts were prepared according to his directions. Almost all of my five hundred yen had gone to pay for the ox cart from Shinkei. The previous night, in the grass, I made a promise to myself, "I must follow this group no matter where it went. No matter what happened. We had to follow."

The white-haired man scanned the crowd around him — the hundreds of exhausted men, women and children looking at him.

He saw me with my children standing in the back of the group. He asked what so many others had already said to me in disbelief, "*Okusan,* are you bringing these three children by yourself?" Then he turned around and looked towards the ox carts. He came up to us, took Masahiko's hand and said, "Let's put this child on the ox cart."

I said, "But..."

He stopped me. "I know. We've already decided on the carts. People have paid their share and you don't have the money. But we'll put this child in." The white-haired man lifted Masahiko and put him on the crowded cart. Then he yelled, "Let's start!" and waved his stick up high.

You can't imagine how happy I was. I took Masahiro's hand. "All right, let's walk," I said to cheer myself up, as much as to encourage my son. I kept my eyes on Masahiko's little face bobbing in the ox-cart ahead. Beyond the cart, I saw large, grey boulders perched on the mountain.

My feet were swollen from the day before. I knew that the soles of my feet were torn and bleeding. Needles of pain shot through them during the night. Infection had spread inside my body, thanks to the muck that had percolated in through the lesions. My feet throbbed.

From the top of the next mountain, we looked down on distant gold colored rivers that flowed straight across our path below. "There's the first river!" someone said.

When we got over the top of this mountain, they took Masahiko off of the cart and we picked our way down the steep path — creeping along this way, it took half the day to get to that first river. The crowd collected at the river's bank and looked at the waters rushing by, daring us to go further. A few people ventured forth and jumped in the muddy water. I watched them closely and saw that the deepest part of the river came up to about my chest. In the middle of the river, these people violently bobbed up and down, as they stepped into deep, hidden cracks beneath the surface. They would suddenly disappear beneath the murky surface of the river, and then pop up, water streaming down their bodies.

With Sakiko strapped on my back, I went into the river, and told the boys to stay on shore. I managed to cross without slipping, by following in the footsteps of those before me. When I reached the other side, I quickly untied Sakiko, put her down on the ground and tied my red rope around my waist. Then I turned around and returned to the boys waiting for me. I picked up Masahiko and went into the river again. My tired arms couldn't hold him long as I waded in — his wet, slick body kept slipping into the water. But once the water was deeper, he felt so much lighter — he was lifted by the river. But the poor boy's arms tightened around my neck as his terror grew, and he shrieked, "Eee, eee!"

I pried Masahiko's desperate fingers loose from my neck, wrapped my arms from behind him, and yelled, "If you cry, I'm going to throw you in the river." We finally made it to the other side. I dragged Masahiko next to his little sister and let go. I turned around and saw my son on the other side, anxiously pacing up and down the bank. I thought, "I don't have the strength to bring Masahiro," and looked to the sky that I hated with all my heart, and took a deep breath.

I threw myself into the river again and heard Masahiro when he called me. "Mommy! Mommy!" He ran into me as I stumbled out of the river. I took off the rope I used to carry Sakiko. I knew my arms wouldn't hold him, and told him to jump on my back.

As he clung to me, I tied him onto my back and I stepped into the river again.

The water beat my legs without any mercy and my bare feet slipped across the stones, invisible beneath the yellow water. With Masahiro so heavy on my back, I could barely keep my balance in the fast current. One misstep and I knew my son and I would drown. This river had already swallowed up a number of people. At one point, I saw through a blade of the icy blue-brown water as it swept over me—I fought back, saying, "No. No. Not now."

Shaking the dirty water out of my eyes, I searched for my children on the bank. Masahiko stood at the water's edge, his little hands stretched out toward me. Sakiko saw me, too. She crawled on all fours to the edge of the river, oblivious to the danger between us. Finally, I got across and reached them. The acrid water I swallowed during those crossings sat heavy in my stomach for a long time.

My clothes dried quickly in the heat as we walked to catch up with the others. By the time we reached the next river, our clothes were dry. I can't remember how many rivers we crossed. Big rivers. Small rivers. Deep rivers. Shallow rivers. At first, I watched the others cross ahead of me, but then we fell further and further behind. So I stopped waiting and plunged in. My eyes strained to gauge the depth and speed of the current in front of me. Finally, I found a sturdy stick by the trail that bolstered our confidence as we maneuvered through the next rivers.

As the sun sank in the west, there were a number of times I was blinded by the sun's rays and lost my balance in the middle of the river. Across the last river, there was a tattered rope bridge, half-rotten and ready to wash away. I walked along the riverside for some distance, looking for another way across. Finally, I thought,

"If this bridge falls, at least we will have the good fortune of all four of us drowning together." We crossed that rotten, swaying bridge ready to die but fate did not choose us that day.

On the other side, I saw the others collapsed across a distant field. The ground lay bare and I saw no evidence of a hamlet nearby. The remains of one house foundation stood amongst a few scattered rocks. Masahiko followed me from behind crying, "My feet hurt, it hurts." When I reached the group, I collapsed — completely exhausted, with no energy left, even to breathe. I felt faint as my body went numb. Nobody was going to help me, if I lost consciousness here. I would be left to die.

When I opened my eyes, I saw a wild rose caught on the front of my blouse. Its thorns had slashed my skin below my breast, and blood shone red through the pale green fabric.

CHAPTER FORTY-SEVEN

A Dead Old Woman

I passed the night collapsed in the field, and woke on August 10th to find a thick morning fog wrapped around us. Both boys were curled up next to me, fast asleep. I didn't remember taking Sakiko off my back, but she was securely in my arms. A memory of that same frightening dream reverberated inside my head...what was that haunting melody?

I saw the dim outlines of refugees clustered here and there, asleep on the bare ground. When the children woke, we munched on *daizu*, and drank what was left in my water bottle. A couple of men moved among the exhausted people—these men had long hair, wore long, ragged pants, and their red skin shone against their black beards. They picked a few small wild strawberries off the ground, swallowed them whole, and nervously looked around as they approached me.

One of them spoke to me. "*Okusan*, who is the *dancho* of this group?" His eyes gleamed above his protruding cheekbones—an

awful, frightening, skeletal face. I didn't say anything and pointed to the white-haired man barely visible through the mist, and he
left me to talk with him.

Some people boiled potatoes with their *hango*, others gnawed
on *daizu* soybeans like us. By the time these scattered people joined
together, a voice called out for everyone to prepare to leave. As
I got ready, the white-haired man approached us, along with the
awful man I just saw, the one who looked like a highway robber.
"*Okusan*, this man will carry your child for you. Why don't you
hire him? Just give him some food as payment."

At first, I was afraid but when I looked at the man closely, I
realized he was still a young man—only twenty-two or so. Was
he one of the many deserters from the Japanese army? He had
already put Masahiko on his back and said, "Let's go." Feelings of
pity came over me—if I had the money, I would have hired him.
But I didn't know what was ahead and knew it would cost at least
thirty *sen* a day for his food. I said, "Thank you, but I'll manage
on my own somehow. I really don't have any money." I had used
up my last hundred yen bill in Masahiro's bag—it was clear, no
one had any money or food or compassion to spare. I turned him
away.

When I stood up, my feet hurt so much I almost fainted.
Gravel had ground into the raw wounds in the bottom of my feet
and now the soles had hardened into a mass of blood, dirt and
stones. "They must be infected," I thought. Fortunately, Masahiro
still had his shoes on. But Masahiko's feet were even worse than
mine—both of his feet were covered with dirt, sand and old blood
clots. How did he sleep so soundly with such feet?

But this was no place for pity. If I let myself think, I would
have hated myself and my desire to survive. How could I be such

a monster — to force this three-year old child to climb mountains with feet like that?"

The group started moving. As usual, we were the slowest and I was terrified we would be left behind. I kicked, pulled and hit Masahiko as he cried, "Mommy, it hurts, it hurts." I was insane — a mad woman who only thought of keeping up.

The road narrowed and soon we were trailing far behind the rest of the people. We were all alone on the trail. "Damn! Serves you right," I yelled at myself as we walked. Ahead of us was another woman driving her two children — they were also slower than the others. I recognized her — it was Mrs. Sakiyama and her boys, Ichiro and Jiro!. Over the past nine days since we left Shinkei, this was the first time I saw someone I knew.

"Oh, Mrs. Sakiyama!" I screamed.

She turned around and cried, "You, you too...!" and we grasped each other's arms with joy.

"We're almost at the 38th Parallel — let's hold hands...we'll get there together," she cried. Meeting Mrs. Sakiyama reawakened my hope, and I suddenly felt a surge of exhilaration.

She berated her son, Ichiro, with renewed energy, "Look. Look, Ichiro — see how Masahiko-chan is walking without whining!" She used rough men's language, too. Both of us walked with new vigor, as we yelled and screamed at the four boys.

From early that morning, flies swarmed around me, torturing us with every step. Perhaps the same flies that had followed me from Heijo. Sakiko had diarrhea non-stop and since I couldn't stop to take care of her — the filth had soaked into my back and streamed down the inside of my pants along my legs. The flies delighted in this stench, but with Mrs. Sakiyama by my side, I no longer cared about them, and cheered myself, saying, "If it rains in the evening—the rain will clean me off. If we cross a river—the river will wash my body. I don't care about the damn flies."

"Water. Water," the boys cried but we scolded them, "We have no more water, children. After we cross this mountain, there will be water. If you want water, you must cheer up and walk, children."

The road suddenly became steep but we drove ourselves harder. A little more, a little farther and we reached the top. From there we saw a flat road in the distance. "Mrs. Sakiyama, are we close to the 38th Parallel?"

"They said it's on the other side of this mountain." As we caught our breath, and walked on, we saw someone lying on the side of the road.

We got closer, and saw it was an old woman, laid on her back with her wrinkled hands pressed together in prayer. She was dead. Her head pointed east, toward Japan, so her spirit could find its way home.

"She must have just died," said Mrs. Sakiyama. Someone had placed a bunch of fresh Chinese blue bell flowers on her.

"They should have buried her. Didn't she have any family or anyone who cares?" I said.

"It doesn't matter whether anyone cares about her or not. It's all the same to a dead person. Nothing matters. Nothing matters now...what the hell," Mrs. Sakiyama said coldly, and passed her by.

Plenty of people died, yet I still despised those people who left a corpse like this. Heartless people who left this old woman out in the open. The flat road suddenly dropped off and before we knew it, we came to an open meadow.

"There's water!"

It was a rice paddy, something that I hadn't seen for a long time. We ran to the rice paddy, got down on our hands and knees, and drank the muddy water. From my back, Sakiko made noises, "Ahh, ahh" She wanted water, too. I took her off my back and cupped the cloudy water and put it to her lips. She drank with relish.

"Mrs. Fujiwara, is that the 38th Parallel right over there?"

"Maybe." I felt better knowing that might be true. "But first, we've got to eat something."

We sat down near the rice paddy, ate some *daizu*, then melted some miso paste with the paddy water in the lid of a *hango* and poured it down our throats.

CHAPTER FORTY-EIGHT

Through the 38th Parallel

We left the road by the rice paddy, and came out to a fine, paved street. Going from a gravel road to a paved one—my hips felt strange as my legs adjusted to a smooth surface after so many miles on a rough one. Nice houses dotted the road side. Korean city children, I guessed from their clothing, ran up and pointed their fingers at us. They cried, "The Japanese are running away. The Japanese are leaving!"

Both sides of the road were littered with things left behind by the refugees ahead of us. A *hango* here, a rucksack there, left on the ground as if they were just slipped off of someone's shoulders. What happened to the people ahead of us? As the skin on our backs tingled, we nervously wound our way through the debris, I recognized a rucksack. "Sato" was written across it in large letters. "It's Mrs. Sato's rucksack," I said, remembering her umbrella.

Mrs. Sakiyama looked around wide eyed. "It looks like we're at the 38th Parallel, after all," she said.

Ahead of us four elderly Japanese walked close together. They weren't really walking, it might be more accurate to say they wobbled and leaned against each other — to keep each other from falling.

When we caught up to them, one old woman said to us in a feeble voice, "Go ahead of us if you can…hurry, hurry — run away. Leave us old people behind and go…" They started chanting a familiar prayer, "*Namu ami dabutsu, namu ami dabutsu…*" Listening to their pitiable chanting, we gave them wide berth and went ahead.

That was the first time I passed anyone. When I realized there were people even weaker and slower than us, a strange energy sparked inside me. This road continued on straight ahead and we saw in the distance — something white. As we got closer, we saw it. What had been in our hearts and dreams for the past year — the sign post for…

We stopped and looked at each other, speechless. Finally, I whispered, "God, this is the 38th Parallel." Our hearts beat wildly and we couldn't say any more. Our eyes followed a white line further down the road. As we got closer, we saw that the white line was actually a white rail alongside a guardhouse, and a railroad-crossing type gate with a large arm lowered across the road. This must be the way across the 38th Parallel.

Several Soviet soldiers with guns came out of the guardhouse. We stopped. The soldiers spoke to each other in rapid Russian, and then one of them came out, pulled a chain, and lifted the gate before us. The soldier used his chin to tell us, "Go ahead."

Oh, I barely stopped my emotions from bursting then. A feeling I would never have again. We went through the gate and as we walked by, one soldier affectionately rubbed the head of each boy. I told myself, "Don't look back. Keep walking straight ahead." We dragged the children across. When we were far enough away so that they wouldn't see us anymore, I breathed a sigh of relief. The western sky was a brilliant red with the sunset. We stopped to admire the sky, then noticed a Japanese group resting in the distance, on the other side of the hill before us.

We panicked. "Oh, no. Have we taken the wrong road?" We jumped into the hillside covered with wild roses, and climbed to try to catch up.

Behind us, I heard heavy rustling sounds. The sound of guns bouncing against leather belts. When I looked back, I saw two Soviet soldiers behind us. In front of us also—two Soviet soldiers appeared. We were surrounded by soldiers.

The sight of their uniforms and guns terrified us. When I think about it now, it seems strange that we were so frightened by soldiers who had just patted the heads our children. Panic filled my head—I scrambled up the hill as fast as I could. By the time we got to the top of the hill, that group of Japanese had already left. The Soviet soldiers following us were also gone.

We dreaded being left behind again. In desperation, we ran to catch up and went down the mountain, and onto a road. By this time, the sun set and it was too dark to see anything. We yelled, "Japanese, where are you?"

In the distance we heard a faint voice, "We're over here." We ran along a narrow rice field road toward that voice. The children also sensed how important this was, and didn't cry as they ran with us. In the complete darkness, we came to a wall. It must have been the wall of a farm. Suddenly, two or three Koreans came out of the building and yelled something. A woman came out, carrying rice balls packed into a *pakachi*, the traditional Korean food container. She pulled out the rice balls and put them under our noses. She said something in Korean, "*Pan mogura!*"

I guessed she said, "Eat the rice." We shook our hands and told them we had no money to pay for it. Then they shook their heads vigorously. "No. That's not it. We want to give you the food for free." They repeated what sounded like, "*Pan mogura. Pan mogura!*" We finally understood them, and with tears streaming down our faces, we devoured the rice balls, each of which were as big as a baby's head. Over the next years, those words, '*pan mogura*,' brought back the warmest memories in my heart—out of all the memories I have of that terrible year.

When we left that hamlet, it was still dark and we headed toward a sound of a large river. There was no moon or stars, and the air smelled like rain was coming. We stood at the edge of the river and shouted again, into the darkness, "Japanese, where are you?"

But this time, our words disappeared into the silent, black hills and no reply comforted us. Where did they go? I didn't know what to do. Are we supposed to cross this river? My boys were on bent knees, about to collapse. I could not go one step further. "Mrs. Sakiyama, please go ahead," I said in a calm voice.

The ominous, black surface of the river gurgled by. Mrs. Sakiyama's silhouette stood before me for a moment, then suddenly she slapped me in the face. Gnashing her teeth as if she were going to bite me, she said, "You crazy bitch, you want to try dying in front of me? Get in the river. What kind of idiot dies with Kaijo camp right in front of us?" With tears streaming down her face, she took hold of my arm and pulled.

"If we go up the river, there must be a bridge somewhere,"

she said. Mrs. Sakiyama's confidence at that moment, felt to me like that of a god. We walked along the bank. I gritted my teeth, and called, "Masahiro. Masahiko," to make sure my boys followed me. Mrs. Sakiyama led us up the river bank—but in front of me, in the dark, a large stone suddenly appeared. I tried to avoid it but couldn't. I fell over and crumpled to the ground. Mrs. Sakiyama kicked my side, and the sharp pain revived me.

"Hello! Is there anyone there from the Korean *Hoantai*?" Mrs. Sakiyama's voice vibrated through my head.

A Korean man's voice came from a distance. "Hello!"

"Help!" I listened to her voice in a daze. 'I'm still alive. I'm still alive.' Three Koreans from the *Hoantai* found us. They saw our desperate condition, and picked up the younger boys, Masahiko and Jiro. Then somebody pulled my hand.

They said, "The bridge is right there. Cross the bridge, otherwise it's dangerous."

I said, "I need water…water," and they brought water to me. After a drink, I stood up shakily, and crossed the bridge as if I was in a dream. When we got out on the road and saw a hamlet, twinkling lamps greeted us. I'm finished. I collapsed right in the middle of the road and Mrs. Sakiyama fell beside me—the older boys, Masahiro and Ichiro, also fell.

I remember people milling around us, but I couldn't see their faces. After a while, a couple of the *Hoantai* people woke us up. I pulled away from them. "Please, let me sleep here." I begged with my hands in prayer.

"Japanese cannot stop here," one of them tried to explain but I said, "I can't move," and refused to get up. Then one of *Hoantai* men suddenly shouted, "Damn! Those bastard Japanese men run off, and leave these pathetic, miserable women behind.

It's always the same. They may think they're civilized but... damn..."

The Hoantai officer's gun rattled as he ran off into the distance. We slept a little on the cold asphalt like creatures dragged there out of the swamp. Then the Korean came back with four Japanese men. He yelled, "Here they are. You bastards think you can just leave them and run off?" He ordered the Japanese men, "Pick up the children and their bags."

Then I heard a loud, familiar voice. "There's no way, I'm going to pick up that brat." When I looked up...it couldn't be? He sounded like Kappa Man—Kappa Man? He was one of the four Japanese men. The Korean officer ordered each Japanese man to pick up a child. Kappa Man had the largest child, my son Masahiro. I saw that he was angry and I was afraid—he's going to hurt my son. This spark of anxiety forced me up. Even though my head throbbed and my legs buckled, I managed to say, "Thank you, Mr. Tokushima...but don't you dare leave my child in the mountains!" I couldn't let Kappa Man beat me.

The Korean *Hoantai* officer heard me and said to the Japanese men, "You bastards try that while I'm here." He helped me up to my feet. "The Kaijo Refugee Camp is at the bottom of this hill, lady. Come on, you can make it." Encouraged by the officer's words, we stumbled forward towards the hill, and followed the men with our children.

"Idiot! We're almost there...Yoshiko, what happened? Come on...Arghh!" said a man. No, it wasn't a man. It was a woman screaming like a man. It wasn't just us—there were other people who were half crazy with exhaustion I crawled up the hill on my hands and feet.

At the top of the hill, I heard a voice. "It's Kaijo! I can see the lights of Kaijo!"

"Don't die. Don't die after making it this far!" That voice came from above to below—then from below to above—like an echo bouncing inside my skull.

"Don't die!" I screamed at Mrs. Sakiyama.

"Don't die!" Mrs. Sakiyama yelled back at me.

In this way, we stood up at the top of the hill. The lights of Kaijo lay before us like an ocean. "It's Kaijo, it's Kaijo," we yelled as tears streamed down our faces. Then I fell down the hill, and rolled headfirst into that ocean of light. Pain shot up my leg when my foot caught on something and I collapsed on a hard surface. I lost consciousness as the lights streamed by.

CHAPTER FORTY-NINE

Rescued by Americans

Something rang in my head. It was a rhythmical tone – over and over against the inside of my skull. As my body tried to float to the surface – something held me down – I was pinned to the ground. From deep inside my brain, I heard ringing and gradually – Masahiro and Masahiko's voices called me from far, far away.

"Oh, the children! Where are my children?" I cried.

I opened my eyes quickly. I was on my side. Masahiro and Masahiko were next to me—they jostled and called me. Between the two boys, I saw a large man's shoes and khaki pants. As my eyes went up his legs—to his face—I saw he was a foreigner...no, not a Soviet. He stared at me lying on the ground.

"Oh...he's American! He must be an American soldier!"

I twisted my body and flipped over onto my stomach. Then I realized I was on a truck—a moving truck. We've been rescued by an American truck. Through my watery eyes, I looked up at the American soldier who stood there. He pointed to my boys crouched next to me, and then pointed to me.

He must have asked me, "Are these your kids?"

I got up on my knees, put both hands in front of me on the floor of the truck, and bowed my head over and over. "Thank you. Thank you," I cried.

The truck sped quickly along the road. So fast that the wind whistled. When I looked around me, refugee women and children like us, filled the back of this truck. Mrs. Sakiyama and her children were also safely on board. The truck passed many Japanese who walked along the paved road. Soon we reached the Kaijo Refugee Camp where dozens of white tents stood, lined up neatly like planted trees. The truck slowed down.

I kept saying, over and over, "Masahiro, Masahiko, we've been saved. We've been saved by the Americans," The boys may not have heard me as they looked — open-mouthed, in awe at the tents. There must have been a hundred of these huge tents.

We got off the truck and were led towards one of them. In each tent, about seventy people were housed. We went into our tent on the edge. The first thing I saw was a beautiful blanket laid out neatly on the cot.

I babbled like a crazy woman. "It's all right...it's all right. We've been saved. We're alive."

I couldn't think. My head was burning hot and soon I was engulfed by the sounds of that rain storm, and that deep, raspy voice of some demon, chasing after me. While the battle raged in my head, my body was strangely calm. I sank into the bed, relaxed and soft. As if this were the end of my life, I went into a deep sleep.

We reached the Kaijo refugee camp on August 11th, the year of our Emperor *Showa 21* (1946), before dawn.

CHAPTER FIFTY

Pebbles of Bitterness

A sliver of morning sunshine shone against the white tent canvas, and someone's form momentarily blocked it—my first glimpse inside Kaijo camp. I tried to get up, but as soon as my feet touched the ground, sharp pain shot up my legs, like nails driven into the bottoms of my feet. Nonetheless, I forced myself to hobble on these pitiful limbs—to get the DDT and vaccine shots we needed. (Back then, they used DDT treatment to kill the body lice many of us had.) The medical tent was wonderful—clean and white. With Masahiko in my arms, I limped slowly to the examination area where a doctor looked at my feet and said, "Hmm... this is terrible."

He asked, "How were you able to walk?"

He had me lie face down on the examining table so he could see the bottoms of my feet. First, he took out a pair of long tweezers and began picking out the stones in my feet. As the tweezers pulled out the stones and dropped them into a metal bowl, they made sounds, "Ping...ping...clink."

The tweezers went deeper into my flesh. The pain sharpened

as if I was being seared by the metal tongs I used to use to pick up hot coals. I clung to the bed with all my strength, and gritted my teeth to keep from crying out, but finally — I passed out from the pain.

When I woke up, I knew that the bottoms of my feet had been completely cleaned out. The metal bowl next to me was filled with a glistening pile of small stones, all coated with dark, thick blood. Bandages covered both my feet up to the ankles.

"These were really awful wounds," the doctor said, and wiped the sweat off of his forehead. "You must not walk on them for a while."

Then he turned to ask Masahiko to be brought over. Poor Masahiko sat there, round eyes filled with tears — he must have seen the whole procedure. Now that he realized that he would undergo the same torture, he screamed hysterically and clung to me. It took all my strength to hold him down while the doctor picked out the stones from his feet.

There was about a hundred meters between the medical tent and my tent. After the doctor pulled the stones out of our feet, I crawled on all fours across this distance every day. Masahiko followed me on all fours, too, crying. I was so humilated, to let people see me like that — a pathetic creature slithering along the ground — and I endured this shame not just to get to the medical tent, but every time I went to the toilet, to get water, to wash Sakiko's diapers. I groveled everywhere.

The shame vied with the joy I felt. After we had gnawed on dried *daizu* beans for so long, the Korean rice gruel they served us twice a day was wonderful, nutritious food. Here I finally stopped feeling afraid. I had clung to the belief for so long that if the Americans saved us, we would make it back safely home, to

Japan—that dream had come true. As I dragged myself in the dirt with Masahiko, I cheered myself up by saying, "By the time my feet heal, we'll be on our way home."

I was horrified at how many miserable women there were like me, reduced to squirming on all fours, like worms. There were dozens of such women in the tent, and I realized I shouldn't think of myself as the only wretched soul. As I crawled across the ground, I forced myself not to cry.

Masahiko, on the other hand, fought me tooth and nail because he didn't want to go see the doctor. That hundred meters to the medical tent seemed interminable—as I held onto squirming Masahiko and desperately scolded him, "Masahiko, stop crying. If you don't stop crying, we can't get to Grandma's." As we struggled and crawled along the ground, I noticed a man rushing towards us from the other direction.

I usually tried to avoid eye contact when I was in this humiliating condition, but when this man went by me, he suddenly stopped and said, "Damn—it's you again."

His words, "You again," bothered me. I looked up. "What the...?" That bald head—Kappa Man—here was that repulsive man in this repulsive place. I wasn't about to let him go this time without saying something.

"Mr. Tokushima," I said, sarcastically sweet. "Thanks so much the other day, for abandoning Masahiro in the mountains." I was ready to fight—that last night, Kappa Man had run off and left Masahiro in the woods, just as I expected. When Masahiro cried in terror, an old man had taken him by the hand out to road where the American truck picked him up.

When I asked Masahiro, "Who was the man who helped you?"

He said, "That old man with the white hair, you know, the one who let Masahiko-chan on the ox-cart. That old man. When the old man put me on the truck, Masahiko followed me. He cried, '*Oniichan!* Big brother!' and the Americans put him in the truck, too. Jiro-chan was on the truck so I knew it was all right. Then at the end, the truck found dead Mommy with Sakiko on the road."

It's true—I was dead at the time. Lying unconscious on the side of the road. When I heard Masahiro's story afterward, I fumed and planned to tear Kappa Man apart limb by limb if I ever saw him again. Here was my chance. I glared at Kappa Man. I would never forgive him.

"Hmm...that brat of yours was pretty heavy," he sneered. He laughed through his nose.

"What? Kappa Man, how can you think you're human?" I didn't care anymore what I said to his face. I crawled toward him. As soon as I got close, I planned to stand up and attack him.

He spat. "You dirty beggar woman. Who's going to carry the brat of a beggar woman?" Just as I got close, the *kappa* leapt back one step, just like the slimy, green turtle-man I named him after.

"Damn!" The blood rose up my head and I grabbed two handfuls of gravel. If I could grab him anywhere, I was going to bite him and tear him apart. I crawled closer but the *kappa* just leapt out the way again.

"A crippled beggar woman, taking a crippled brat out for a walk. Isn't that darn sweet?"

"Damn!" Furious and helpless, I flung the stones at him. But they bounced around him as he stood there laughing. The pebbles fell harmlessly and gently, like a soft spring rain.

CHAPTER FIFTY-ONE

The Lawyer who Pretended to be Mad

There was a family in my tent who claimed they came from my hometown, Nagano—a lawyer and his wife with two children. Maybe because of this connection, they asked me, "Where's your husband?"

When I told them my husband had been taken away to the *gulag*, a Soviet labor camp in Enkichi, the lawyer suddenly interrupted me with a nasty laugh. "Your husband was a fool," he declared.

He continued. "Ever since Manchuria, I've outsmarted the Soviets—pretended to be mad, insane. No matter what happens, I'm all right. You see, I can pretend to be crazy. Who's stupid enough to be taken away to Siberia? Not me!" He laughed with a self-satisfied air.

This man was horrible. I was so shocked, I didn't speak with him after that. But he kept talking to me, and called my husband a fool. "I'm a lawyer, you see, and lawyers wouldn't get themselves in such a bad situation like your husband did," he boasted.

The lawyer's wife was a piece of work, too. When the restrictions on refugees buying goods were lifted, that woman went out and bought everything she could lay her hands on. Of course, the Korean gruel ration was too good for them now. They had their white rice cooked for them somewhere and brought it back to the tent. They bought cans of food, sweets — there was no end to their purchases.

You see, they were trying to get rid of all their Korean money. On the third day after I met this lawyer and his family, they spread out their paper money on their beds. They made three thick stacks of Korean bills. Each stack was so thick the lawyer couldn't hold it in one hand. This tactless man counted his money in full view of seventy pairs of eyes. They were both crazy, just as he had described himself.

But I had to admit — he was no fool to have gotten this far with so much money. There must be some truth in his bragging. He said things like, "I worked for the Manchurian Railroad and the Manchurian Bank." They got into Korea with a huge amount of money. And then they managed to change it all into Korean money. How did they get through all these inspections, and the check-points at the 38th Parallel? There was no explanation. I was dumbfounded.

The old lady next to me whispered, "*Okusan*, what do you think he's going to do with all that money?"

It would be interesting to see what happened to them after this. But I was too busy trying to take care of my children. My boys gawked as the lawyer's family ate their fill of delicacies, and then throw away half-eaten morsels. This family tormented my boys with their gluttony. I tried to turn them away and pleaded with Masahiro and Masahiko, "Be patient a little bit longer. When we get to Grandma's house, I'll give you lots and lots of bowls filled with mountains of white rice."

But my boys still watched the lawyer and his family longingly. Finally, I gave up and snapped, "Don't stare at people eating!"

CHAPTER FIFTY-TWO

We Reach Giseifu

Every day, more refugees poured into the camp, like the waves of the ocean, lapping the shore. Every time I saw a new group of ragged, starving people, they reminded me of myself — it was awful. After about five days, I decided we had to leave. My feet hadn't healed yet — in fact, the entire bottoms of my feet were still infected and gory. Even the nurses turned their faces away in disgust when dressing my wounds. But I wanted to go home — even if it was just a matter of one day sooner — I wanted to be on my own country's soil.

There was a big reason for this desire — my baby. In camp, Sakiko's fever and diarrhea worsened. I knew how bad it had been to force this baby — who was not even a year old — to eat my chewed up *daizu* beans, and drink *miso* stirred with muddy water. But there was nothing else I could have done. And even after we reached Kaijo camp, my breasts didn't produce milk so I only fed her watered down rice gruel. I believed Sakiko's survival depended on how soon I could get home.

I found an ox-shoe made out of straw on the ground, and tied it on my right foot. On my left foot, I tied on a broken *zori* sandal that someone had thrown away. With Sakiko on my back, Masahiko on my hip, Masahiro beside me, and a bag in my left hand — we followed another group of refugees out of Kaijo camp.

The two kilometers to the Kaijo train station were difficult to walk but, at least, nothing chased me from behind. Shame, rather than fear, was what burned in my heart this time. I was so sad, letting people see me like this — a ragged, limping woman with three emaciated children. Humiliation and determination was what I felt as we got on the train.

Blood and pus oozed through the bandages on my feet, and stained the rough sandals dark red. After the train reached Keijyo, a larger town south of our former camp, we were met by a 'Japanese Rescue Group.' They gave us socks and some hard biscuits. But I found no one from my *dan* — Mrs. Sakiyama, Mrs. Daichi, and Mrs. Sato had all disappeared and I lost track of them.

Back on the train, the summer evening sun shot its last beams through the window on my left. Trying to cool off a little, I put my face outside, and suddenly realized, "The evening sun is on my left, we must be heading north. Where are we going?" I started to panic.

I asked the other passengers, "Where is this train going?" But the other passengers were calm and puzzled as to why I was suddenly so distraught.

"*Okusan. Okusan*, the train is going to Giseifu," a man nearby told me.

"Where is Giseifu?"

"It's a little north of Keijyo. It's on the way to Genzan."

Genzan was much farther north. "Why are we going there?" I'm sure I sounded upset.

"Why do you ask why? Didn't you get on the train to go to Giseifu?"

"No. I want to go to Fusan, where we can catch the ship to Japan."

"So it's all right then," he said. He must have thought, 'what a strange woman.' The people around me suddenly burst out laughing. Now I had no idea what was going on.

"*Okusan*, wasn't the refugee camp at Kaijo full? That's why we've been moved to the refugee camp in Giseifu. We're going to wait there until we hear about the ships leaving Fusan for Japan."

Something must be wrong with me. I should have known. I was no longer a *fuku dan-cho*, representing my group so I hadn't paid attention to where the next stop was. But if I wasn't alert, something terrible might still happen to us. Back when we reached the Kaijo refugee camp, the tension in my nerves must have gone slack—and I stopped thinking. I reminded myself, "We still have a long ways to get home."

A full moon shone on the mountain of Giseifu. There was about three kilometers from the train station to the Giseifu refugee camp. Aided by the light of the moon, we took our time to get to the tents. Now nothing frightened me and I walked happily down the moonlit road. I smiled at myself. "How funny I must look with the cow-shoe on one foot and the broken sandal on the other!" I carried Masahiko on my hip, limped one step, then another. As long as I'm calm, the children won't cry.

Every time an American jeep went by, I called out cheerfully to them.

CHAPTER FIFTY-THREE

A Can of Corned Beef

The Giseifu refugee camp had about fifty tents. The medical tent in this camp was even better prepared than the one at Kaijo. The food was wonderful. They brought in loads and loads of hot Korean rice and for the first time since the end of the war, we ate our fill. There was so much white rice that some was thrown away! At the Kaijo camp, we only ate Korean *kayu* soup, diluted with hot water. I realized that the simple food at Kaijo taught our bodies how to eat again. Suddenly eating rich food in Kaijo would have been like putting a person suffering from hypothermia into hot water — dangerous and deadly.

At Giseifu, the rations were opulent. They delivered *miso* soup with *wakame* sea vegetables. But on top of that, they gave each of us a can of corned beef along with vegetable salad, a pound all together each day. I opened the glittering can of corned beef, and ate it, trembling with delight. Masahiro and Masahiko also ate it ravenously. For Sakiko, I chewed some of the meat for her, and she ate the softened food quickly. This was a terrible mistake — even as we looked at the empty can, my stomach began cramping. Before I could even make it to the toilet, I threw up—Masahiro and Masahiko also threw up. Our stomachs didn't have the strength to digest this sudden glut of rich food. Many of the other refugees also weren't able to keep this food down. We were the poor people, the ones who suffered malnutrition—beggars, as Kappa Man called us. People who were dressed decently, those who had shoes, didn't throw up.

I exchanged our cans of corned beef for the vegetable salad. But we still ate well. The children stopped whining about food. They took naps and were satisfied. But even then, I made a mistake that was almost fatal. I felt sorry for the children so I let them eat as much as they wanted, even though the diarrhea started again. Our stomachs were at battle with our bodies.

The camp doctor warned me, "If you let them eat, they will throw up. If they don't throw up, they will have diarrhea. It might sound strange but you've got to take care of your bodies by eating less." But I ignored him and let the children eat. I just went to the doctor to get more medicine for the diarrhea. Finally, the doctor said, "Young woman, do you know what *Kwashiorkor* is?"

He said, "*Kwashiorkor* means even if the child eats and eats, his body cannot take in nutrition. In fact, the stomach grows weaker. When there is diarrhea along with *Kwashiorkor*, your children are in the second stage of starvation. Such children may seem healthy and eat dinner one evening—then be dead the next day. Just like that. " He woke me up.

After that, I forced myself and the children to eat less. Now the children were unhappy again. They knew there was food but I wouldn't let them have it. They begged and cried, especially Masahiko.

The mornings began with Masahiko complaining about food,

but one morning, the children cried, "Mommy, my eyes! I can't open my eyes!" Our eyes were covered with some sort of discharge, a hard, crusty pus that sealed the eye lids. The doctors put stinging eye drops in our eyes. Then they applied a purple medicine on the ulcers and scabs that covered the children's bodies—more DDT for the lice, and vaccine shots over the next several days.

This time, there was no mistake. The trains were heading south. I decided it was time for us to leave again. In the morning, as I sat in the train facing forward, the sun shone in from the left—the train went south.

CHAPTER FIFTY-FOUR

Social Decency on the Train

It felt like whenever we got on a train, it rained. Our train moved very slowly as it poured outside. The windows were closed, but rain still leaked inside here and there. With the summer heat, rain, stale air, and crowding—we Japanese were forced into this hellhole, a purgatory where any civilities and manners were just faint memories. Hatred and selfishness filled our souls. Any humanity we had left was pressed to the bottom of our beings. Like maggots crawling over a dead body, we squirmed in our seats.

Masahiro and Masahiko had severe diarrhea when we left the Giseifu camp. The train ran on and on—who knew how long it would be before the next stop? Of course, the boys soiled their pants, and the air around us stank with their flatulence. The stench collected in the train car and never dissipated. "It stinks! It stinks!" people yelled.

I shrank and mumbled, "I'm sorry. I'm sorry."

As the complaints got louder and more incessant, I could no longer bear to take on all of criticism alone, and turned on my son. In a loud voice, I scolded him, "Masahiro, you're six years old!

You should know better!"

A little ways down the car, there was a family — a couple with three older daughters. This father was especially horrible. He bellowed, "Can't you do something about it? You're bothering everyone with your stink. Hurry up and do something!"

"I'm sorry. As soon as we get to a train station, I'll clean them up," I said.

He yelled back, "Who knows when we'll get to the next train station. Do something! Do something now! Think about all the other people here."

I meekly replied, "Yes, but this child only has the pair of pants he has on. If I throw it away, he'll have nothing to wear. Please be patient. I'll wash him when we get to the next station."

He only yelled louder, "Can't you get it through your thick skull, woman? I don't want to hear any excuses. You're the type who doesn't care about common social decency, aren't you?

"What?" I said.

He continued, "How can you call yourself a mother when you let your child shit in front of other people?" As he said this, the man turned to his wife and daughters, and pointed at me with his chin. "Isn't that so?"

Then the whole family looked at me with utter contempt and smirked, "Look at that pathetic woman."

The three daughters all had their backs to me, and they raised their large rear ends as if to avoid being contaminated, and turned to glare at me. When I saw the arrogant look in those girls' eyes, something snapped in my soul.

I yelled, "You are the ones who have no social decency! We haven't always been this pathetic. You see us now in this horrible condition and you bully us in front of everyone. Is that your idea of social decency? Of course, I would love to throw away my son's filthy pants, and put on a clean pair. I...I feel so awful that I want to die. Everyone—look—see how ashamed my son feels. Tell me what I should do."

That man became silent. Then he turned, and said to his older daughter, "Fumiko, give them something to wear."

She opened her large rucksack and began digging through the contents.

I said, "Stop that. I don't want anything from you. I'm not going to accept your charity now—even if I die. I am not a beggar. If you really have any social decency, you would shut up, and breathe in the stink!" I said this with tears burning in my eyes, then turned to Masahiro who looked at me with a frightened expression.

He was old enough to remember this shame but I tried to comfort him. "Masahiro-chan, it's all right, it's all right. When the train stops, I'll wash you clean." Saying that, I broke down and cried.

The train car became quiet and the other passengers looked at me with a mixture of puzzlement, pity and indifference. The sorrow of having children. As a mother, I was miserable, but the children—the children—were so much more wretched than I was.

CHAPTER FIFTY-FIVE

Hundred Yen Magic Trick

When the train finally stopped at a station, I got busy. I washed the only diaper I had, wrung it out and put it back wet on my poor baby. When we left Giseifu, I bought some food for us with the last twenty yen I had. Of course, I couldn't buy bread or rice balls that cost five yen apiece. All I could afford for the rest of the trip was apples. They cost ten yen for six—I bought twelve apples with my last twenty yen. After the train ran the whole day, it stopped in the middle of a rice field. We were there for a day and a half. Vendors from nearby farms started gathering as soon as they saw our train.

Rice dishes, bread, *daifuku* steamed rice dumplings, there was everything. The passengers fought each other to buy the food from the vendors. Again, I tortured my hungry children here with a terrible experience. An awful ordeal—one that has probably been seared into their souls. I forced my starving children to watch others eat.

The man I fought with sent his grown daughters out to get

food, one after the other. They bought bread, holding the rolls in both hands, and rice piled high in their *hango* containers. But he wasn't satisfied. "Isn't there some *sake* somewhere? No? Go find some…if you tell the vendors, they'll bring some to sell." The man sat there like a mountain, and ordered his daughters around.

After a day and a half, the train started again. Finally, we headed towards Fusan. When the train doors closed, I felt a wave of relief. I closed my eyes to try to get a little sleep, but those girls in front started making noises and woke me up.

"It's not there…it's here," they shrieked with laughter. They were pulling out the seams on the patches sewn on their father's shirt. Earlier, I noticed his shirt wasn't even worn that much, but patches were sewn all over it. The daughters picked off the stitches on these patches. When they pulled out the thread, a folded hundred yen bill fell out. That's what amused them.

This was more interesting than watching magic tricks. They did the same with their mother's collar—a hundred yen bill popped out. Five more bills came out of their father's hat. It looked like they had finished their magic tricks but there was one task left. The woman who appeared to be their mother spoke. "You girls, take the money out from that spot."

"But…," the daughter looked bashful.

"It's all right. It's all right to take everything out now."

"But, mother…"

"It's all right."

What an odd conversation. The oldest daughter looked around to see if anyone was watching. She put her hand down the front of her pants and rustled about. Then something ripped from deep inside her pants. She pulled it out and started picking at a piece of folded money as if she were picking at bugs.

I see. They must have sewn money inside the crotch of the pants. I was impressed. These three girls quickly performed their magic tricks until the mother said, "Is that all?"

The train started speeding up. My only thought was, we've got to get something to eat in Fusan soon. Over the past four days on this train, my little family of four survived on the food I brought—twelve apples.

That day, there was no more food—we only had water to drink from the morning. The hunger pangs we suffered on that train were worse than those we felt since Sensen, and when we crossed the 38th Parallel.

CHAPTER FIFTY-SIX

At Fusan

The train's brakes screeched in protest at the last stop. We reached Fusan on the evening of August 26th. From the train station platform, I was excited by the glitter of the dark ocean right before us — but there was no time to linger. Everyone was herded into a large warehouse with reed mats laid on the floor, our sleeping places. Dinner was served — big, white rounds of *daikon* root floated in rice gruel. I don't remember what it tasted like — we were so hungry, we ate like starving dogs, then collapsed to spend one night in the warehouse.

The next morning, a clear hot summer day greeted us, and we were shocked to see the azure ocean before us. It had been years since I last saw the sea. Two big cargo ships floated in the harbor; the white uniforms of their crew shone crisply in the sunshine.

I took the children out onto the walkway and put the diapers to dry on the concrete wall. Then in the warm sun, I stripped the children naked one by one. Their dirty pale skin stretched over thin, bony limbs and distended stomachs. We couldn't bathe so I used a rag to clean them. I rubbed their thin bodies, and flakes of dirty skin flew down into the ocean below. As I watched these bits float away, I prayed our suffering would also fly away, never to return.

After noon, a walkway was lowered from one of the ships. Thin, yellow smoke poured out of its smoke stacks. When the shadows of people moving about on board multiplied, I felt my heart quicken.

I said to the children, "Masahiro, Masahiko-chan, we're going to get on that big boat and go back to Japan! Look—look. We're going to cross that big ocean." The boys were wide-eyed with excitement as they looked at a sight they had never seen before.

I held up my baby and faced her toward the ship. "Sakiko-chan, look! We're going to get on that boat!" I pointed to the ship but her half-open eyes remained glassy, motionless—and her body was limp.

We received DDT treatments again. Finally, we boarded a very large cargo ship. The long line in front of us shrank back little by little and a plank-way was lifted up, which led up to the ship's deck. The ship's crew helped me with the children by grabbing their arms and lifting them onto the deck. Once we were aboard, they led us to a large open hatch-door on the floor. I looked down to see a big opening beneath my feet, and we climbed down a ladder one by one. A beautiful two story platform had been built inside the belly of the cargo ship to house hundreds of refugees.

We were assigned on the top level. When I realized—we don't have to walk anymore—we don't have to go someplace—my energy suddenly drained from me. The loudspeaker announced,

"All aboard," to signal our departure, and everyone gathered back on deck. A long mournful wail blasted from the ship's horn as our ship slowly moved away from the dock.

Some people cried. Some people waved. Some howled. Everyone expressed their emotions at that moment in his or her own way. There were screams of jubilation with the excitement of knowing — we survived! We're alive! But I had no tears left to cry. Quietly, I took off the straw cow-shoe on my right foot and the broken sandal on my left foot. With all my strength, I flung them into the ocean. What a wonderful feeling. The summer heat penetrated the dirty bandages around my feet as I walked across the deck.

A last look at those mountains — mountains I hoped to never see again in my life. We went to the hatch-door and climbed down the ladder to our assigned spot in the ship's hold. The rumble of the ship's engines comforted us as we lay down to sleep.

CHAPTER FIFTY-SEVEN

Fat Fujiwara and Thin Fujiwara

I'm suffocating in a dark ocean, strings stuffed in my brain unraveling into reality. Wait. The water is rocking around me. My chest feels heavy. I can't breathe. I want to get to the surface.

As I struggled to get up, gradually I woke. I took a deep breath. Morning is here, I thought as I came out of my first sound sleep in weeks. The ship was still and silent. Had we arrived in Japan? It must be Hakata Harbor. I had to see and climbed up to the deck. It was early morning when I first saw the harbor—quiet yet full of ships like ours, anchored in place. The green pine trees and the lush, black mountains were proof that we arrived in Japan.

At first, I didn't see evidence of a country defeated by war. But when I looked around, there they were—several black carcasses of ships on their side in the water. Ugly, gutted and dead. The smoke stacks of the city also stood silent, and emitted not a single breath of smoke. Hakata Harbor was a quiet as a country lake.

A small boat gently approached with the red and white Japanese Red Cross flag fluttering from its stern. From the center of ever widening ripples across the still waters, the reassuring putter of the boat's engine rolled forth. Soon, I looked down from the deck to see the small boat pulled up alongside our huge ship. Several white-uniformed women climbed up on board. It had been years since many of us had seen such bright red lipstick and permed hair. The women caused whirlwinds of excitement among the refugees as they went into a tent set up on deck. Traces of perfume lingered behind them, and we eagerly tasted the air. That fragrance — was that evidence of the new Japanese woman? And it reminded me that I was a woman, too.

The first welcome ceremony to greet us home was a rectal exam. A long line formed for that demeaning experience. The line continued into the ship's hold. One by one, each person went into the tent, pulled down their pants, and got down on all fours to be examined — like a sick animal.

As I stood in the women's line, I heard a man talking in a loud voice in the men's line on our left. He said "Enkichi" a number of times. That's the name of the Soviet labor camp where my husband was sent — the husband I had tried to bury deep in my heart. I listened in and gathered that this man returned from Enkichi. When I saw him talking, I guessed from his dirty uniform and dark weathered face that he was a soldier, a deserter.

When the rectal exams were finished, the nurses left on the Red Cross boat — it bounced along easily on the quiet surface, as it sped away leaving a small wake. The ship's deck returned to its former state of chaos — chattering, and sounds of washing.

For the next few days, I walked around our large ship, searching for that man with the dark face. On the fourth day I found him sitting on a big coil of rope.

I asked, "Excuse me, may I speak to you? Did you return from Enkichi?"

He looked suspiciously at me. "What d'you want?" He got off the coil. He was a tall man and I shrank even smaller as he towered over me.

"My husband was taken to Enkichi. I thought maybe, you might know him."

"Is that so?" His face suddenly softened. As I had thought, this man was a soldier and was a prisoner-of-war at Enkichi. When he told his captors he knew something about cars, he was sent to work in the vehicle maintenance shop for Chinese Communists' Eight Route Army. Somehow, he managed to get out of the prison and found himself all alone. Then he crossed the Tomanko River, joined the *hikiage* refugees there, and crossed the 38th Parallel.

He said, "Yes, there were a lot of Japanese prisoners with the Chinese Eighth Route Army. When was your husband in their hospital?"

"Around February. He was definitely in there until February," I said.

"February? I got to the Eighth Route Army around May. What was his name? Your husband."

"Fujiwara."

"What? Fujiwara? I know him. I know him well. Is that guy your husband?" His voice grew louder.

"Did you know him? and...and what was he doing? Was he well? What was he saying?" I was thrilled.

"Hey, you can't ask me all those questions at once," he laughed at my sudden excitement. "Mr. Fujiwara was well known among us Japanese prisoners. He got special treatment. He worked for their Wireless Electricity Office. He had a white band around his arm and often hung around headquarters. At mealtimes, he got to eat with the officers of the Eighth Route Army. While we were dirty and greasy, he always dressed well. But he was quite a fat fellow. So fat that when he walked, he would huff and puff."

"Wait a minute, my Fujiwara is thin," I said as I remembered how my husband looked when I said good-bye to him on the train in Sensen.

"Thin? No way. He was as fat as a sumo wrestler. His must've been paid pretty good. Among us Japanese, he was the only guy who was fat."

I could understand that my husband might have worked at the Wireless Electricity Office. He knew a lot about electricity and machines. I hoped that he might survive by using his knowledge. But how could he be fat? Maybe that wasn't my husband. I tried to find some way to connect my husband to this fat Fujiwara. "Did you talk with him?" I asked.

"No. They kept us busy, and if they caught us talking, they beat us — we lived in different dorms and ate at different places. Once in a while I ran into him at the john, and just have time to say, 'Pretty hot, isn't it?' "

My hope waned — maybe it wasn't my husband. I turned to Masahiro and Masahiko who had been craning their necks, listening to our conversation. I asked, "Of these two boys, did he look like one of them?" I looked at that man's face with hope, and pushed the boys in front.

"Let's see...he might've kind of looked like him," he said uncertainly as he put his hand on Masahiko's head. Although he wasn't confident, my hope revived again.

After that, every time I ran into the dark-faced man on deck, I tested him with more questions like, "Did he walk with a limp...

did he have a habit of cupping his chin when he thought?" But this dark-faced man's answers were wishy-washy. I also asked him whether he knew of malnourished men who got fat. He shook his head. "Usually, they died — so I don't know."

But I didn't give up. I looked for signs of hope everywhere. Every day, I saw the ship's doctor who treated my feet. I asked him. "Doctor, can a man who was starving thin become fat?"

The doctor put down his tweezers and thought. "I suppose he could get fat. As long as he gets good food. It doesn't matter if he was malnourished. If a man recovers and eats a lot, he'll get fat." The doctor looked at my face with curiosity. I became hopeful and told him about the dark-faced man and his story about my husband with the Eighth Route Army.

The doctor said, "It does indeed sound like that man is your husband. The fact that he had special treatment, and did important work would be big reasons for your husband to be alive. Which boy does your husband look like?"

"Everyone says he looks like Masahiko. This child. They say he looks like him." I rubbed Masahiko's head as he sat on the table with his legs swinging.

The doctor continued, "And the dark-faced man said right away that he thought this Fujiwara looked like your son? Hmm. That Fujiwara must be your husband." The doctor turned his swivel chair half-way around to ask a white-coated assistant. "Hey, you...do you like mysteries? How would you solve this problem?"

The young man replied dryly, "There's no definite proof. I think you're talking about two different people. The reasons I think so are..."

Suddenly, a harsh, high-pitched female voice called out from the back, "Excuse me, doctor. When are you going to see me?" I was so wrapped up in this problem, I forgot all about the next patient waiting.

"Ha ha. Shall we solve this mystery tomorrow?" The doctor laughed in a friendly manner.

I left the laughing doctor, with Masahiko's hand in mine and headed back to my spot in the ship's hold where my oldest was waiting. I knew Masahiro got tired when I left him in charge. Often I'd find him asleep when I got back.

As I climbed back down the ladder, my head was full of images of my husband as a fat man and as a thin man. I couldn't help but try another fortune-telling game with myself. I decided — if I find Masahiro asleep that would mean that the fat Fujiwara was really my husband. But if Masahiro was awake, that man was not my husband.

As I climbed down the ladder, I peeked through the steps and saw Masahiro. He was wide awake, staring at someone eating something.

CHAPTER FIFTY-EIGHT

Woman with Children

A large number '3' marked this part of the ship's hold — where the four of us slept on a thin reed mat laid on the metal platform. This huge hold was divided into three levels — we were on the top, and when I looked up — I saw a single, dim electric bulb that hung from the middle of the ceiling, day and night. That light bulb was the only sympathetic soul I felt in that metal box.

Immediately on our right side, an unfriendly childless couple glowered at us. On our left side, a single woman, about twenty-two or twenty-three years old, kept to herself and ignored us. Frightening sounds filled that space every night — anonymous male voices cursed and swore, women moaned and complained. And then there were the pitiful mothers with children, women like me.

My fear of the dark started that year. The fear I felt in northern Korea compared to the fear I felt on this ship were from different origins, but when nightfall came I invariably felt uneasy and a cold dread spread through my body. When everyone started coming down the ladder to get ready to go to sleep, my nerves started to tighten.

In the dark—jeering, mocking voices terrified me—faceless men yelled, "Shut up! Stop letting the kid cry!" Poor Masahiko and Sakiko suffered from bleeding skin ulcers. Most of the children who crossed the 38th Parallel were plagued with these sores—symptoms of malnutrition, I was told. Their entire bodies were covered with them, and when they dried, big scabs formed. At night, when the children quieted down, their mottled skin seemed to get unbearably itchy. Each time the children moved in their sleep, or tried to relieve the itchiness—crusty scabs tore off, thick pus oozed out, sticking their skin to the mat. Then when their skin tore away from the mat, the children cried in pain.

I tried to hold Sakiko and Masahiko so that if they cried, I muffled their cries against my chest. When they finally fell asleep, another scab would get torn, and they cried even harder. An invisible thug would then yell, "Be quiet! Why are you letting your kids cry? Get a needle and sew that mouth shut!" They said such terrible things all through the night. By morning, I was convinced someone would hurt us.

There were other woes—twice a day they gave us rations of rice gruel, but children under five only got a half-portion. Our family of four only got three small portions. Our total ration just filled my *hango* container. Knowing every meal was short one ration tormented me—such injustices consumed me as we waited on that ship.

In the mornings, as the boys licked the empty *hango* after our first meal of the day, my head still throbbed from all the angry voices the night before. My frustration and anger grew with each day we were on that ship. Up until then, at the refugee camps, I hadn't faced the rule of half-rations for children under five. At the Kaijo Refugee Camp, Giseifu Camp, and in the refugee center at Fusan, each person, no matter the age, received one ration. But on this *hikiage* ship, a child under five got only a half-ration. Who decided that rule? Did the other refugees decide that? Was it the ship captain? At every meal time, I obsessed over these questions.

One morning after our first meal was done, as people came and went up the ladder through the hatch onto the deck where they washed their *hango* containers—I noticed the *hancho* came down with a load of books and magazines donated by the *Hikiage* Returnee Aid Office. The *hancho* was a sunburnt man, designated to distribute such items to our group. He handed the reading materials out one by one, and said, "Please return these without getting them dirty," and stepped between the people sitting and sleeping everywhere.

"Excuse me, may I have one book?" I asked.

He looked at me and my children. "No. I can't lend them out to women like you, with small children. You'll get the books dirty—so you can't have one," he said as he turned away.

The unfriendly neighbor next to me raised his hand, "Sir, may I please have one?" The *hancho* promptly handed him a book.

I couldn't stand this injustice. I asked again, "Please, I'll be careful with the children. Let me have one book. Please. I want to read a book very, very badly."

The *hancho* looked at me with disdain. "*Okusan*. Everyone wants to read a book. If you have time to read a book, you should use that time to keep your children from crying. Do you know how much trouble you've caused everyone here in this section? People can't sleep at night, and besides that, you stink."

"We stink?" I said and felt my face burn.

"Yes, your kids stink! They've had diarrhea the whole time. You've got to think about how you're bothering everyone— right?" The *hancho* then looked at the unfriendly man next to me —my neighbor and his wife nodded in agreement.

I was not going to give up. Keeping my temper in check, I said, "I'm sorry. You're right. Maybe I'm not doing enough about the stink, but can you please lend me a book? Did the ship captain make this rule?"

But my question further annoyed the *hancho*. "Of course, he made this rule. Before you get all high and mighty with me, you should take a look at yourself and think about what a nuisance you are."

I held back my tears as I watched the *hancho* walk away. Everyone hated me for having children during the entire past year. Now I was horrified to realize that until I got safely home with my parents, my children and I would continue to face this never-ending grudge from my fellow countrymen. All right. One more try. I turned and asked my neighbor in a small voice, "Sir, after you finish, would you lend that book to me?"

"After my wife...," he started to say, but then said, "No. No, people with children aren't supposed to have one..." He frowned and pulled the book back close into his chest.

I had had it, and said, "Are you saying you won't lend it to me? All right." I left Sakiko on the mat with her brothers and stood up unsteadily. I went up the ladder and went to the ship captain's office, located deep in the middle of the ship.

I shouted up to the captain in his office, "Why can't people with children borrow books?" The ship captain was startled when I suddenly spoke. He turned his face and looked at me. His glasses gave him a scholarly look.

"What are you talking about?"

When I explained how poorly I had been treated, he looked at my body up and down, and said, "Is that so? I'll look into the matter," and quickly turned his attention back to something else.

That's it? That's all he's going to say? Looking at that ship captain's face, I knew he wasn't sincere. I couldn't accept that—I just couldn't back down. As I stood there unsteadily, finally I ended up saying things I know I shouldn't have. I blurted out, "I bet you only care about yourself. You only care about women and children who are related to you. I wonder what you are really going to do about our problem."

He slowly turned back to me and his eyes narrowed inside his glasses, "What do you mean, what am I going to do about your problem? I just told you. I'll look into it—the food portions that are given to children."

I said, "What do you mean exactly by 'look into' the problem?"

"'Look into' means 'look into'," he said.

"I don't understand what you're saying. Tell me in concrete terms, what you're going to do," I persisted.

Exasperated, he said, "Oh, shut up!"

The captain finally lost his temper. As I walked away, he said in a loud voice, "That woman's crazy. Look at her. She's filthy and her shirt's ragged."

I've never been so humiliated as a woman. For me, being called dirty was worse than a slap in the face. In my entire life, I've never experienced such inhumanity as that of the captain who mocked me. Did he know this was the only blouse I had? I was so mortified, I couldn't cry. I still tremble now as I remember his voice. I didn't accomplish anything—during those twenty days on that ship—there was no change in the rations for the children and I never got even a magazine.

* * *

One humid evening in the ship's hold, I overheard this conversation.

"Are you going up there again tonight?" The single woman lying next to me whispered in a conversation with another woman a couple of bodies over.

"Yeah. I'm thinking of going."

"Is it fun?"

"Sure, it's fun. I'll bet you don't even know what a crew cabin is like. There's white sheets on the bed…and a nice blanket laid on top…and you can even cook a proper meal in there," boasted her friend.

The woman who was talking with my neighbor looked young, her voice was childish — high-pitched and sharp — but her words were anything but. She was also on her own, I guessed.

My neighbor asked, "How do you cook rice in the crew cabin?"

The child-woman said, "There's something called an 'electric hot plate'. You put the metal *hango* with rice and water on top of the hot plate, and before you know it, white bubbles appear and beautiful rice is ready in a snap. And there's canned food. Canned salmon is delicious, you know—there's no color like it—juicy red meat—the color of lipstick, packed in tight."

"Did you get to eat some?" My neighbor asked as she swallowed her saliva with a gulp.

"Of course. I put it on rice and poured soy sauce on it. And I mixed it like this…" It was unbearable listening to her fantastic story.

"Can you take me with you next time?" my neighbor begged.

"Well, maybe…but I promised him I'd come by myself. And the crew cabin is small. We can't have a crowd in there. This time I'm going to learn a song that's popular in Japan now. He said he'd teach me. And I've forgotten something there…"

"Forgot something?"

"Yeah. I left my slip in there the other night," the child-woman said.

"What?" my neighbor gasped.

Not surprisingly, my neighbor was shocked. But the child-woman didn't seem to care. If people were listening in, her attitude was like, 'so what?'

"Take me sometime with you, all right?" my poor neighbor pleaded.

"Yeah, sure. Sometime."

"For sure. All right?"

That child-woman nonchalantly ended the conversation as my neighbor and I watched her leave and go up the ladder. When the child-woman disappeared, I saw through the hatch that it was dark outside.

The summer heat clung to the humid night air. I took off my one blouse and carefully laid it aside. A jagged tear across the back of that blouse gaped accusingly at me. I lay down and covered my bare sweaty breasts with a dingy spare diaper. I closed my eyes to go to sleep. I thought, "I can't let that hole to get any bigger." Soon, we'll land in Japan. I heard there was unbelievable chaos on the trains at home. And I only have this one tattered blouse to wear for the many hours it would take for the train to reach my home in Nagano. That blouse was my one precious shield so every night, I took it off. Tears filled my eyes as I felt shame engulf me—I felt like trash. My dirty bare back stuck to the rough reed mat beneath us.

Every hour or two, I woke up to take Masahiko and Sakiko to the toilet up on the deck. Both of them had diarrhea. I only had four diapers so I couldn't change Sakiko often. This was my never-ending battle to lessen the stink people had to inhale. Masahiko woke me with a tiny voice. I felt badly for forcing such a young boy to be so cautious. I scolded him so harshly each time he cried, that now he stifled his voice and looked at me with guilty eyes. I woke up immediately, put the sleeping Sakiko still naked on my back, and carried Masahiko with one arm because his feet were still too tender to walk on. I used to leave Sakiko with Masahiro when I took Masahiko to the toilet, but ever since the neighbors complained when Sakiko cried, I took her with us. At least four or five times a night, I took both children to the toilet like this.

Little Masahiko walked barefoot across the 38th Parallel for me—and now he paid the price. The bottoms of his feet were badly infected and he still couldn't walk on them. But my feet weren't much better. When I climbed the ladder too quickly, needles of pain shot up from my feet right into my brain. Many times, I had to stop as I climbed the ladder. I clung to the railing, crouched in agony until I caught my breath—finally, I'd make it up to the deck and go to the toilet. Because it was night, the toilet attendant wasn't there. But neither was the bully who said, "Women with children should have more cleaning duties because their kids make a mess."

It was past midnight. When I looked out from the dark deck, I saw the eerie red lights of the other boats floating in the Hakata Harbor. In the dark corners of the deck, furtive couples of young men and women entertained themselves. Just then, the moon came out from behind the clouds and illuminated the side of a woman near me. The blanket covering their knees looked as pale as alabaster in the moonlight.

* * *

In the morning, that flag was put out again. Its snapped in the wind and signaled for a boat to come pick up a person. The people on the ship used that flag to signal to the shore—'someone has died again.' A small boat came up alongside our ship, announcing its presence with the sound of an engine. My boys watched fascinated—as a large metal lift rattled down and lifted the small boat up to the deck. Eventually a box about the size of a large kerosene oil can appeared from our ship's hold, and was placed on the small boat.

"It's a child again today," someone said.

I lost count of how many children were taken away like this. The poor, young souls who made it to Japan only to perish before they set foot on the motherland. Their small corpses probably covered with sores and scabs, like those on my children. The only reward for these children who had gotten as far as Hakata Harbor, were the rough, wooden coffins they were taken away in.

"Mommy. What are they doing with that box?" Masahiro asked.

"It's probably going to be burned at a crematorium.'

"Why?"

"Why? Because people who die in Japan are burned."

Masahiro looked at me horrified. "Am I going to get burned up if I die?"

"Yes. Everyone here does," I said—then, realizing my mistake, added, "So you can't die. All right?"

Masahiro didn't move, and stared in silence at the small boat with its dead passenger being lowered with the wench.

The longer we stay here stranded on this ship, the more young children are sacrificed. Why don't they let us land? Why can't we move? Even during the terrible two weeks in the Korean mountains, we had the ability to walk, so we still had hope. With every agonizing inch, we got closer to home. On this ship, cold hatred and despair surrounded the four of us, and we were trapped. The green pine trees of Japan beckoned in front of us, yet we couldn't move. I thought, "I might have to send Sakiko off soon—tomorrow or the day after tomorrow—in one of those small wooden boxes." More suffering, much more suffering, lay before my little family.

CHAPTER FIFTY-NINE

Beelzebub's Invitation

I was sick of life, but I didn't want to die either. That intense drive to stay alive I felt in Sensen—no longer radiated within me. The adrenaline that drove me through the 38th Parallel was gone. Just as I didn't cry when we left the harbor of Fusan, I didn't cry when we arrived at Hakata Harbor. My body was sapped of all emotion. Perhaps that was the first symptom of reaching extreme physical exhaustion.

By this time, the soles of my feet healed so that I could almost stand and walk normally. But I still felt out of breathe when I climbed up and down the ladder. When I peeled off the socks I was given at the Giseifu refugee camp, my feet revealed their ugly history. The bottoms of my feet were swollen blue-white and the hard skin snapped like a metal can when I pressed it with my finger. As much as possible, I lay still and kept my eyes closed.

My mind was filled with Japan as I went about the dreary daily chores, laundry and meals. I imagined that my relatives would praise me for bringing my children back home safe. But with my husband gone, what was 'family' for me and did it exist anymore? Would I live out the rest of my life as a deranged widow?

As we got closer to the day we would disembark from this ship, I agonized more and more about my future. During the day, these thoughts were tolerable—they were kept in check by the mundane events of daily life: a white seagull flew over the ship, fish gathered below when I washed the diapers, ships filled with returnees increased and decreased in number, and the line of waiting ships before us grew shorter.

But at night, these same worries transformed into monsters. I'd close my eyes and as soon as I fell asleep—the storm started toward me. No matter how high I climbed, the mountain of red mud grew faster. In the reflection of the blue-green water of the rivers, I saw myself sink deeper and deeper—feet first and felt myself drown. The squall intensified and from inside the storm—furious piano music and a man's deep voice chased me so that I sank into a thick, black fog. For hours, through this whirlwind of sound and darkness and terror, I ran with the children—ran away from that man's voice which finally grew distant. When the piano music also faded, my mind settled into an exhausted sleep.

"Tonight I'll have that same nightmare," I thought as I closed my eyes. My heart beat faster as it knew the terrifying sensations approached. It didn't matter that I had crossed the 38th Parallel, reached the Kaijo refugee camp, the Giseifu camp, the train, and even this ship to Japan—that dream still whispered at me, like Beelzebub latched on my back. He laughed and said, "I think I'll have a little fun with her tonight."

I tried to fight back, and shouted, "All right, go ahead. Give me your best shot." Then he grinned his yellow teeth at me from his perch on my shoulder—he knew how tired I was. The thick deep voice frightened me but I thought, "If only I could remember the name of that piano melody, I would be all right."

Almost every night, the refugees held a talent show on deck to pass the time. The hold, where I lay, was quiet because most people, in an effort to forget the summer heat, went to watch the talent show at that front deck. I watched the others in the hold as I lay on my mat.

A melody drifted quietly in the distance—perhaps from a radio in a crew cabin. The radio music got louder and softer when the wind changed direction. As soon as one song ended, the next one began.

Suddenly, a song made my chest tighten painfully—that song, that music...has something important to do with me. I stood up and put my feet on the ladder so quickly dizziness almost overcame me. I went up the ladder to the hatch. From there, I heard a man's deep baritone voice. That was the voice. The man's voice that tormented me night after night—and the sharp and haunting piano melody.

I went out on the deck and saw lights through the round window on the ship's bridge. The radio blared through an open cabin window—then I remembered—the name of that music. In Japanese I called it—'Beelzebub's music.' It was Schubert's Opus 1 (D. 328) for voice and piano, where a baritone singer describes a terrified child pleading with his father to save him from a supernatural being, called *Der Erlkönig* in German.

My husband was very fond of Schubert's music and often played this record. When he played 'Beelzebub's music', the drama and emotion moved me deeply. Even then, as I listened on the deck of that ship—the music was beautiful.

Now that I recognized Beelzebub's music, I was relieved and suddenly felt lighter. Once I recognized the name of the voice and music in my nightmares, I felt as if a heavy weight was lifted off my chest. I sat on the edge of the door hatch and listened peacefully to the rest of the radio broadcast.

The stars sparkled in the dark blue sky beyond the four cables that ran from the mast to the railing. The scene before me was like a gorgeous fabric, cables woven with stars. Beneath the stars, our planet moved, indifferent to my existence. A comet, a falling star, disappeared into the horizon and reminded me of my husband. I couldn't help but wonder — was he still alive?

I made another bargain with the spirits. 'If I see three falling stars — before a particular bright star moved from the left to the right of the mast — that would mean that my husband was alive.' And then I promised I would never play this game again. Such games with the gods were not good for me or anyone. And I knew it was an insult to my husband's spirit, whether he was alive or dead. This would be my last time.

Then I faced upward and opened my eyes wide to see as much of the sky as possible and waited for the heavens to tell me my fortune. It was a still night. The mast stood tall as the celestial bodies quietly moved across the sky. Just when my star disappeared behind the mast, two spectacular falling stars appeared — then a third falling star appeared and disappeared into the ocean horizon.

CHAPTER SIXTY

The Four Thousand Yen Carrier

The day of our landing finally arrived. A *Hikiage* Assistance official came on board and explained the landing procedure to us in detail. He said, "After the DDT treatment in Warehouse number 3, you will line up in single file and go to Warehouse 5. Here there will be an inspection of your belongings. When that is done, you go to Warehouse 8, and you will receive your evening meal."

We nervously jotted down notes in pencil after each of his announcements. Then on a lighter note, he continued, "There will probably those of you who are unofficially 'married'. If you break up upon landing, that doesn't concern us. However, you might want to formalize your relationship with a marriage license here in Hakata." Somebody laughed.

The speaker was in his mid-twenties, hair stiff and shiny with pomade, and he wore a red necktie and wide shoes. This dandy must have been a soldier a year ago — fighting like a tiger in a jungle somewhere. I looked at the pockmarks on his face. Is this what happens to a man after one year away from the war?

He went on, "...next, we will talk about the money you can take back—each person will be allowed to exchange and bring in up to one thousand yen in Japanese money. That's one thousand yen per person. If you have less than a hundred yen, the government will provide you with a hundred yen payment per person, to cover the travel expenses home." Everyone tensed up as they listened.

"For detailed information on the trains to your hometowns, please read the Temporary Train Schedule for Returnees."

These officials had thought of everything, and must have repeated this speech for every refugee ship that came in every day—over and over. His words flowed smoothly, like water over a flat board. After the *Hikiage* Assistance officials returned to their boat, we headed back to our sleeping area below deck, my mind crammed with the information. On the way, Masahiko said, "Mommy, look." He stopped us to lean from the bannister and watch another boat dropping anchor. The boat stopped with a loud rattle of the engine, and floated in a mass of bubbles. Everyone on that boat leaned precariously over the deck railing to wave.

"Excuse me, *Okusan*." Someone tapped me in the shoulder. When I turned around, I saw the familiar face of a man who was a fellow passenger. "*Okusan*, do you have any money?" He spoke in a low voice so as not to be heard by the others.

"No, I don't." What an odd thing for him to ask, I thought.

"Is that so? That's good. I have a favor to ask of you," he said. "You are a family of four so you have to right to disembark with four thousand yen—Can I ask you to carry four thousand yen for me? In return, I'll give you a hundred yen for your trouble. And of course, the four hundred yen the government would have given you."

He continued, "In other words, I'll give you five hundred yen in total. This way, you'll make some money and it'll be a help to me. What do you think?"

I was impressed. What a clever scheme. But I turned him down and said, "I'll stick with the official four hundred yen payment from the government. I don't want to be responsible for other people's money."

He persisted. "Well, then. I'll give you two hundred yen thank you money. So all together you'll get six hundred yen," he said.

"What?"

"How about it, *Okusan*?"

I said, "I'm sorry. We can get home with the four hundred yen payment from the government," I said and turned away. What a pest. He followed me all the way back to the hatch, and raised his offer again—to seven hundred yen. But I left him.

When we got back to our sleeping spot, the unfriendly neighbor couple were whispering something to each other. I sat down and the woman said to me, "*Okusan*, can we ask you something? This is a small gift for you…" She brought some hard biscuits out of her bag, and offered them to me. I was surprised because until now, this woman had not even bothered to say one word to me. When I looked up, her husband spoke.

"Excuse me, *Okusan*, would you please carry four thousand yen for us? I'll give you two hundred yen as thanks. In other words, we'll pay you the four hundred yen that's due you from the government, plus two hundred extra. Six hundred yen all together. "

This man tried to be friendly now, but that only made him look more sordid. "Oh that business. Somebody else on deck already asked me to do the same for eight hundred," I lied.

"Eight hundred yen? All right, I'll pay you a thousand yen. Yes, that's what we'll do. How about it?" he said.

"I'm sorry, I've already decided," I said smugly. Turning them down felt delightful. I stood up and said to Masahiko, "We might land tomorrow, so we'd better go see the doctor." I snubbed the nasty couple and went up the ladder to find a man waiting for me at the hatch door. It was the lawyer.

"*Okusan*, I have a favor to ask of you..."

Dirty scoundrel, I thought and interrupted him, "I know what you're going to say. You're going to ask me to hold your four thousand yen for you. Then you're going to offer me four hundred yen thanks money. Together with the four hundred yen that's due me from the government, you're going to give me eight hundred yen all together. Am I right? "

He laughed. "Mrs. Fujiwara, you're very clever. Actually, that is what I meant to say." His oily voice continued. "Hey, since we're both from the same hometown, I'll make a better offer. How about I give you a thousand yen all together? You'll make six hundred yen profit."

I shot back, "So you can make three thousand yen?"

He laughed and raised his hands in surrender. "I'm no match for you, *Okusan*! All right. How about I give you one thousand two hundred yen? And I'll do all the paperwork for you." He assured me that I wouldn't even have to handle the money.

I said, "All right. All right. Just give me a thousand yen. Anyway, someone else is going to pester me so I want to get this settled quickly." I remembered the face of this lawyer when he counted his hundred yen bills at the Kaijo camp. His words, "...since we're both from the same hometown," reverberated in my mind.

The next morning, the ship was abuzz with talk of the landing. A crowd gathered on deck around the chalkboard. I stuck my head between the people to see what was going on. Everyone was looking at a the message on the board. It said in big white letters: THIS SHIP WILL DOCK TOMORROW, SEPTEMBER 12TH, 9 A.M.

I called my boys, "Masahiro-chan, Masahiko-chan, we're landing tomorrow morning! Then we'll get on a big train and go back to Grandma's house." I hugged them both close to me and felt so happy to be able to finally tell the truth that my cheeks burned.

I thought, "Tonight will be our last night on this ship. Never again do I want to cross these dark waters." That night, I couldn't sleep for a long time. I listened to people excitedly chattering all night, and thought of my parents and my brothers and sister. "Will I see them?" My husband's gaunt face also came to mind. I lay flat on my back and closed my eyes. My lips naturally mouthed that melody I heard in northern Korea—the Shooting Star is Alive.

I'll meet you again, dear
I will definitely meet you again, dear
Look again tonight,
the shooting star is alive

As I sang that song to myself over and over, a tear rolled down the side of my face, left a long thin trail into my ear, and then dripped down to the mat beneath us. I became calm, as if my husband were with me, and fell into an deep easy slumber.

CHAPTER SIXTY-ONE

Landing Day

NO. 648 HIKIAGE DOCUMENT

Name: Tei Fujiwara   .

Date of Birth: November 6, 1918   .

Hometown: 13018-ban, Suwa City,

          Nagano Prefecture, Japan

Address: (before the evacuation)

House Unit #21, Government Compound #8,

Shinkyo City, Manchuria

Occupation: none   .

Number of Dependants: 3   .

_____   .

Hakata Returnee Processing

Today: September 12, 1946

          Hakata Harbor

          Sept 12, 1946

Department of Welfare

Head of the Hakata Returnee Office   ____

_____   .

I felt exhilarated — my second life began on September 12th when the walkway was lowered. My first steps into Japan was on shining white concrete and I remember how it hurt the soles of my bare feet. We were herded from warehouse to warehouse in a confusion of procedures, and I didn't know what was what. Finally, we were directed to a dormitory and as we walked by a fence, Masahiro and I both noticed something strange.

"Mommy, there's a Japanese lady walking over there," Masahiro said in a loud voice. She wore a silk kimono with a traditional wide *obi* belt, and like Masahiro, I was amazed. I expected all Japanese women to look like me — miserable and in tatters.

I am a Japanese woman, and the poor refugee in front of me was also a Japanese woman. But Masahiro and I were shocked to see the beautiful lady dressed in a silk kimono — she was like a different species from us. When I think about it now, I must have been a pathetic sight — barefoot and emaciated. We were taken to the dorm facilities with an oddly picturesque name, *Matsubara-ryo* — 'the dorm with pine trees.' There were neat rows of temporary buildings with simple wood plank floors and a gravel pathway between the units. I went inside one and was very grateful to find a water faucet and a toilet nearby. We drank our fill of the water from the faucet. And we didn't have to wait in line to use a faraway toilet!

Here I was issued the official *hikiage* document, a crinkly, single sheet of paper — the only tangible evidence of everything we endured over the past year. Then they distributed all sorts of things: children's clothes, biscuits, wooden *geta* clogs, food coupons, and a blanket. I placed everything on the blanket and rolled it up into a bundle so I could carry it. It was heavy like a precious treasure box.

Since we left Sensen in August, this was the first time we slept with real bedding. In Matsubara dormitory, there were no *matsu*, no pine trees, just a warm breeze.

That night, I looked out into the harbor. There were still many ships, full of refugees like us, waiting in the port. They floated peacefully on the surface, and glowed gently like the phosphorescent sea algae that drifted aimlessly out at sea.

CHAPTER SIXTY-TWO

The Second Day after Landing

The next morning, I awoke with one more worry on my mind. The money I was supposed to receive from the lawyer who had agreed to handle the paperwork in return for my 'carrying' his four thousand yen. He assured me I didn't have to do anything — but I lost track of him in the confusion of the landing. He owed me a thousand yen 'thank you money' and the four hundred yen the government would have given to penniless families of four, like mine. He must still be somewhere in the Matsubara dorms but I didn't have the energy to go from building to building and search for him. As I enviously watched other families counting their government payments — crisp one hundred and ten yen bills, I began to regret making that arrangement with the lawyer. "I should have just taken the government payment," I thought.

"That was a mistake, to try to make a little money — too late now. Oh, well. No sense regretting it now. If that lawyer escapes before me on the trains, I'll have to deal with it then." At least, I was not as miserable as I was back in Korea. I still had time to find him—a day and a half until the train for my hometown, Suwa City, departed. For food, I still had the biscuits they gave me.

In the middle of the Matsubara dorm complex, they served cups of free green tea to the refugees. I missed the taste of tea over the past year and relished trying a cup, but when I walked across the hot sand to where they were serving the tea, I saw a long line. If I waited for my turn, we would get terribly hot in the sun, so I decided to make do with just water. On the way back from the water fountain, I noticed a couple of barbers cutting hair for a long line of men. As I casually glanced across the crowd, a man suddenly turned his back on me. That movement caught my eye.

"How rude," I said to myself. "Wait...it's the lawyer." I walked up to him and grabbed his shirt.

"Mr. Fujita, I guess you've been found," I said.

The lawyer turned around and pretended he saw me for the first time. "Oh, Mrs. Fujiwara. It's you. I looked all over for you," he said..

I said, "Oh, really? Is that why you turned away after you saw me?" I pulled on his shirt. "Step out here."

"Please wait a moment. It's almost my turn," he said.

"You don't need to wait. Give me my money." I spoke in a loud voice so everyone in line could hear.

The lawyer cringed. "Oh, that. I looked for you everywhere. I went to each dormitory room and I looked for you."

I made sure everyone heard my answer. "Well, good for you. Please give me back my money," I said.

"I don't have it right now. My wife is holding it for me," he mumbled.

I couldn't stand it any longer. My chest was burning. "Mr.

Fujita, do you intend to be a criminal now that you're here in Japan? Or are you just going to pretend to be crazy like you did in Korea?" The lawyer stepped out of the line, took my elbow and walked me away from the other men who listened in.

He became pale as he tried to quiet me. Once we were out in the middle of the road, I let him have it. I yelled, "You want to run away, right? Go ahead and run. I'll scream 'thief, thief' and come after you. Remember, you're in Japan now. Look, look over there. The *hikiage* officials are watching us. If you think you can run away, go ahead and try it."

The lawyer raised his hands to admit defeat and said, "Please, don't make such a fuss. To tell you the truth, your money and my money, I lost it all in the chaos yesterday…"

"You're still telling lies, are you?" I said with all the fury I saved since landing.

"No. It's the truth. I can give you four hundred yen, the same amount as the government payment owed to your family. Won't you give me a break?" he pleaded.

I was so exasperated I couldn't speak. I thought about dragging him to the *hikiage* officials to demand that he give me the thousand yen he owed me. But, at the same time, I was repelled at the thought of having to deal with this conniving creature any longer. "I can't stand the idea of talking with you anymore. Give me the four hundred."

He looked around, groped through the papers in his pocket, and fished out his money. He said, "All right, here's four hundred yen," and handed me four hundred yen bills.

As he slunk away, I shouted, "Mr. Fujita, I hope you don't get killed — people here might not be such easy victims."

"What?" He stopped and turned around in surprise.

"I hear there are more desperate people in Japan after the war," I said, thinking of all the people who survived the war.

The lawyer looked frightened, hunched his shoulders, and ran into the crowd to hide himself. He must think I'm a miserable refugee like everyone else. I was sure there must be an even more wretched victim crying somewhere. Someone left destitute by this bastard. Clutching my four hundred yen, I went back with my head held high to the dorms. In a few hours, we would get on the train for home.

As I made my way through the crowds, I noticed a small man standing on a crate, speaking to a group. About forty or fifty women and children gathered around him, weeping. So I stopped. When I took a closer look, I recognized these people — it was the Miyamoto *dan*. The man on the crate — was none other than Kappa Man. Coming closer, I saw tears sparkling on his ruddy face. He said, "After this *dan* breaks up and you all go back to your homes, please don't forget all the hardships we suffered together over the past year...I won't either." He wiped his eyes with the back of his hand. All of the Miyamoto *dan* women sobbed as they listened to him.

Kappa Man. Until the very end of journey, here at Hakata Harbor, this *dan* stayed together. And here they all were. All of them together for their farewells. I had to admit, there was no group like this. Out of the ten groups that started in Sensen, this Miyamoto *dan* might be the only one that got through to the end intact.

I wondered if the reason for their success might be the Kappa Man's leadership skills. He himself declared at the *dancho* meeting back then, "If a person doesn't put his own *dan* first, how can he think about others?"

Kappa Man might be considered decisive and independent by some, but as far as I was concerned — he didn't deserve to live. It's true I couldn't accuse him of not being dedicated to his group but I crept away so as not to run into him again. I imagined how he would humiliate me if he saw me.

"Hey, you woman *dancho* from Meterological Station," he would yell. "What happened to your *dan*?"

This would be my ultimate disgrace. To be discovered by Kappa Man here and to be spoken to in this way. I'd have to answer, "Where is my *dan*? Why…they're nowhere."

I didn't know where they went. They should have come on the same ship with me, but as I searched all around me, there was no one from my group.

CHAPTER SIXTY-THREE

From Hakata to Suwa

The government arranged for freight trains to pick up the thousands of *hikiage* refugees who poured into Japan — we boarded ours in the middle of the night. And of course, I expected rain again when we got on this time — but the Japanese skies were kind to us. In exchange for the good weather for our first train ride, we were royally treated to the stench of horse manure. In the freight car, evidence of the previous equine passengers was piled high everywhere we stepped. This miserable ride stopped at Moji town, and we got off what would be our last freight car in our long journey.

After we waited a long time, we boarded a regular passenger train for Tokyo Station. But of course, we wouldn't be so lucky to get any seats in this packed train. We found some space in the aisle near the toilets and passed the night on the floor.

I worried about Sakiko. That morning before we left Hakata Harbor, I took her to a clinic near the Matsubara dorms, and the doctor said, "I can't imagine she will live more than a day or two."

As we sat on the dirty train floor by the toilets, I tried to breast-feed her, but she made no effort to suckle. Only her closed eyes showed any traces of movement. I wondered what sort of dream she was having. My tears fell on her as I gazed at her wan face — and willed her to hear me, "We've made it this far...we've made it this far..."

At Itozaki, dawn arrived, and using the food coupons, I bought two *bento* lunch boxes. At least the boys were happy and ate. People who got on at Okayama gave the boys a couple of pears. Their curiosity obvious, the passengers wanted to hear all about the *hikiage*. One man leered at me. "We heard bad things happened to the women over there," he said as he looked down at me. I knew very well what he expected to hear.

When we arrived at a large station and got off to switch trains, we saw a student with a big megaphone who walked around, shouting in a breaking voice, "Dear everyone who returned from overseas. I really, really feel for you all. This has been a long, hard journey. You are almost home now. I congratulate you from the bottom of my heart."

"Mommy, what is he saying?"

"Masahiro, it's nothing." I had gotten tired of explaining. In any case, this student with the megaphone sounded very unreal. To hear a young man walking around shouting such things. It was nine p.m. when we reached Nagoya.

We switched to the Chuo Line. Suddenly we were surrounded by a crowd of students dressed in traditional navy-blue school uniforms. They took my bags and guided us to a waiting room.

"*Okusan,* your baby doesn't look well," said a medical student with a stethoscope around his neck. He brought out his supplies and gave Sakiko an injection. I don't know what that was but it seemed to help. Her little face flushed pink and she gave a weak cry.

"What schools are you from?" I asked the students. Their uniforms were all different.

"We're with the Japanese National University Student Association." At that time, I didn't know what the Association was. At Nagoya, my opinion of students completely changed— after that strange first encounter with the student shouting through the megaphone. One of these students told me that the next train would leave Nagoya soon after eleven p.m. Of course, I didn't get any seats again.

But this time, a student actually apologized. "I'm so sorry, *Okusan*," the student said as he glared at the men who had grabbed the seats ahead of us. "Those people are so rude. They're all *ringo no yamiya*."

I was touched that he felt responsible for their behavior.

"*Yamiya*?" I asked.

"Oh, you don't know about the *yamiya* yet. Basically, they're people who operate behind the law—black marketeers, in other words. They're everywhere now." His comment reminded me of the lawyer.

We reached Shiojiri at four in the morning. The platform was still dark and there was another student group, of young men and women this time, who waited for us. They reached out to take my bags. Someone carried Masahiro and someone else took Masahiko. We all climbed the stairs to the platform for the next train.

I had no idea what was what but I followed them. A train was waiting for us—its sign said: Leaving Shiojiri Town, Destination: Shinjuku, Tokyo. This time, we actually got to sit down in real passenger seats! After the train left Shiojiri station, I learned that these kind students were from the regional chapter of the Japanese Youth Association. Some of these young people had come out to help from the distant countryside. They tried to take care of me, and asked, "Do you need anything to eat....?"

The Tokaido train line and the Chuo line are so different. I was so grateful for my country, for these trains, I trembled with happiness. I was getting very nervous. In two hours, I would see my parents. What shall I say to my brothers and sister?

My thoughts were interrupted by a sharp voice. "You're from Manchuria, are you? Must've been real tough," an elderly woman in the seat in front of me peeped over the top of her seat. She spoke with a heavy country accent, "Awful tough...with a little one like that...hey, sonny, isn't that something?"

A young soldier sitting next to me who she called "Sonny" nodded his head and said, "Yup. yup."

The old woman continued, "*Okusan*, you must be awful hungry." She reached into her *furoshiki* bag, pulled out a rice ball and placed it in my hands, "....have an *onigiri*...go on, have one...really, it must've been awful tough." The old woman looked at us as tears poured down her face.

The soldier she called "Sonny" looked annoyed and poked the old lady on the side. "Knock it off, leave her alone," his eyes said. The old woman noticed the soldier's poke and said, "What, Sonny? You, dummy! This lady...don't you see the little baby? Look. Look. Poor thing is so thin...it's awful." She started crying again. I was grateful but embarrassed.

We were going to reach Suwa soon, and I didn't want to talk with this teary old woman any longer. I carefully wrapped her *onigiri* and returned it to her. I pretended to go to sleep.

The train went into a tunnel and I knew, after this tunnel, we would get to the valley near Suwa, my hometown. I wondered, "Would my dear parents and kind siblings be waiting for me?" My nerves throbbed with anticipation.

CHAPTER SIXTY-FOUR

Finally, My Parents Embrace Me

After the train went through the town of Okaya, the big Lake Suwa came into view, and in the morning fog, the surface of the lake glimmered like jewels beneath a veil. I emptied the water bottle to dampen a cloth and wiped Sakiko's face. Until last night, she was almost too hot to touch, but now her skin felt cold and clammy. The only evidence of life was a feeble movement of her head when I wiped her tiny face. Her pale lips let out no cry, not even a whimper. When I lay her down on the seat next to me, her eyes remained closed.

I turned my attention to the boys. "Masahiko-chan, we're almost at Grandma's house. Let's clean up, all right?" His neck was thin and bony, and his head looked like a ghastly, round lantern. His huge eyes peered out of his emaciated face. "At least, he is too young to remember," I thought.

I then turned to my older son. "Masahiro-chan, we need to clean up your face." He was so wasted, he lost his balance and fell each time as I tried to wipe his pale face. As his mother, I felt responsible for his terrible condition. With food, his body might heal, but would his spirit?

I asked for his forgiveness. "Masahiro-chan…Mommy treated you very badly. I'm very sorry. I won't scold you again, ever. When we get to Grandma's house, I want you to eat lots of rice and grow up big and strong." Masahiro, as my oldest, had borne the brunt of my emotional storms over the past year. He was my trustworthy companion, my brave little man, the only one I could lean on. I felt such sorrow for my maternal sins—I burdened this six year old child with so much pain and suffering. Would he ever forget?

The train ran on through the morning fog. "Hurry," I urged the train. I stepped out into the aisle to try to calm my nerves and the train finally arrived at Kamisuwa—Upper Suwa. The four of us got off the train to step onto the platform where three Youth Association students waited for us.

The town of Suwa was hushed in the morning, as if asleep, nestled in a white blanket. Standing on the platform, I looked around. Nothing's changed. Everything was just as I remembered. The slightly metallic smell of the hot springs, the fragrant flowers, and the faint shadows of mountains before me. This home that I had dreamed of for so long.

"Nothing has changed," I sighed.

The students took us to a room marked with a hanging sign—WAITING AREA FOR HIKIAGE RETURNEES. I stepped one foot into the waiting room and gasped. *A ghost stood there.* She stared back at me with wild grey hair, an unrecognizable face tinged blue and black, cheekbones jutted out under sunken eye sockets, and a chest flat and bony. A faded, sweat-stained shirt hung across her sharp shoulders, below that a pair of frayed pants torn at the knees…and two swollen legs, like white wax candles, stuck out. At least she wore proper *geta*, wooden shoes. On her back, a limp baby that looked dead; and she held hands with two boys about to collapse. My reflection in the big mirror that advertised the local hot springs, *Suwa Yu*, was the first image I saw of myself in over a year. I was horrified even more than frightened. "A ghost from the graveyard," I thought.

I left the children in the waiting room and went to find a phone. Across the town square, the Sanmi Cafe was open. Good. I knew this shop owner well.

"Excuse me," I called out as I entered. The proprietor, a woman who hadn't changed at all, came out with a feather duster in her hand. She jerked back when she saw me.

"What do you want?" she said. She didn't recognize me.

"I'm Tei from South Suwa." When I said this, she looked and looked again, and her face changed expression.

"My goodness. It really is Tei…what happened?" She stood there with her eyes wide open and held the duster frozen in mid-air.

"May I use your phone to call my home?" I asked.

She suddenly snapped to attention. "Please, please go ahead," and pointed to the phone by the clerk's desk.

I tried to reach the phone but didn't have the strength to step up on the raised floor around the desk.

"Ma'am, I'm sorry. Can I trouble you to call the Chimura's next door to my parents' house and tell them to let my family know to pick me up?" I knew my parents didn't have their own phone yet.

"Yes, yes. Right away. I'll call right away," she said. She picked up the phone and instructed the operator to connect her.

"Hello. Hello? Is this Chimura residence? Oh, this is the Kimura's? No. No, I don't want the Kimura's, I am calling the *Chimuras*!" She was angry with the operator. "What a nuisance! Hello? Hello?"

I left the flustered cafe owner to deal with the telephone operator, and went back to the train station room where my boys waited.

The students gave me my final instructions and handed me a clipboard. "Excuse me. Please write your name and address here." After I wrote my information, I looked at the top of the clipboard. It said, HIKIAGE LIST.

I realized, "These are the people who made it back." My heart thumped while I scanned the list for my husband's name. Once, twice, three times. His name wasn't there.

I sat down on the wooden chair and waited for my family. How was I able to sit there so calm and dry-eyed? I was amazed at myself.

Running footsteps. "They're here." I turned towards the door. "Oh, damn!" The cries came from my two younger brothers who rushed in—first Kohei, the older one, and then Ryohei with his student uniform. The two of them stopped and stood there at the same time. They didn't say anything—I didn't say anything. We waited for the other to break the silence first. It had been four years since we last saw each other.

Kohei was a soldier who made it back as *hikiage* refugee from the battlefield. Ryohei was still a university student who had stayed in Japan. I was elated that both of my little brothers were alive and had grown into fine men.

"Big Sis!" the girl who ran into the room was my younger sister, Reiko. There was no trace of the school girl I last saw four years ago. She had grown into a beautiful young woman. We screamed and she jumped at me. She yelled something as she held me with her strong arms. I completely broke down.

Then more voices cried out my name, "Teiko…dear Teiko." My parents. I heard them but my eyes were so full of tears, I couldn't see anything.

I pried myself loose from my sister Reiko's arms and loosened Sakiko from my back. I managed to blurt out, "Quickly, quickly — take my baby to the hospital."

After my parents, my younger brothers and my sister found us — my eyes failed me. I suddenly no longer saw anything in front of me. I got light-headed, lost my balance and collapsed. My baby, Sakiko was taken and wrapped in a blanket Reiko brought, Masahiro rode piggyback on Kohei's back, Masahiko was on Ryohei's back. All the children were taken care of.

"It's all right now. It's all right now," echoed inside me. My consciousness gradually faded.

My father's voice. My mother's voice. "Get a hold of yourself, Teiko. Here, grab hold." My parents held me from both sides and we walked through hazy town.

"It's all right if I die. This is all right. I can die now," I said to myself. My mind was clear again as if everything else had been swept out. Only the words floated through my mind. "If I keep walking into that fog, deep into the fog, maybe I'll find my husband. I don't have to live any longer." I put my head into the clouds, wisps of white film, and sank into its sublime depths — deeper and deeper.

AFTERWORD

Author's Notes from 1976 and 1984

(From edition dated 1976) With my book coming out [again] in the paperback edition, I decided to read the words I wrote so long ago. Even through it's been more than twenty-five years since everything happened, these words immediately ignited my memories of the *hikiage*, the repatriation. Every experience still vivid and painful. Terrible dreams woke me the other night…they haunt me even now. The terror of that time raced through my mind, and when my own screams jerked me out of sleep, waves of sadness washed over me. I wiped the tears off my face and tried to go back to sleep, but felt sick at heart.

The next morning I casually said to my husband, "You know, last night, I just couldn't get to sleep…" I hoped he would make a joke and laugh it off because he knows that I'm usually a sound sleeper, but instead he gravely said, "Is that so?" He knows I am reading my book.

Three months after the children and I returned to Japan, my husband came back from Enkichi in northern Manchuria [a Soviet labor camp]. I can imagine how horrible that year must have

313

been for him but he never says a word about it. Now that we live in this peaceful time, he never revisits the past. But I wonder, "How deep are his wounds from that time?"

I think he's working on a novel in his office now. It's probably a historical novel, not a memoir. He's only written once about his own *hikiage* experience. In his many works, he doesn't reveal even a shadow of his own feelings about the experience.

Even though I put my own memories on paper soon after I came home, he refused to do the same. Although he read my book, he was a reluctant listener to my stories. Before I knew it, any talk of the *hikiage* became taboo between us.

My eldest son, Masahiro, who was five when we fled from Manchuria, is now thirty-five. He studied mechanical engineering at university and is now employed by a large car maker. He became a father himself but he also never speaks of that time. Whenever any mention is made of that year, he becomes silent, gets up from his seat and leaves the room. Something terrible was burned into the soul of that five year-old boy.

I feel so sorry for him. I still remember the emaciated little boy who tried to comfort me by saying, "Mommy, I'm full, eat my potato so you can breast-feed the baby." And this when he hadn't eaten anything himself for three days! That day he proved the incredible capacity of his young heart. So I am resolved to not speak of that painful time in front of him now.

My son, Masahiko, was only two at the time, just a toddler when we left Manchuria. Last year, he returned from the US where he taught mathematics for three years at an American university. [University of Colorado] Now he is teaching at a Japanese university. I used to think that my second son was too young to have any memories of that year. But just the other day he said,

"Why am I so afraid of rivers? Whether I'm in Japan or in America, no matter how small the stream, I can't help but feel uneasy before I cross..." I looked at his face and wondered.

It must be from that time. When I crossed that chest-high river in Korea, he clung to me and howled in terror. As I held him with one arm, I feared losing my balance and screamed at him not to cry. That terrible day must have left its imprint on his subconscious. These last years, I thought he was so happy, so carefree, enjoying his life in the States. He expects the world to only offer him wonderful things. He approaches life with gusto, but now I see that the terrible year did wound his subconscious. His body remembers.

My daughter, Sakiko, was just a newborn then. Now she is thirty years old. She studied literature in college so I thought she might write, but she chose the path of marriage and now, she is a busy mother of two boys. She scolds her children, "Now, now, don't be picky eaters. When I was little baby..." The *hikiage* doesn't seem to pain her at all and she eagerly listens to my stories and reads my words. She lives her life as a mother and doesn't hesitate to compare herself to me. She says, "I wonder whether I could have survived that time like you did?"

Once I recovered, I tried to raise my children with my heart and soul. Perhaps they suffered more than their friends who remained in this country during the war. But to raise them as normal children, I needed more than the normal effort. I can't coddle them, it's my responsibility to give them this story, this unhappy burden.

Maybe my story is my way to apologize to my children. When they were so young, I was so deep in despair that I almost forgot I was alive. But now as I watch them grow one by one into adulthood, I look through half-closed eyes and wonder if my story matters. My children have all left me far behind as they go out into the world. Is this all there is to life?

Sadly, I think I must sort out my memories alone, and I cannot really tell them of my painful experiences. Perhaps this is a natural process, just as dead leaves become soil for the next generation. I find it hard to talk anymore about the past. I tell myself to keep the sorrow locked in my heart. I must not chase after the children anymore, to tell them what happened.

I've resisted the urge to say to them, "Look at what I endured for you." When we finally reached my home in Japan, I was so sick, confined to bed for such a long time, I believed I was going to die. That was when I wrote this memoir for my children. I said things on paper that I could never tell them directly. I hoped that when they grew up after my death, my stories would encourage them during hard times. Then they would see how I gritted my teeth to endure, and how they, too, suffered and survived.

I wrote what I believed would be my last testament to my children. But I survived. And those words were no longer a will. They became this book. I have nothing left to give to the world but this book. Now I try to quietly live my life, not bothering anyone, and pray for my children.

From edition dated July, *Showa Era 59* [1984].

My book, *Nagareru Hoshi wa Ikiteiru* has now gone into its 46th printing. This is a rare phenomenon for any book and when I heard about it, I was incredulous and extremely happy. Words I wrote thirty-four years ago are still in print. This is proof that people continue to read it.

When they told me the news, I immediately told my husband, because I knew he would be the most happy for me if he were here. He died four years ago. But in the forty long years of our married life together, we hardly ever talked about that experience, the *hikiage*. For both of us, the wounds were too deep and painful. The subject became an unmentionable topic in our life together.

That was not to say our life was idyllic — far from it. Although we were in the same house all day, he wrote his novels in his room, separate from me. There were many times when we got on each other's nerves — over stupid little things — like whether the breakfast soup was too salty or not, whether the window is too high or too low. We often fought and I was always the first one to lose my temper. I'd throw things — a handy tangerine would fly across the room, or the chopsticks would bounce off of the furniture, but even at those times when I was furious, some things I never said.

He already knew what I'd been through without my having to remind him. To say such things to his face would be like stabbing an opponent in the back — after he had already surrendered. To tell him how heavy that burden was in my soul was something I could not do to him. So he died before I said anything like that.

The day my husband died and left me alone, I opened my arms towards the heavens in grief, and collapsed onto the ground in tears. I really thought about following him into the grave that day.

But I still have the three children my husband entrusted to me... They all live close to me. When my husband died, they came to comfort me. Now we regularly gather to eat together. The meals are noisy and cheerful. Sitting with my children and grandchildren, I wish my husband could be by my side to see how happy we are. This kind, healthy family is the most wonderful legacy he left for me.

I am sixty-five years old now and know that this book is likely to be the most valuable heirloom I leave behind. For the years left to me, I must treasure this book, and live as best as I can until the day I join my husband in the next world.

July, 1984
Tei Fujiwara

About the Author

Tei Fujiwara was born *Taisho Era 7* (1918) in Nagano Prefecture, graduated from *Kenritsu Sukuwa Kojoo*, married in *Shōwa Era 14* (1939), transferred with her husband in *Showa Era 18* (1943) to a position with the *Shinkyo Kanshodai* (Shinkyo Meteorological Observatory) and went to Manchuria, China.

Her journey home, the *hikiage*, began in *Shōwa Era 20* (1945). After returning to Japan from *Shinkyo,* Manchuria, she reached her home in Nagano, barely alive. Her husband is the writer, Jiro Nitta.

昭和31年の藤原一家。前列右から著者，咲子，
夫（新田次郎），後列右から正広，正彦。

Glossary of Names, Places, and Terms

Names

藤原てい　　*Fujiwara Tei*　　Fujiwara family name. First name Tei, and her children, age at the beginning of journey:

正広	*Masahiro*	eldest son (5)
正彦	*Masahiko*	second son (2)
咲子	*Sakiko*	daughter (one month old)

大地　　*Mr & Mrs. Daichi*　　*dan* members who are old friends, with baby and teenage daughter *Seiko-chan*

藤田　　Mr. Fujita　　the scheming lawyer

藤原 作平　　Fujiwara Sakuhei　　Tei's uncle-in-law, head of the Meteorological Observatory, Japan

ゲンナージ　　Gennage　　Soviet soldier friend

五味　　(Old Man) Gomi　　Distant relative of Tei's husband, teacher

本田　　*Mrs. Honda*　　*dan* member

保坂 団　　*Hosaka dan*　　Hosaka *dan*

かっぱ　　*Kappa Man*　　(see Mr. Tokushima and Kappa)

倉重　　*Mrs. Kurashige*　　*dan* member with one son

　　　　Kuniko　　Mrs. Kurashige's younger sister

木本　　*Mrs. Kimoto*　　dan member with beautiful voice

金　　*Mr. Kim*　　Korean man, member of the Korean *Hoantai*

水島　　*Mizushima*　　*dan* members, Mr. wears glasses, Mrs. suffers insanity

宮本　　*Miyamoto Dan*　　Wealthy *dan* led by Kappa Man

長須　　*Mr/Mrs. Nagasu*　　*dan* member, older proud bossy couple

　　　　Hisako　　daughter (5)

成田　　*Mr. & Mrs. Narita*　　Third *Dan-cho,* sickly man,

talkative wife and son, Daikyo

大江	*Mr. Oe*	Second *Dancho,* older former manager
	Old Woman Oe	Mr. Oe's older sister
王谷	*Dr. Oya*	Japanese Association medical doctor
朴	*Mr. Park*	Korean person
崎山	*Mrs. Sakiyama*	dan member, poorest, morose with

two boys Ichiro (6), Jiro (4) and newborn

佐藤	*Mrs. Sato*	*dan* member
柴田	*Shibata*	*dan* member
田中	*Mr. Tanaka*	Japanese Association official
多谷	*Mr. Taya*	most recent head of the Meteorological Station
東田	*Mrs. Toda*	*dan* member

and *Tamio,* step-child

徳島	*Mr. Tokushima*	Also called *Kappa Man,* (see Kappa)

leader of the 宮本団   Miyamoto *dan*

戸野	*Mr. Tono*	first *Dan-cho*
ブラースチイ	Veraschy	Soviet soldier friend
和達	*Mr. Wadachi*	former head of the Meteorological Station
山岸	*Mr. Yamagishi*	Also called Old Man Yamagishi, senior

Japanese Association member.

Places as they appear in original memoir:

安東	*Anton*	Manchuria
千村	*Chimura*	Japan
鎮南浦	*Chinnanbo*	Northern Korea
長白山脈	*Chohaku Mts*	Chohaku Mountains, Northern Korea
延吉	*Enkichi*	Enkichi *gulag* camp, Soviet Union

元山	*Genzan*	Northern Korea
議 政 府	*Giseifu*	Southern Korea
奉天	*Hoten*	Manchuria
仁川	*Jinsen*	Southern Korea
平壌	*Heijyo*	Northern Korea
鳳凰城	*Hojo*	Hojo, Manchuria (meteorological station)
上諏訪	*Kamisuwa*	Japan
開 城	*Kaijo*	Kaijo Refugee Camp, near 38th Parallel,

Southern Korea

海 州	*Kaishu*	Northern Korea
京 城	*Keijo*	Southern Korea
満州	*Manshu*	Manchuria (now Northeast China)
門司	*Moji*	Japan
名古屋	*Nagoya*	Japan
劉家河	*Ryukaga*	Manchuria
岡谷	*Okaya*	Okaya, Japan (big lake)
岡山	*Okayama*	Japan
鴨緑江	*Oryoko*	Oryoko River on the border of Manchuria and

Northern Korea

連山関	*Renzankan*	Manchuria
三味食料店	*Sanmi shokuryouten*	Sanmi Café in hometown Suwa, Japan
宣川	*Sensen*	town in Northern Korea where Tei's *dan*

lived for a year

沙 里 院	*Sharin*	Northern Korea
市辺里	*Shihenri*	Northern Korea
新 渓	*Shinkei*	Northern Korea
新京	*Shinkyo*	"New Capitol", Manchuria where Tei's family

lived for two years, and the journey begins

新幕	Shinmaku	Northern Korea
塩尻	*Shiojiri*	Japan
大連	*Tairen*	probably in Manchurai
豆満江	Tomanko	Tomanko River, on border of Northern Korea and Soviet Union
通化	*Tsuka*	Manchuria

Group Names and Other Terms Used in Memoir:

朝鮮人	*Chosenjin*	Korean people
恒年誤差	*hisashinengosa*	constant year error
団	*dan*	designated group (rhymes with 'run')
団長	*dancho*	head of the *dan*
八路軍	*Hachirogun*	Eighth Route Army (Communist Chinese Army)
	fuku dancho	assistant head of the *dan*
微分記号	*bibunkigo*	differential symbol

$$\partial$$

風呂敷	*furoshiki*	a large square of cloth used for wrapping
デマ	*dema*	demagoguery, propaganda
合	*go*	a Japanese cup = about 150 grams of Japanese short grain rice.

飯盒	*hango*	small metal food pot with two compartments

引揚げ	*hikiage*	end of WWII Japanese repatriation
保安隊	*Hoantai*	'Hoantai' the local (Korean) police force
積分記号		integral sign ∫
一貫目	*1 kan*	unit of measurement = 3.75kg
関東軍	*Kantogun*	Kanto Army Division, Japanese Army
かっぱ	*kappa*	Japanese mythical part-man, part-turtle creature.

粥	*kayu*	rice gruel
マクワ瓜	*makua uri*	melon
満州銀行	*manshu ginkou*	Manchuria Bank
満銀	*mangin*	Manchuria Bank (shortened name)
観象台	*Kanshodai*	Meteorological Observatory (Manchuria)
気象台	*Kishodai*	Meteorological Observatory (Japan)

オンドル　　　*ondoru*　　　　　*ondol*, Korean traditional heating system which uses direct heat transfer from wood smoke to the underside of a thick masonry floor.

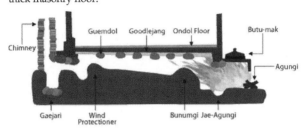

温飯屋　　　*onpanya*　　　hot food shop

里　　　　　*ri*　　　　　Japanese unit of distance (3927m)

.41 ri = one mile.

ヤポンスキー *Yaponski,*　　マダム ハラショー *Madam harashu*

Russian words heard by Tei

赤十字　　　*Sekijuji*　　　Japanese Red Cross

青年会　　　*Seinen Kai*　　　Japanese Youth Association, Japan

社務所　　　*shamusho*　　　shinto (Japanese religion) shrine office

一升　　　　1 sho　　　　unit of measurement= 1.8lit

疎開団　　　*sokaidan*　　　evacuation group

Songs/poems

黒い瞳よ 今 いずこ Where is My Dark Eyed Love?　　name of Japanese song

佐渡 おけさ　　Remote *Sado* Island　　　name of a traditional Japanese song

Lyrics of song at Tei's song at the New Year's party:

小諸なる 古城の ほとり、　*Komoro naru Kojo no hotori*

雲 白く 遊子 かなしむ　*Kumo shiroku yushi kanshimu*

Franz Schubert's Opus 1 (D. 328) inspired by German poem by *Johann Goethe*
depicting the cries of a child killed by a supernatural being, the *Erlking*.
Tei calls this music 魔王の声 *maonokoe* "Voice of Beelzebub"

畳み	*tatami*	Japanese traditional flooring mat, also used to show room size

zori   traditional Japanese sandal

For More Information:

Please visit the book website at:
http://www.nanamizushima.com/.

Discussion Questions

1. Why does Mr. Fujiwara refuse to leave with his family when they leave Shinkyo?

2. How did members of the *dan* group get along? In what way is the *dan* a microcosm of Japanese society in general?

3. Is there any gender difference in the ways they dealt with the *hikiage* experience?

4. How did the *dan* members react to the announcement of the end of the war?

5. How does the issue of "race" surface in this narrative?

6. What was the group's reaction to the death of Tamio Tōda?

7. Why does the narrator hate to see other Japanese peddling soaps or promoting the *chintonya* band?

8. Under the severe conditions such as those described in the narrative, how did the family relationships change?

9. What do you think about the narrative strategy to completely circumvent larger (geo)political themes and opt for more personal dynamics within the group?

10. Are there critical opinions concerning the Japanese nation-state in the narrative? Why or why not?

11. Why has this book continued to be a bestseller in Japan for so many years?

Printed in Great Britain
by Amazon